IMAGES
of America

DOWNEY

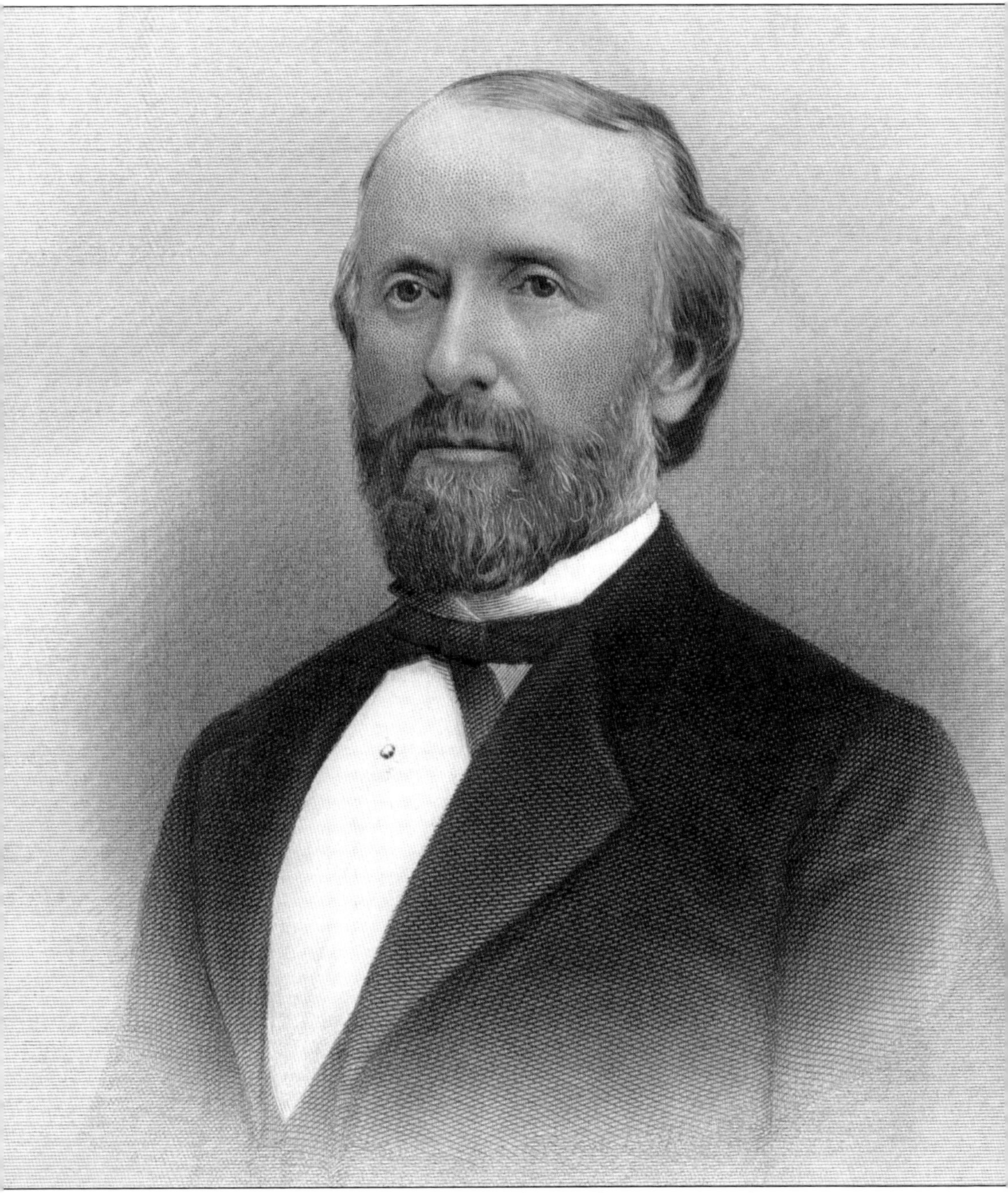

John Gately Downey served as governor of California from 1860 to 1862.

On the cover: A group of Downeyites returning from an excursion to Long Beach on July 4, 1912. They are parked in front of Hull's Drug Store and the Los Nietos Valley Bank on Crawford near Second Street. (Courtesy of the Downey Historical Society.)

IMAGES
of America

DOWNEY

Larry Latimer and the Downey Historical Society

ARCADIA
PUBLISHING

ISBN 978-0-7385-7164-5

Published by Arcadia Publishing
Charleston, South Carolina

Printed in the United States of America

Library of Congress Control Number: 2009932657

For all general information contact Arcadia Publishing at:
Telephone 843-853-2070
Fax 843-853-0044
E-mail sales@arcadiapublishing.com
For customer service and orders:
Toll-Free 1-888-313-2665

Visit us on the Internet at www.arcadiapublishing.com

Dedicated to Mr. John Vincent and the Downey Historical Society. And, to the "pioneers" who endured an arduous journey to a new land and a new life. This book is dedicated to their spirit, perseverance, and hard work.

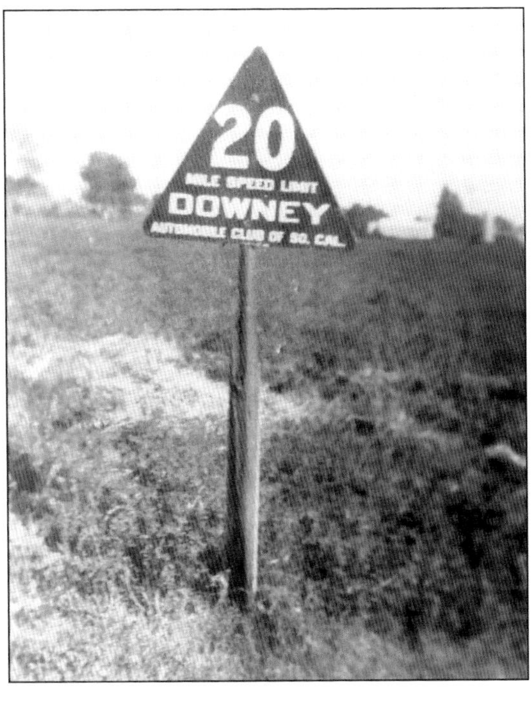

Remember when the speed limit was only 20 miles per hour on that old country road? Read ahead and take a trip down some old country roads in Downey, California.

Contents

Acknowledgments

Great thanks are deserved by my incredible wife, Rose, for her patience and support during this long project, and my parents, Warren and Cleo, for their wisdom and understanding. I would like to acknowledge the Downey Historical Society for developing such an incredible archive of information for all to visit. Very special thanks go to John Vincent, Bob Thompson, and Donna Honeycutt at the History Center for their helpfulness in uncovering resources and material.

Thanks also to Joyce Lawrence and Barbara Callarman for their devotion to Downey history; Marge Swain Lewis for her photographs, stories, and guidance; Jerry Blackburn for his vision and ability to inspire; and George Redfox, Bill Hansen, Bill Kirkwood, Lash Stevenson, Arlene Hoffmeyer, Albert Ball II, and Laurel Cochrane.

My deepest thanks go to Birdella Ball Stock, who shared her family story and photographs. I also want to thank my editor, Jerry Roberts, for his help. I must also acknowledge two books, *The History of Downey and Vicinity* by Easter Bangle Morrison and *The History of Downey* by Russell Quinn. Special thanks are deserved by the Aerospace Legacy Foundation of Downey.

Most of all, we owe a debt of gratitude to the early pioneer families who laid the foundation of modern day Downey—a nice place to live.

The photographs in this book are courtesy of the Downey Historical Society unless otherwise indicated.

INTRODUCTION

The history of Downey follows the westward expansion of our nation after the Civil War and the arrival of the transcontinental railroad to a new town called Downey. Many of the first settlers and pioneers migrated along the numerous dusty trails heading toward Lexington, Gallatin, and College Settlement, within a fertile valley between the San Gabriel River and the Rio Hondo. The Shoshonean Indians had lived here in large families for many generations. In 1837, author Hugo Reid described a village called "Carpenter's farm" along the west bank of the Rio Hondo. Lemuel Carpenter and his Native American wife, Espiritu Uribes, settled down here to begin a family. Espiritu died during the birth of their second child, and soon after, Carpenter moved to the Santa Gertrudes side of the river. This was part of the Manuel Nieto Land Grant, 300,000 acres of pristine Southern California land. In 1834, after division among the Nieto heirs, a portion of this grant between the banks of the San Gabriel River and the Rio Hondo became Rancho Santa Gertrudes. After the death of Espiritu, Carpenter married Maria de Los Angeles Dominguez, a niece of Josefa Cota Nieto, granddaughter of Manuel Nieto.

After Carpenter's death in 1859, John Gatley Downey acquired this property at auction for just $60,000, purchasing what would become modern-day Downey and much more. With over 17,000 acres, this smart Irish immigrant and seventh governor of California knew exactly what could be done with this fertile real estate. Southern California would offer the right climate and setting for the massive ranchos to transform into miles and miles of agriculture predominated by large citrus groves, ranches, and dairies. The Los Nietos Valley, which included Downey, was considered the "garden spot" of Southern California.

Of those pioneers who settled in this area, most had seen that Downey offered land at "$10 an acre with ten percent per annum interest . . . the best land for homesteads and vineyards in this section of the state," according to a poster from the 1870s. It was not until 1873 that John Downey and partner James McFarland subdivided these 96 acres of land, which became the center of a community called Downey. Known as the Tract of the Downey Land Association, it was located 10 miles from the sea and 10 miles from Los Angeles. Maston "Duke" Crawford bought 400 acres known as the "Pettes Tract" from John Downey in 1874. The boundaries were interesting and were as follows: "Commencing at 1st and New Streets thence east to New San Gabriel River; north on New St. to north line of A.L. Balls place, thence east to San Gabriel River. Judge Crawford had the land surveyed into 40 acre tracts." (T. R. Crawford 1924) Crawford acted as Governor Downey's agent in town. Downey and Crawford developed a great friendship. Judge Crawford managed most of the affairs of this growing city.

Thus begins our visit to the good old days of Downey, filled with beautiful orchards, farms, ranches, dirt roads, floods, schools, old homes, hospitals, churches, and much more. Travel through time and visit the people and places that are the story of Downey, "Future Unlimited."

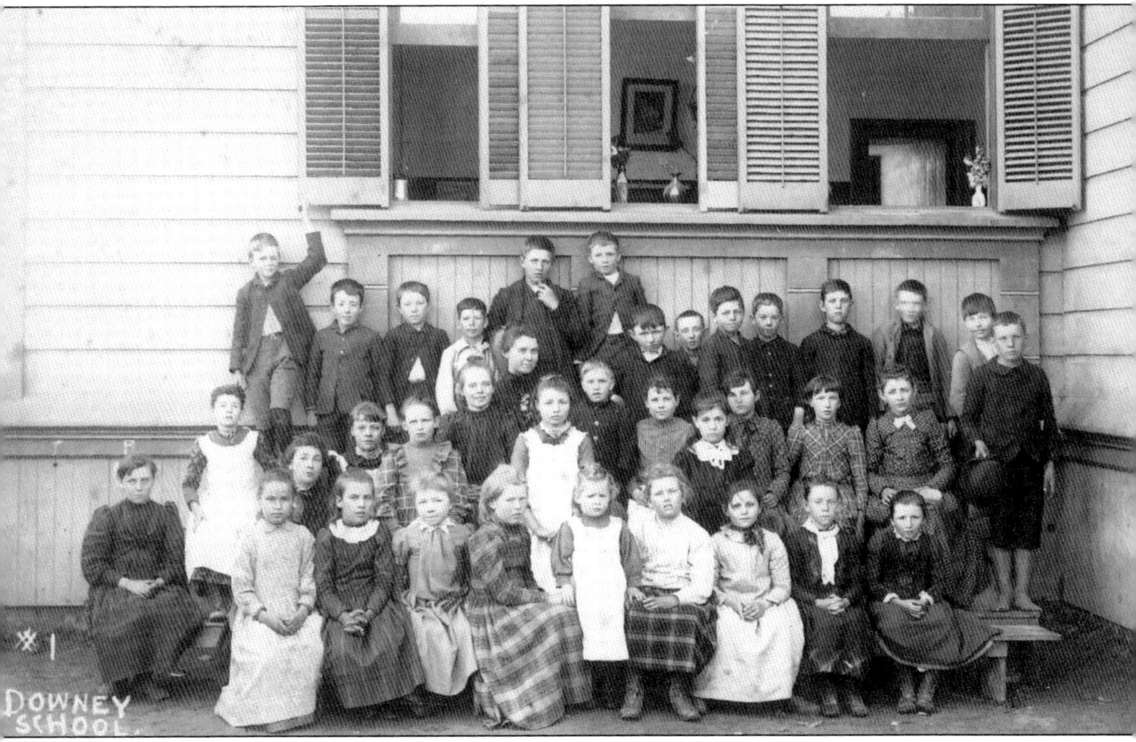

In *History of Downey and Vicinity*, author Easter Bangle Morrison wrote in 1939: "Each generation, no doubt, has said: 'This is the greatest age in the history of man. Surely none greater will ever be,' and yet, looking back in the light of this present day, we know that human intellect hath wrought more superior wonders with each passing decade. Our admiration mounts higher and higher as we realize the wisdom of the Eternal God and the latent potentialities within the human mind, awaiting but the transforming power of circumstances to bring them forth with courage and perseverance." This 1891 photograph of Downey Grammar School shows Mrs. Crawford's class.

One

The Early Years of Downey and Vicinity

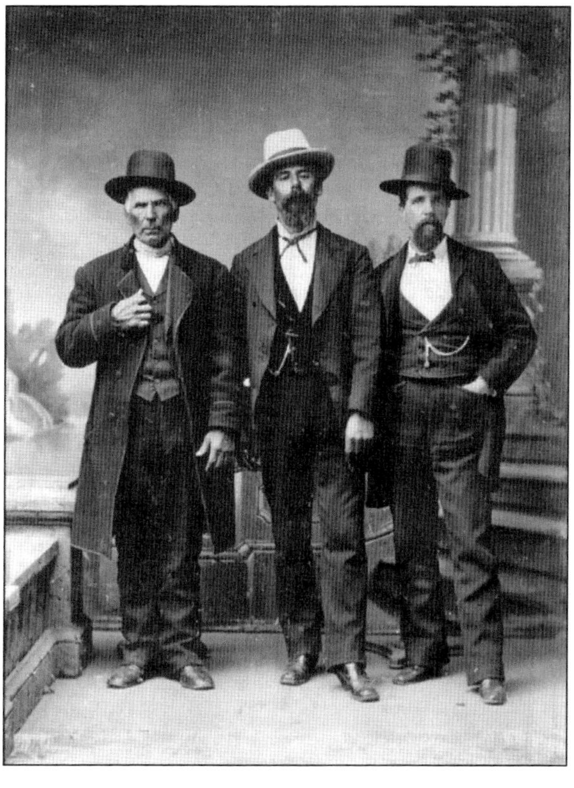

This portrait depicts Jose Ruiz, Gov. John Gately Downey, and Miller of Miller and Lax law firm in Los Angeles. California's seventh governor was also the founder of Downey and was instrumental in building the economic foundations of early Southern California. Downey oversaw the transition from large cattle ranches to small fertile farms that attracted settlers, many from the South. Based in Los Angeles, Downey was involved in banking, agriculture, real estate, transportation, trade, oil, and more.

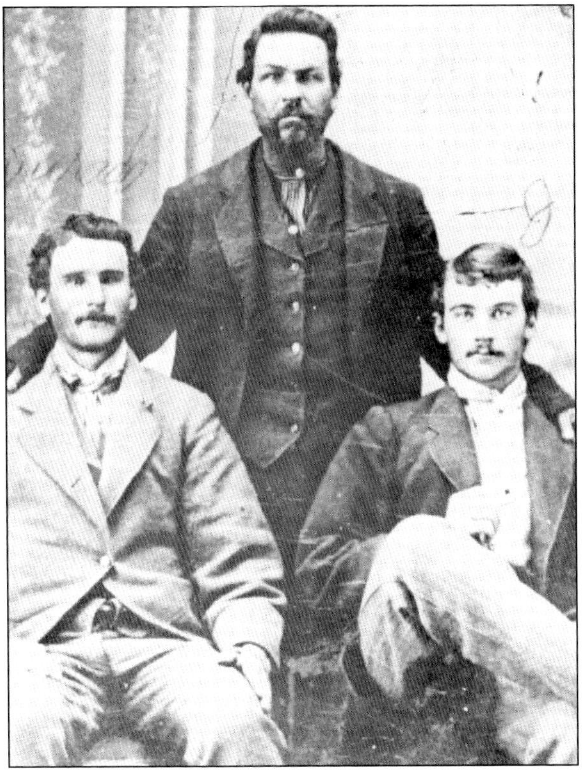

The three young men of Los Nietos at left are James Carpenter (the "J" is for James), Benjamin Carpenter, and the nephew of Lemuel Carpenter, who acquired Santa Gertrudes Rancho from the Nieto heirs in the 1840s. Benjamin Carpenter was a mountain man who had a home in Los Nietos.

Samuel Carpenter purchased the No. 16 brand, below, from the Nieto heirs. The cattle roamed Rancho Santa Gertrudes with this brand, issued in 1839. The No. 17 brand was originally owned by Manual Nieto's widow and was assumed by Lemuel Carpenter in 1855. When McFarland and Downey took control of Rancho Santa Gertrudes, their cattle were herded onto land bearing the brand (No. 18) of Ramon Yorba, which was assumed by James P. McFarland and John Gately Downey on September 18, 1854. The "J" at the top belonged to James Carpenter.

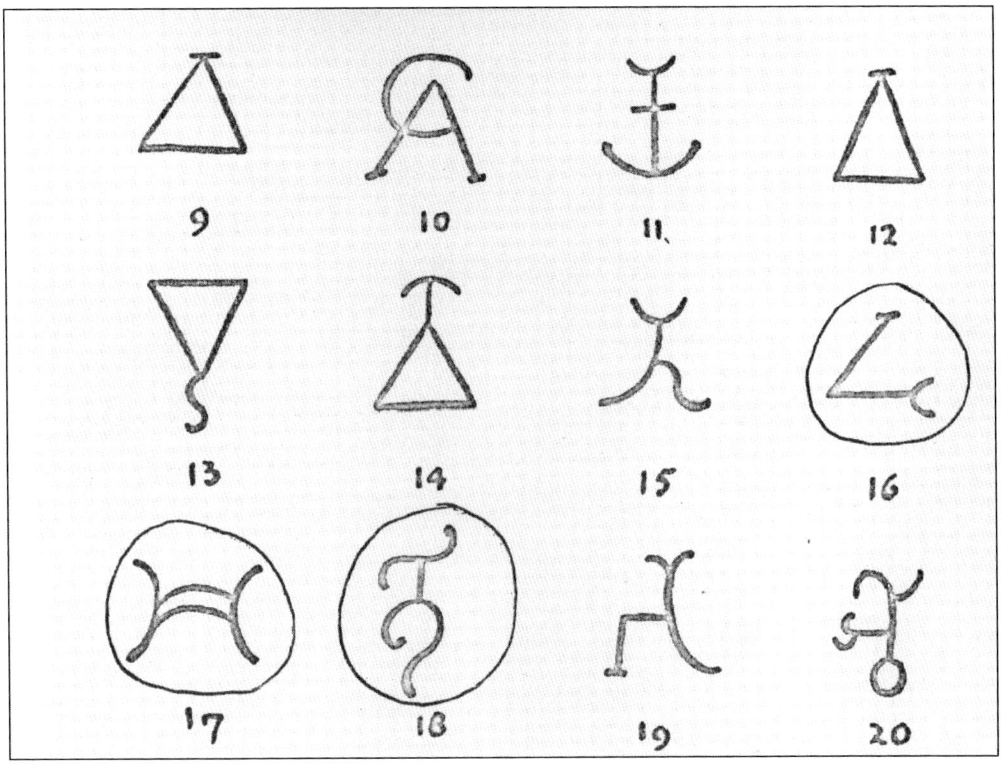

Downey and vicinity were once owned by Lemuel Carpenter, who came to California from Kentucky during the winter of 1832. He founded a soap factory on the bank of the old San Gabriel River. After his first wife, a Native American woman named Espiritu, died in childbirth, Carpenter married Maria de Los Angeles Dominguez. In 1843, he bought Rancho Santa Gertrudes from Maria's aunt. This photograph shows their oldest daughter, Maria Refugio Carpenter.

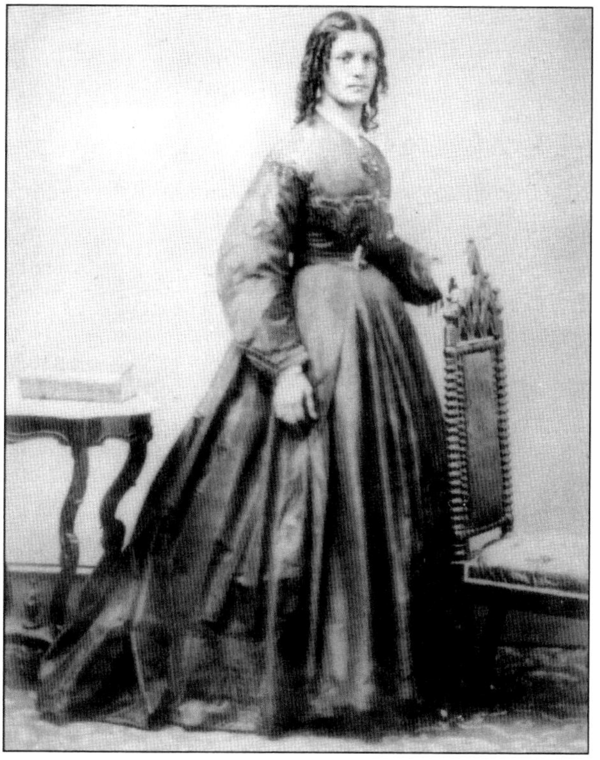

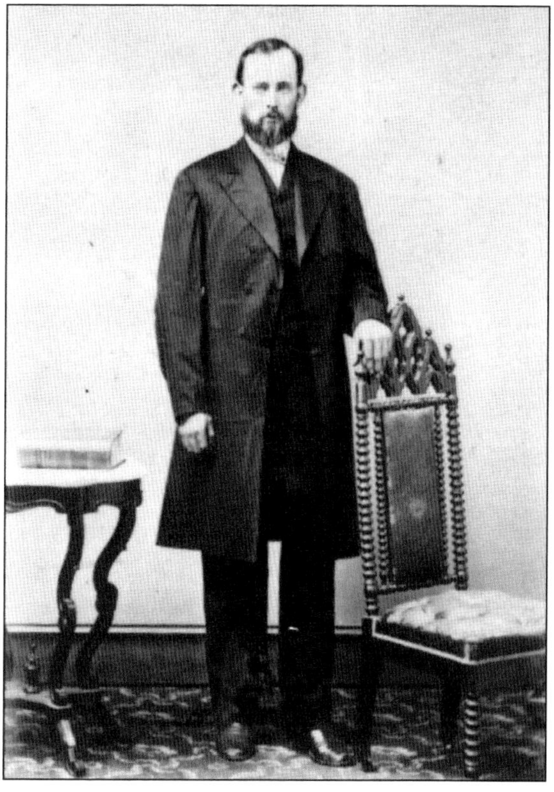

Joseph Edward "Ed" Pleasants and Maria Refugio Carpenter were married on July 15, 1868. Pleasants was the son of James and Lydia Pleasants. After Lydia's death in 1848, James and Joseph set off for the California Gold Rush in 1849. By 1851, they had moved to Pleasant's Valley in Solano County. After moving again in 1858 to William Wolfskill's Rancho Lomas de Santiago in the Santa Ana Mountains, Pleasants became Wolfskill's foreman of the rancho.

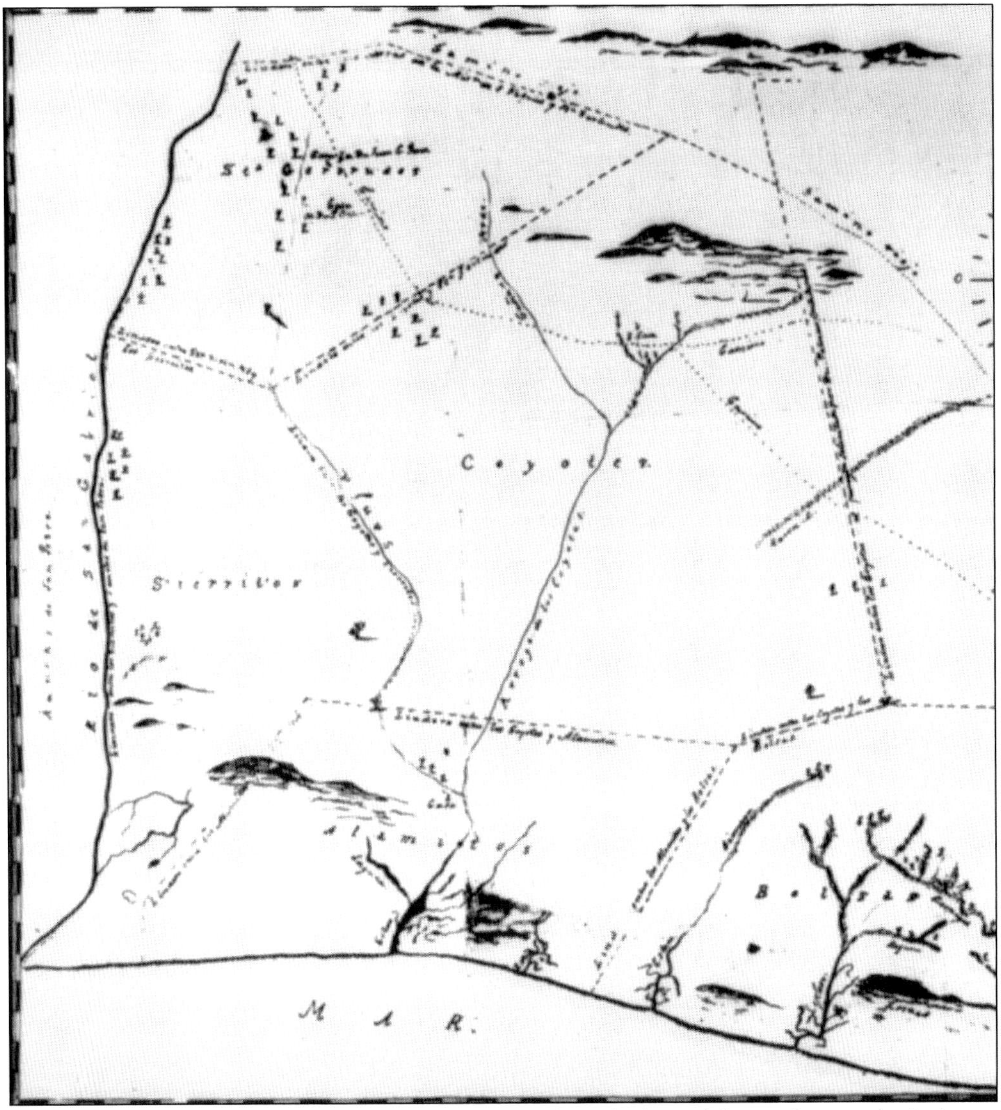

The Nieto Land Grant of 1795 provides an early snapshot of Alta California. Previously the home to peaceful Shoshonean Indians drawn to the fertile coastline of Southern California, this area became the home of California's missions, giant ranchos, and eventually the cities and farms of pioneers heading west to a fertile "paradise" between two rivers. In 1784, Spanish Governor Pedro Vegas divided up much of the land into large grants. One of his loyal soldiers, Manuel Nieto, was granted 300,000 acres comprising all of "the land lying between what is now the Rio Hondo River and the Santa River east and west; and from Mission Highway on the north to the Pacific Ocean on the south." The Mission Highway paralleled today's Whittier Boulevard. By today's standards, the Nieto family land would encompass the cities of Downey, Norwalk, Pico Rivera, Lakewood, Long Beach, Signal Hill, and Huntington Beach. In 1834 the land was divided up among heirs and became six huge ranchos: Los Alamitos, Los Cerritos, Los Bolsos, Palo Altos, and Santa Gertrudes. Enormous herds of cattle and horses roamed the ranges of these lands. Joseph Cota, who was the widow of Manuel's son, Antonio Nieto, inherited much of modern day Downey and Norwalk. Rancho Santa Gertrudes is in the upper left section of the map near the Old San Gabriel River.

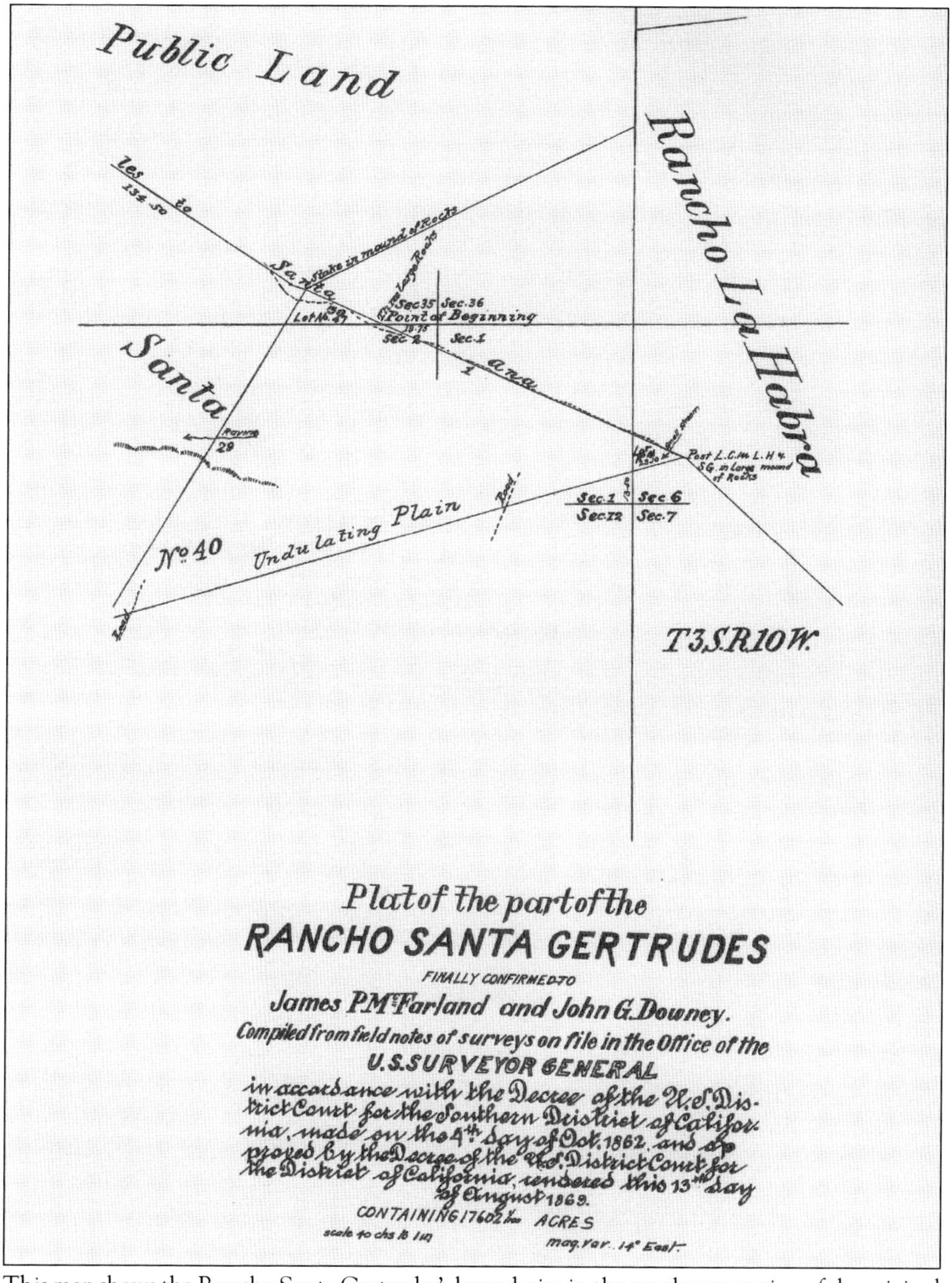

This map shows the Rancho Santa Gertrudes's boundaries in the northwest section of the original Nieto Land Grant. In today's terms, to the west is the Rio Hondo near Whittier Boulevard Crossing. South where the Rio Hondo and the Los Angeles River come together, and eastward to the new San Gabriel River and northeast to La Habra. The northern boundary paralleled the old mission trail back to the Rio Hondo. Lemuel Carpenter had a soap factory on the river bank at Jaboneria and married Josepha Cota Nieto's niece, Maria de Los Angeles Dominguez. Carpenter purchased Rancho Santa Gertrudes in 1843 for $4,000.

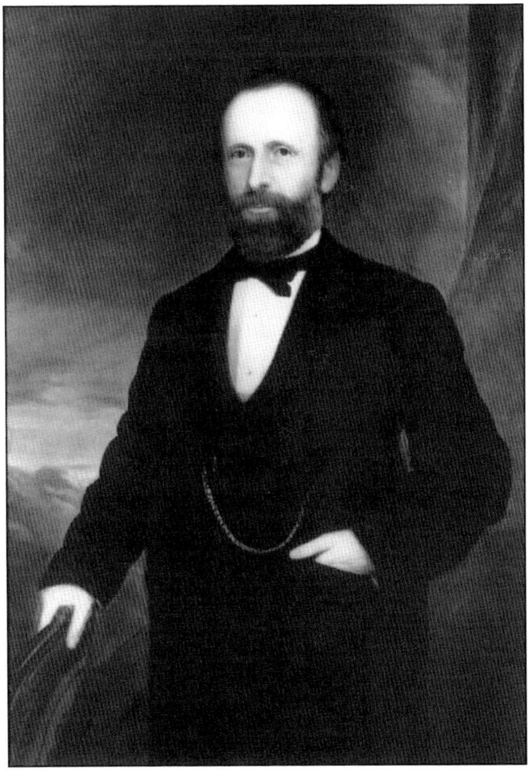

John Gately Downey was born in Roscommon County, Ireland, in 1827. He attended Latin school in Maryland and ended up in Washington, D.C., as a druggist's apprentice. He operated drug stores in three states before coming to California during the Gold Rush. In the early 1850s, Downey moved to the pueblo of Los Angeles where he became an American citizen and married a Californio. Elected to the Los Angeles City Council, he helped found the Sisters of Charity, which provided hospital services and care for orphans. In 1854, Downey purchased 2,400 acres of Rancho San Pedro with Benito Wilson and Phineas Banning. From this property, the Los Angeles Harbor area was created. By 1855, Downey was elected to the state legislature, and in 1859, Downey and his former druggist partner James P. McFarland purchased Lemuel Carpenter's 17,602 acres of Rancho Santa Gertrudes for $60,000 at a sheriff's sale.

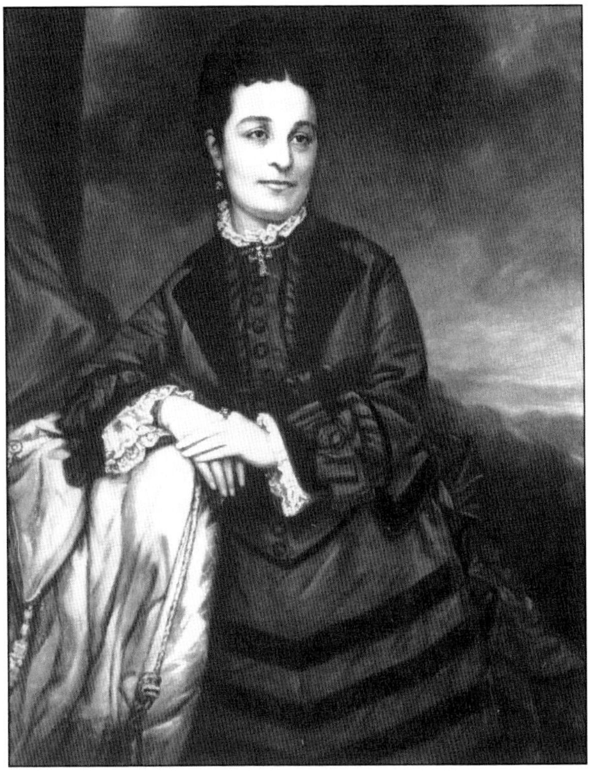

Educated, beautiful, and refined, Maria Guirado moved with her family from Guaymas, Mexico, to Whittier, California, in 1833. In 1852, she married John Downey, who became California's governor in 1860. After Downey left office, he and Maria returned to Los Angeles where Downey helped found both the Farmers and Merchants Bank and the University of Southern California. Maria Downey died in a train accident in the Tehachapi Mountains on January 29, 1883. John Downey survived the crash but suffered a nervous breakdown afterwards, having lost the love of his life.

Maston Duke Crawford was born in North Carolina, migrated to Mississippi, came to California in 1869 via the new transcontinental railroad, and joined the Downey Land Association as John Downey's attorney and agent. Crawford raised a family and built one of his two homes near today's Rio Hondo Country Club, owning most of the land along the river. His other home was on 53 acres near Fifth and New Streets. Many citizens wanted to call the town Crawfordville, but by Judge Crawford's recommendation the name became Downey. Crawford Street was named after M. D. Crawford but was changed in the 1930s to Downey Avenue.

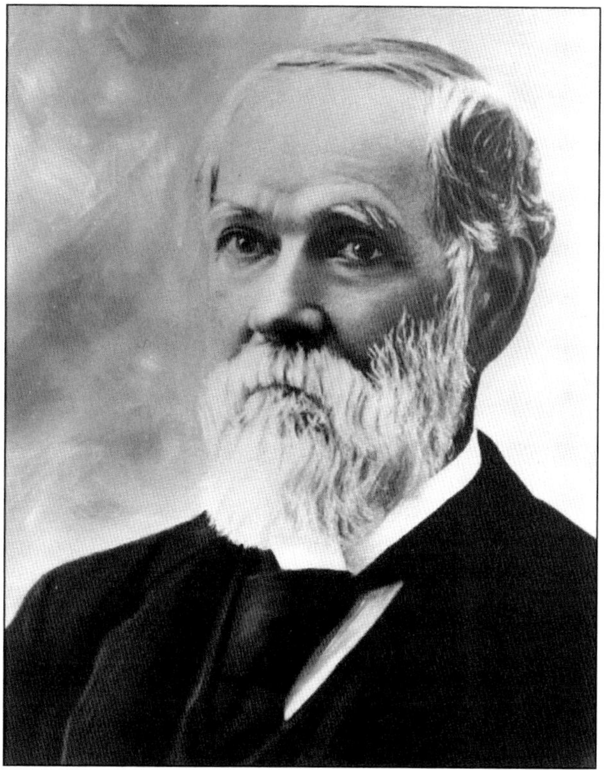

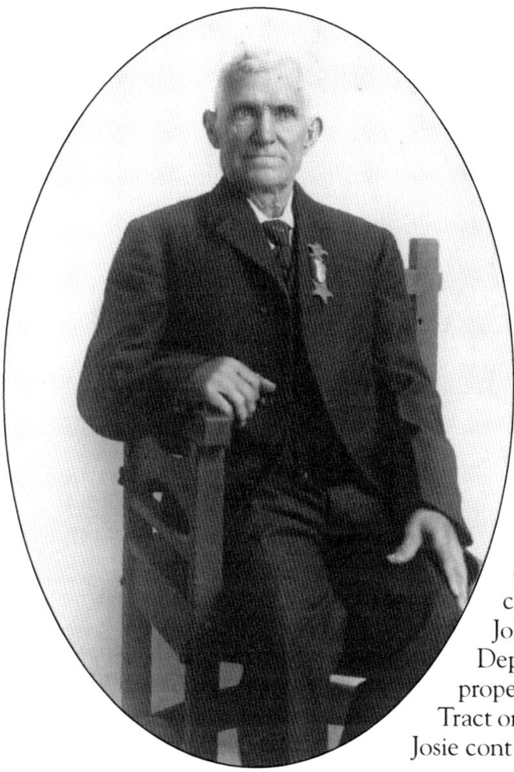

James Stewart was born on March 19, 1835, in Ireland. His wife, Sarah Pullen, was born August 27, 1842, in Missouri. The Stewarts came to Downey in 1873 and raised nine children. Their oldest daughter, Jennie, married John Hansen, a local carpenter at the Downey Depot. James Stewart purchased the first lot of property sold within the Downey Land Association Tract on September, 23, 1873. His daughters Mary and Josie continued to live on the property into the 1940s.

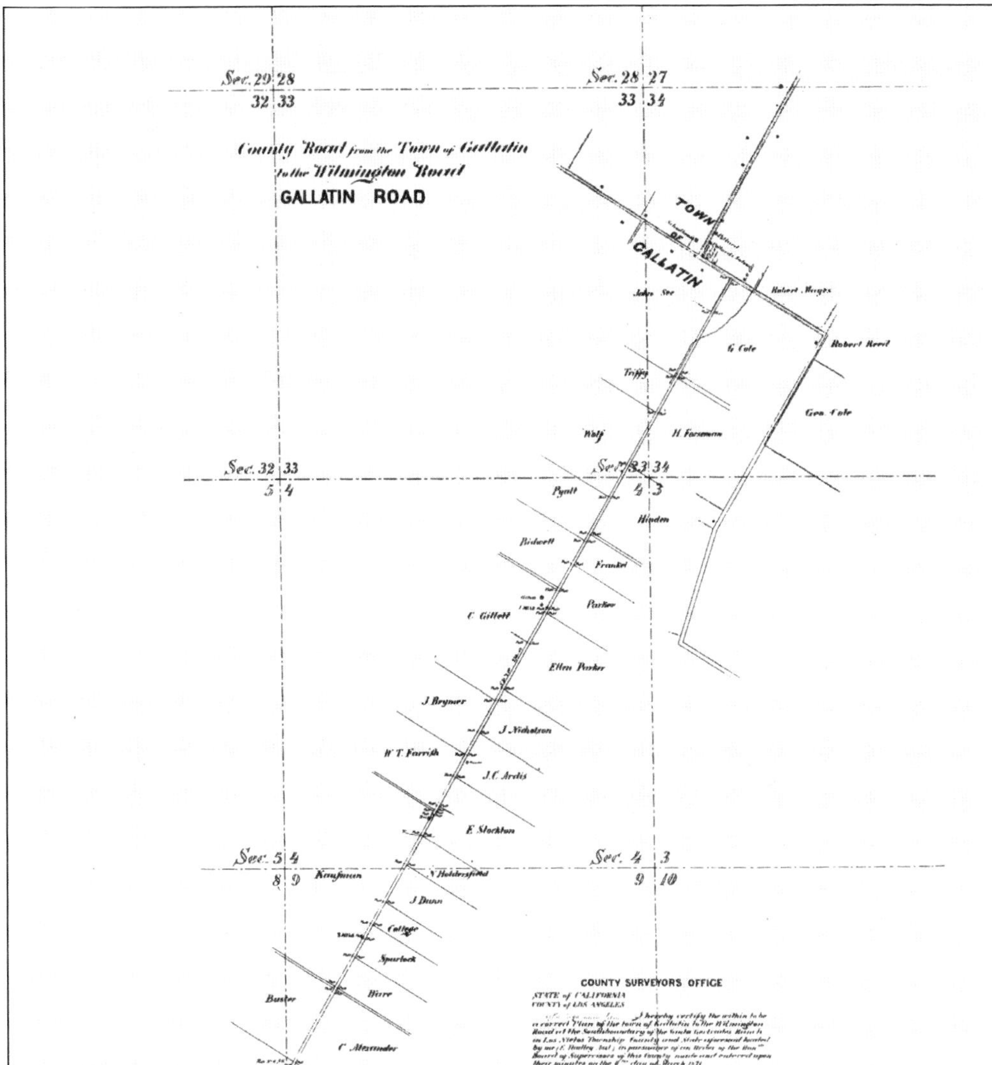

This April 1871 map from the Los Angeles County Surveyor's office shows a grid of North Downey near Gallatin Road. Notice the name "Robert Mayes" in the upper right corner. Mayes was an early Downey landowner with a ranch northeast of Florence Avenue and Lakewood Boulevard. Also shown is the location of the old Gallatin School House. The names listed are those of the early pioneers and landowners central to the growth and development of Gallatin Settlement and eventually Downey City.

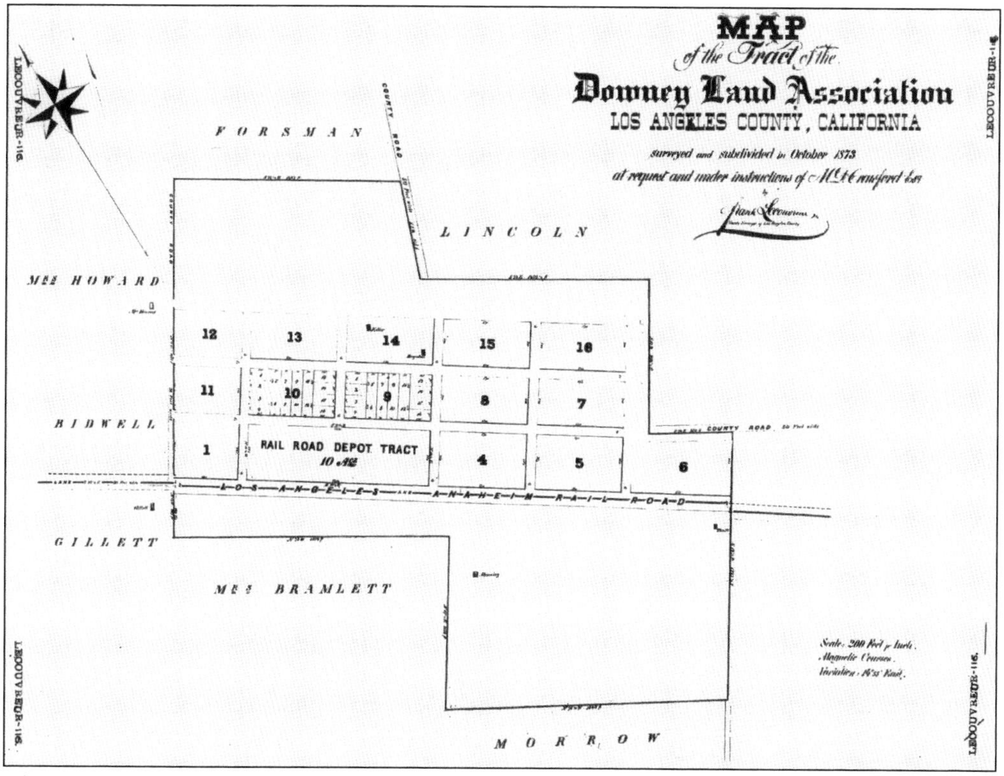

This map was filed on October 13, 1873, by Frank Lecouvreur, Los Angeles County surveyor. This "Tract of the Downey Land Association" became the center of Downey. James Stewart, who worked for the Southern Pacific Railroad, bought the first one-acre plot. His land and home were on the south side of the train station. Soon, merchants from Gallatin and College Settlement followed, and Downey City took shape. By 1874, around the new depot stood a hotel, two churches, three schools, and a newspaper office.

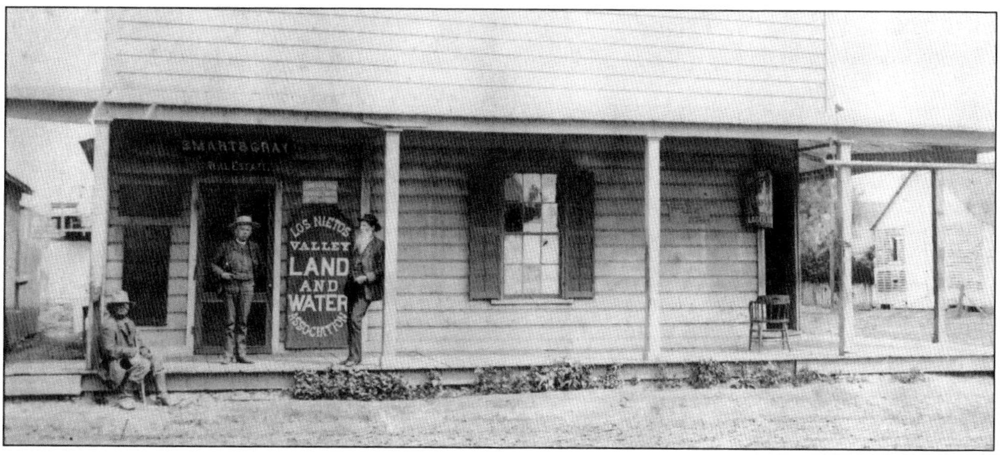

This rare 1890 photograph of the Los Nietos Valley Land and Water Association was taken on the northeast corner of what is today Firestone Boulevard and Downey Avenue. The famous "Indian Joe" sits at left. Harvey Gray stands in the doorway, and the bewhiskered Dave Smart leans on a porch post. Smart and Gray were officers of this real estate venture. Benbrook's saloon is on the corner.

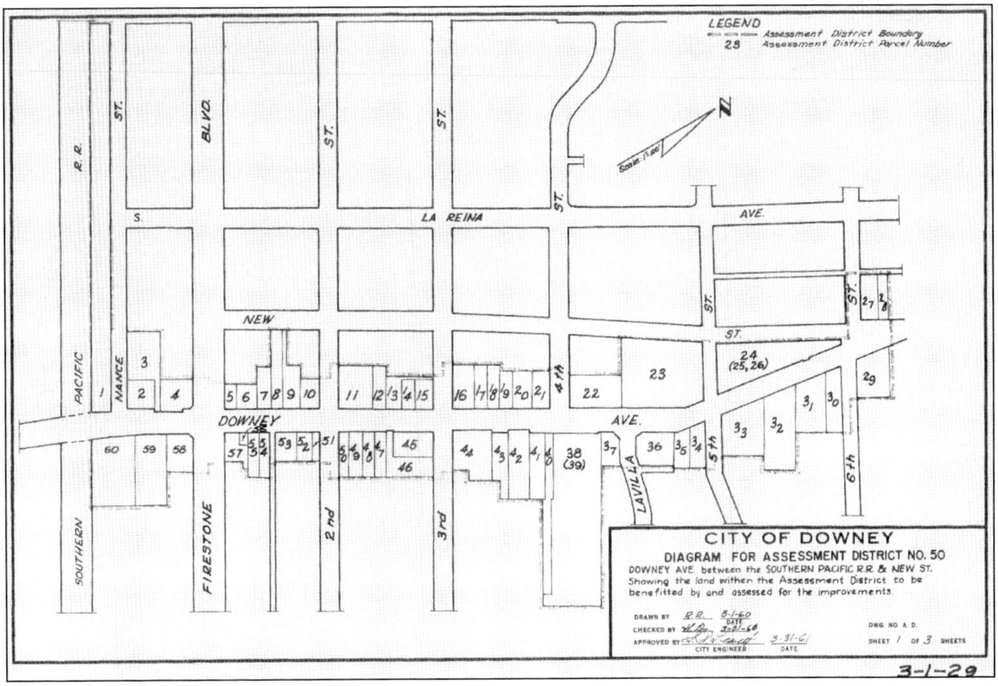

This 1960 City of Downey assessment map shows an extended layout of the original Downey Land Association from the Southern Pacific Railroad tracks to Sixth Street. The original layout was First Street (Firestone) intersected by Venable Street (also known as Depot Street and La Reina Street), Crawford Street (Downey Avenue), and Dolland Street (Dolan Avenue).

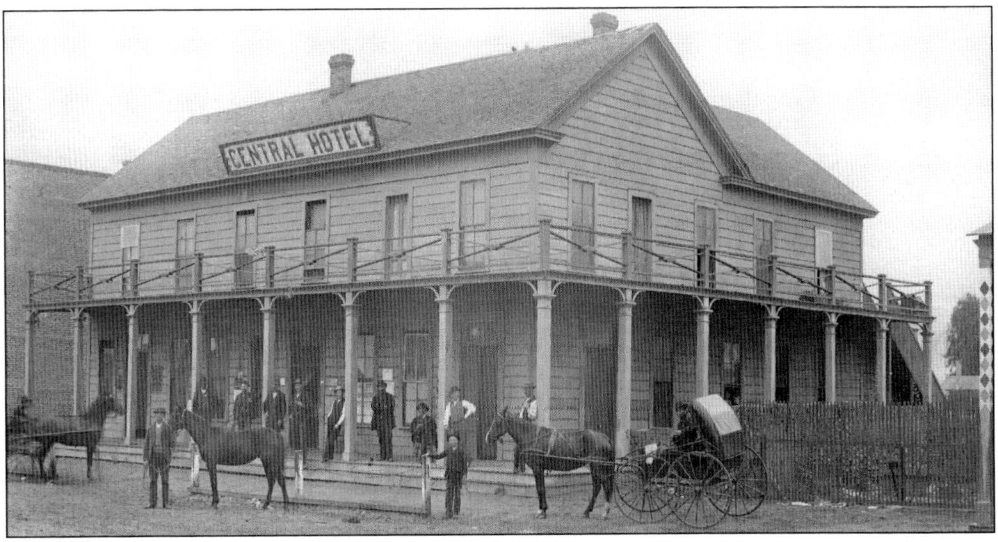

Downey and Crawford built the Central Hotel at Venable (La Reina) and Front (Firestone) Streets. After an 1877 fire, the Central Hotel was moved just north of Jennison and Greenings Merchandise store. Visitors and friends gathered on the hotel's wide veranda. The man holding the colt in this photograph is hotel owner Gene Ruddock, and the man in the buggy is Elbert Pratt Beckwith. Henry Roemer had a barbershop in one corner of the building, and H. S. Redfield operated a jewelry counter in the opposite corner. Ruddock also worked as an apprentice with James C. Rives at the *Downey Signal* newspaper in 1883. Fire destroyed the hotel in November 1900.

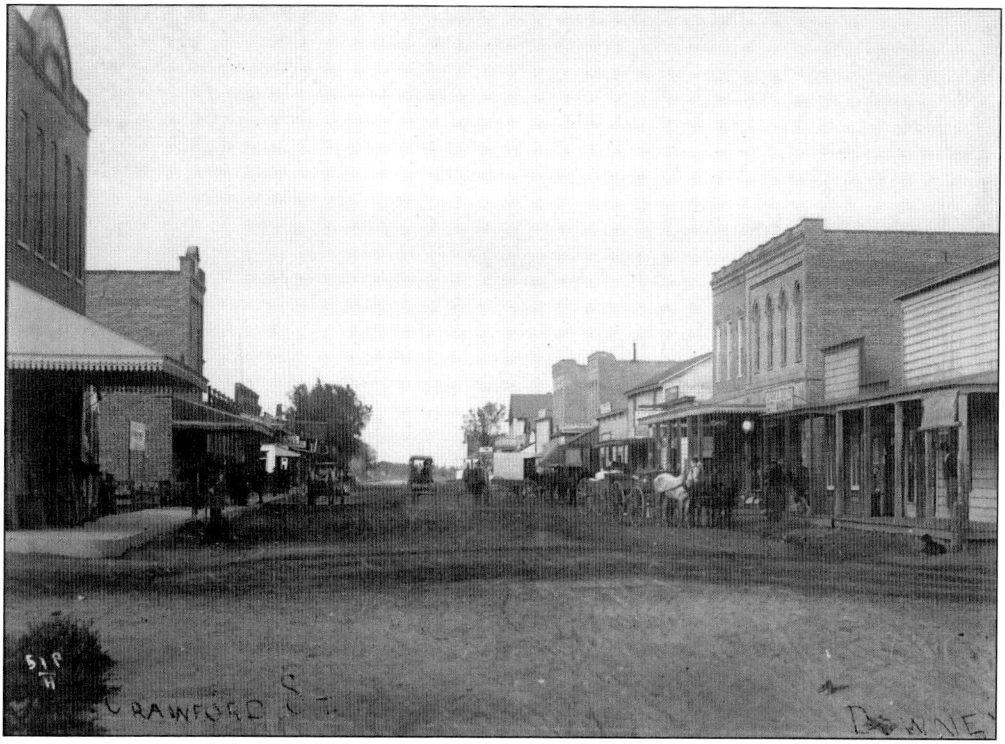

This photograph of Crawford Street from the late 1880s shows that the horse and buggy was essential transportation around the turn of the century in Downey.

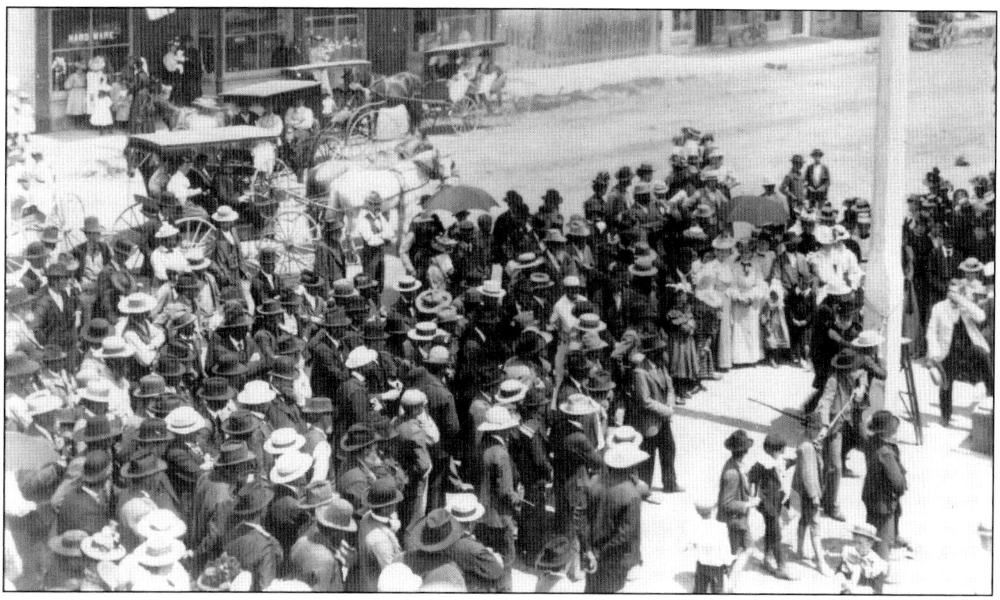

The patriotic 1898 rally above was held on Crawford Street near Second Street and featured the raising and dedication of this flagpole. More than two stories high, the pole remained a meeting spot for many years. William Dickinson's hardware store stands in the background. Downey's first women's club, originally known as the Friday Afternoon Club, was founded that same year.

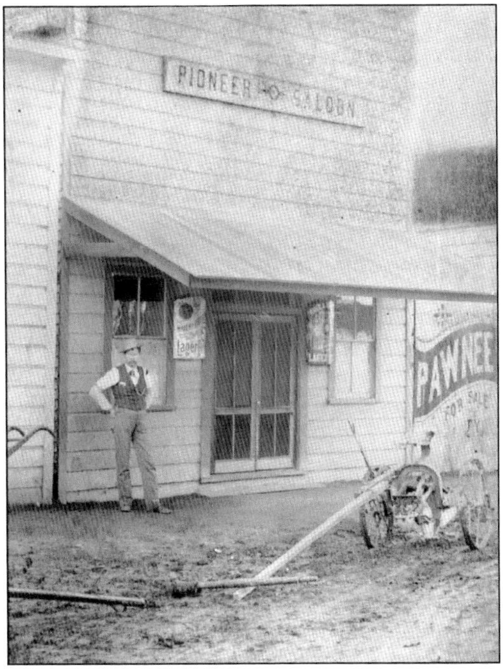

Lou Pollard's Pioneer Saloon, left, stood on the east side of Crawford Street between the alley and Second Street. Pollard moved his business from Gallatin to Downey Lot 2, Block 8, on September 1, 1874. He later sold the saloon, locally called "The Sting-ray," to George Click. Pollard also ran a livery stable next to the saloon. J. A. Mitrovitch and Dave Smart also ran Downey saloons.

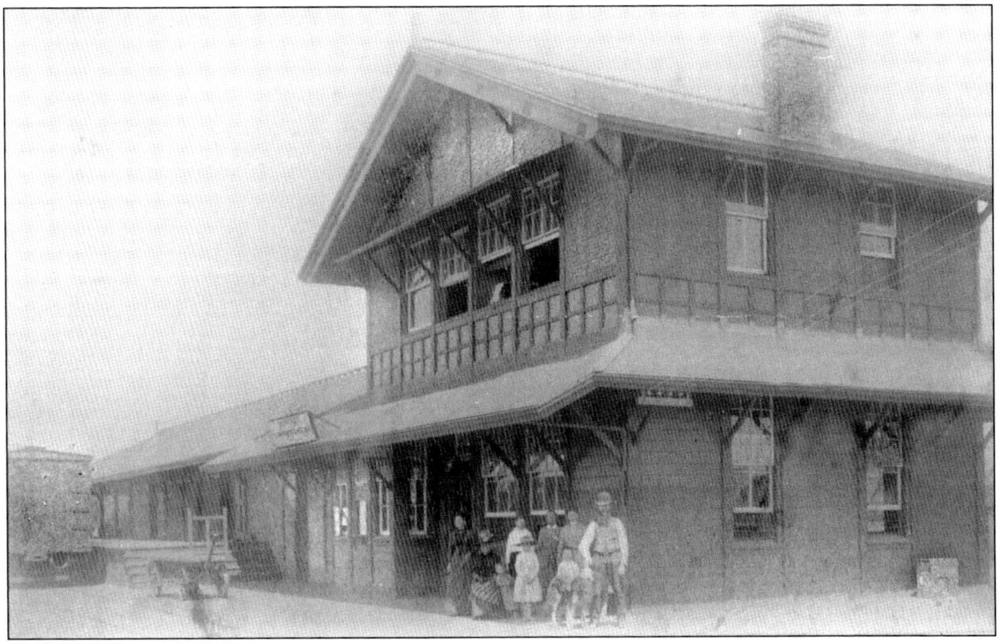

John Kirby Banks (right) came to Downey from Texas. He first settled in College Settlement, owning an apothecary shop selling pills and patent medicines. As the railroad came to Downey, Banks, like other merchants, moved closer to the first depot. He built one of the first homes on Third and New Streets near the depot. Banks served as stationmaster for over 20 years. He and his wife Clementine had five children. On the left is Bell Cheney, Clementine's sister, her mother, and Mrs. Anderson, John Banks's sister. Banks is holding the family dog, Bango. The depot was on today's La Reina Street, which was formerly called Venable Street after Judge J. W. Venable, and, for a time, Depot Street.

John and Clementine Banks's daughters are shown here, from left to right: Willie Amanda Banks, Olivia "Ole" Banks (d. 1882), Belle Banks, Augusta Romayne Banks, and Lizzie Harter Banks. Lizzie Harter lived a long life (1886–1985) along with her sister Belle (1879–1971). Clementine was converted by Brother Spurlock of a Los Nietos church. She and John were married by the minister on January 8, 1873. Clementine, born January 9, 1857, died in 1888, at 31 years of age.

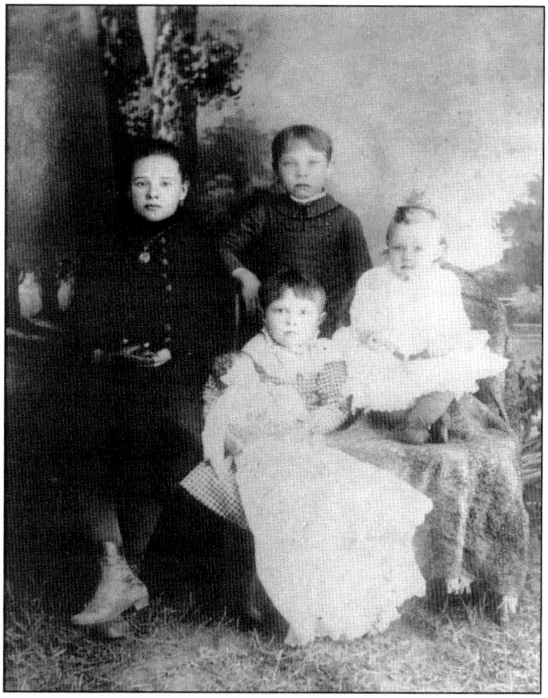

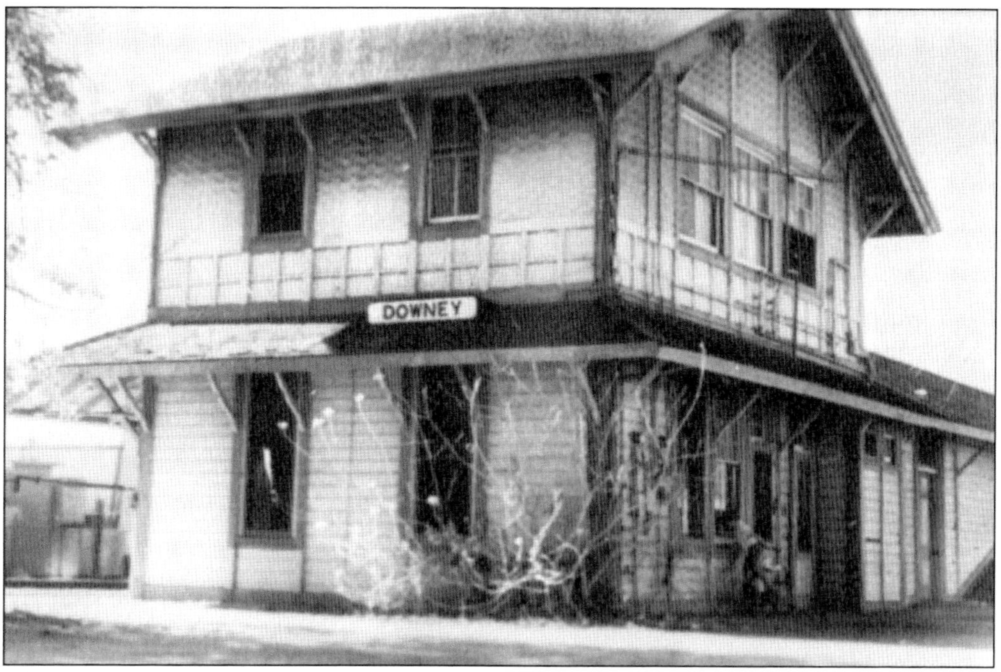

The original 1874 Southern Pacific depot burned down, and in 1888 a Mr. Knox built this replacement for a total cost of $12,000. In the new depot's first six months of service, the depot clerks sold 11,790 passenger tickets. Exports during the same period were 7,991,105 pounds. This 1960s picture shows a Downey boy on his Stingray bicycle, peering into a depot window. The train to Los Angeles, the "Dinky," cost 15¢ and only took 20 minutes. Passenger train service was discontinued in the 1920s, and the depot was torn down in the 1960s.

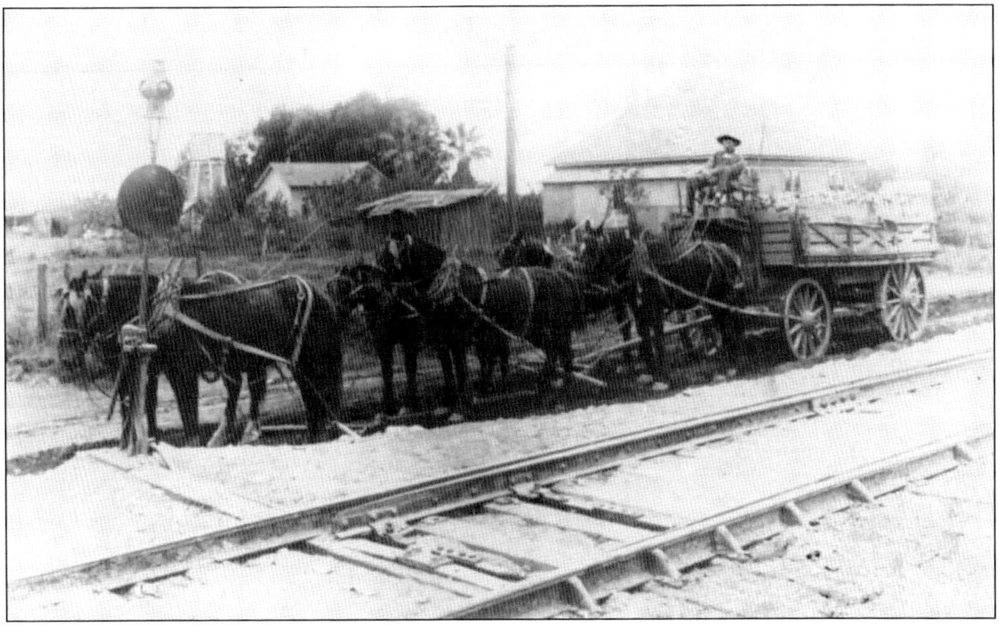

This photograph features a wagon load of sugar beets on the way to the railhead and thus to market. Ed C. Lewis, son of local pioneer Ed. W. Lewis, owned land from Woodruff to Clark Streets, and from Imperial Highway to Foster Bridge Road. Over the years, the Lewises farmed sugar beets, corn, alfalfa, walnuts, and Klondike strawberries. In 1915, Ed C. developed 25 acres on Foster Road and Ardis Street, establishing the Golden Gate Ranch. He served eight years on the Alameda School District Board.

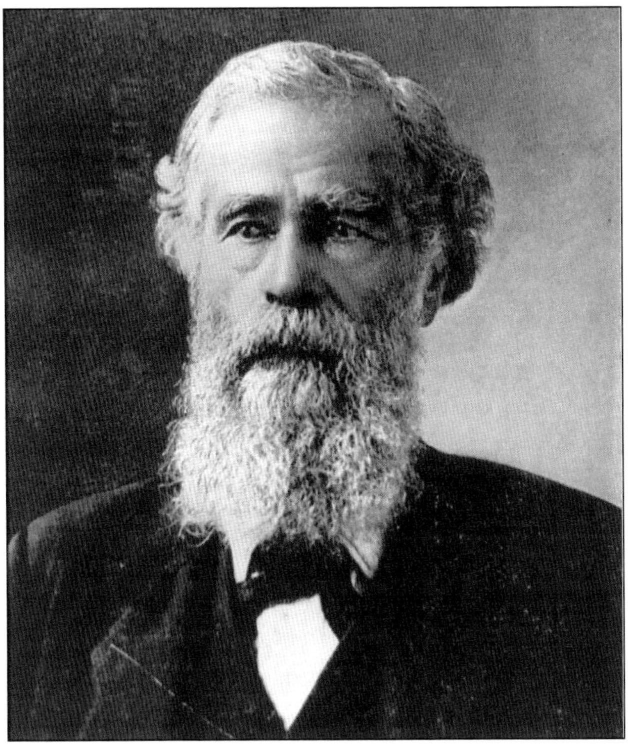

On April 22, 1865, former governor John Downey issued the first land grant of his Rancho Santa Gertrudes to Joseph Hartley Burke, who had obtained his Downey property in a trade with ex-Governor Downey for some land in Los Angeles on Main Street near Fourth Street, where Burke had operated a wagon shop. The Burke home was on Rives Avenue south of Florence Avenue, near what is now Irwingrove Street. The property bordered Florence Avenue and extended south to a point between Fourth Place and Third Street, was bounded on the east by Rives Avenue, and on the west by Old River School Road. Downey reportedly said to Burke, "Go and pick what you want and come and let me know where it is located."

This report card belonging to young Martha Cornelia "Judie" McKellar (sometimes spelled McKeller) was issued in May 1875 by the Silver School District. Silver School in Downey was so named because when one looked across the river from the west either the water or the willows looked like sheets of silver. The first teacher was Miss Branson, who lived with a Mr. and Mrs. J. H. Burke. The school was near the corner of Paramount Street and Florence Avenue, on land donated by Allen Neighbors, whose nearby ranch was along Tweedy Lane. Judie's father was Daniel Henderson McKellar, who raised a large family in Downey. Sisters "Judie" and Josephine McKellar grew up to become Downey teachers. "Miss Judie" lived in Downey from 1870 to her death in 1961 at age 105.

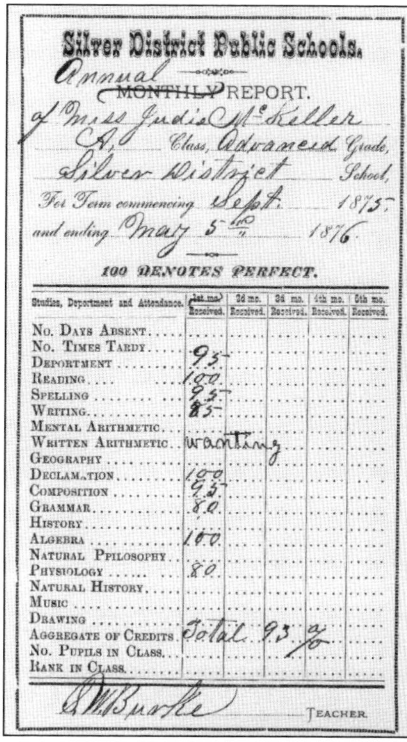

Silver District Public Schools.

Annual ~~MONTHLY~~ REPORT.

of Miss Judie McKeller
A, Class, Advanced Grade,
Silver District School,
For Term commencing Sept. 1875
and ending May 5th 1876.

100 DENOTES PERFECT.

Studies, Deportment and Attendance.	~~1st mo.~~ Received.	2d mo. Received.	3d mo. Received.	4th mo. Received.	5th mo. Received.
No. Days Absent					
No. Times Tardy					
Deportment	95				
Reading	100				
Spelling	95				
Writing	85				
Mental Arithmetic					
Written Arithmetic	wanting				
Geography					
Declamation	100				
Composition	95				
Grammar	80				
History					
Algebra	100				
Natural Ppilosophy					
Physiology	80				
Natural History					
Music					
Drawing					
Aggregate of Credits	Total 93 %				
No. Pupils in Class					
Rank in Class					

O. W. Burke Teacher

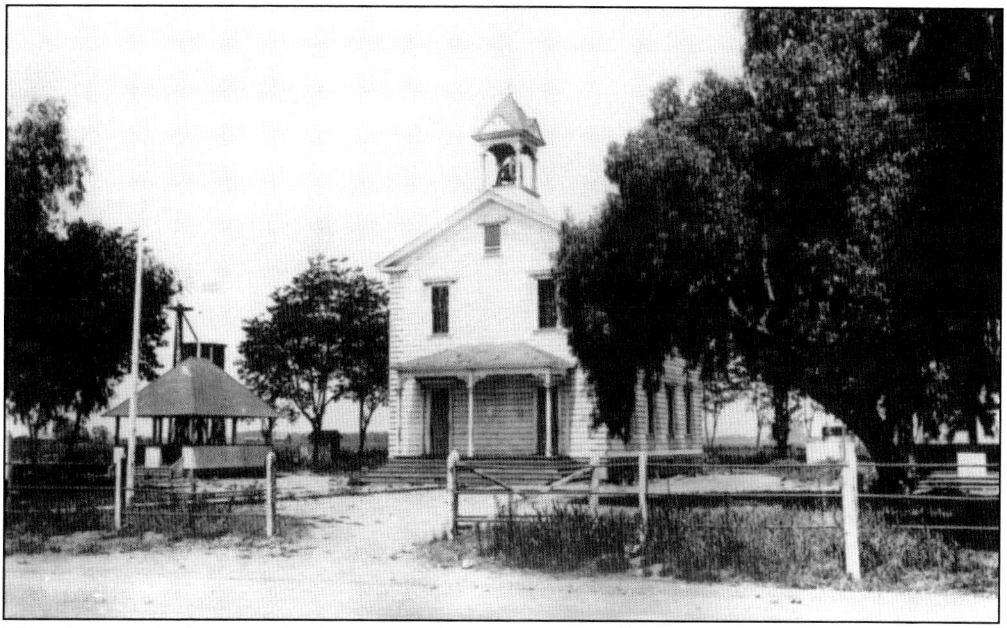

This photograph shows the Gallatin schoolhouse in 1906. A farming community made up of small country homes with lean-to front porches and kitchens, like College Settlement to the south, Gallatin had its own local school, stores, butcher, blacksmith, livery, town hall, boardinghouse, and saloons. By 1913, the old schoolhouse was torn down; it was replaced by a tile-and-stucco building in 1915. After the 1933 earthquake, this second Gallatin Elementary was condemned and a new school built in 1936.

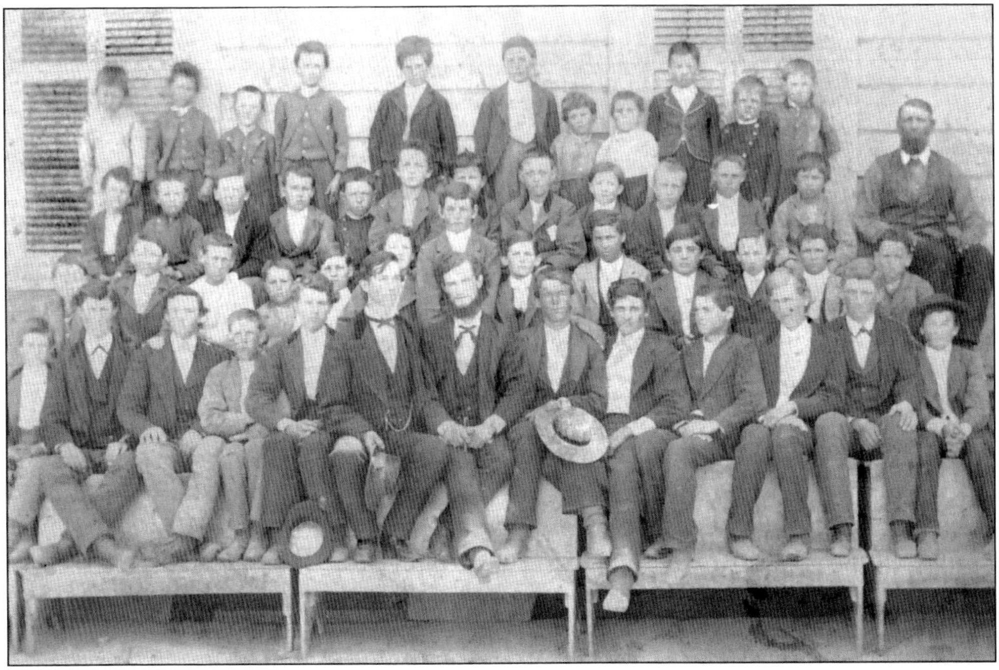

The first Downey school was on the northwest corner of Florence Avenue and Tweedy Lane. This 1874 photograph shows the boys of Gallatin School, of the Silver School District, the 11th district in Los Angeles County, covering Los Nietos Township, which became Downey and vicinity. Joseph Burke sponsored the building of what became Gallatin School on October 21, 1871.

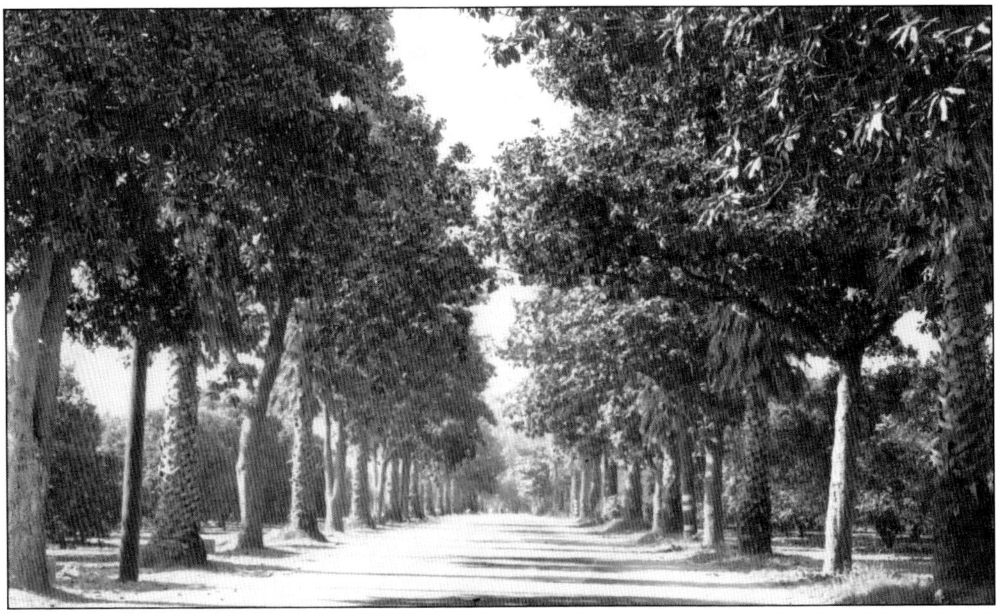

Tweedy Lane is shown here around 1913 with its trademark palm trees, bordered by miles of orange groves. Named for the large pioneering Tweedy family, this road later became known as Telegraph–Jaboneria Road. It connected Telegraph Road with Carpenter's ranch and Carpenter's *jaboneria* (soap factory). Upon arriving in Southern California, former South Carolinian Allen Neighbors raised a large family on Tweedy Lane close to Florence Avenue (Easy Street).

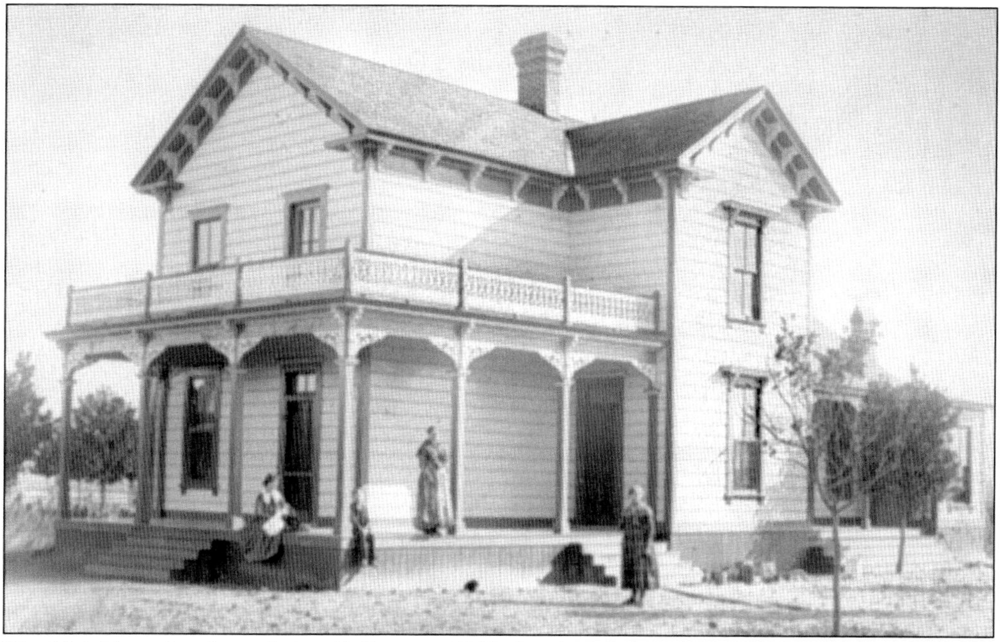

The Neighbors family settled in Gallatin in 1865. South Carolina–born Allen Neighbors was one of the earliest pioneers in this area of north Downey. He gave to his community and donated land and materials to build Gallatin School. The Neighborses owned about 50 acres, of which 20 were planted with walnuts. They built their home on Tweedy Lane near Florence Avenue. Neighbors and his first wife Pricilla Burrow had three children: Celia Cheney, Sara Fuquay, and Nancy Rose. His second wife, Elizabeth McCann of Tennessee, bore seven more

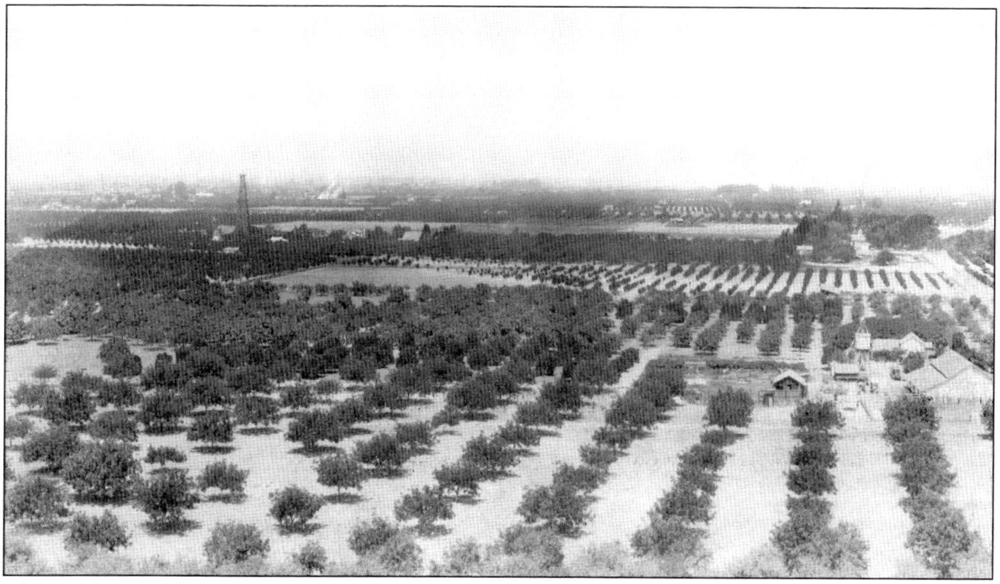

This is the North Downey ranch of William H. Morrow. Morrow, from Missouri, was in the well-boring business. He married Margaret Brookshire, the daughter of farmer James Brookshire, who lived near current-day Brookshire Avenue and Cherokee Drive. Their son, William Jr., operated a livery.

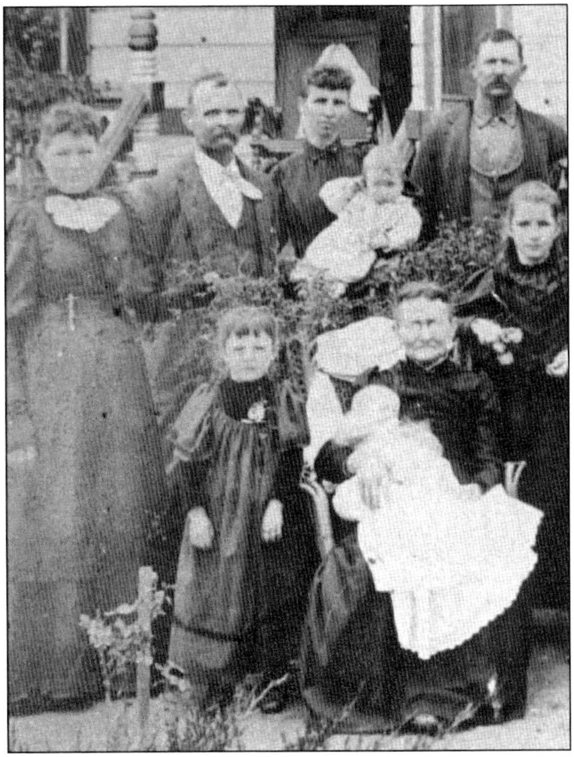

James Brookshire built his Downey home in the 1890s. Brookshire Avenue, named for the family, was originally called Church Street because of the Nazarene church and another church nearby. For many years, Church Street ran north to the southern edge of the Ball ranch. Family members pictured in this photograph are, from left to right: (first row) young Sarah B. Leffingwell (standing), and three unidentified people; (second row) Margaret Brookshire Morrow, James Brookshire, Emma Hamner Brookshire holding an unidentified baby, and an unidentified man.

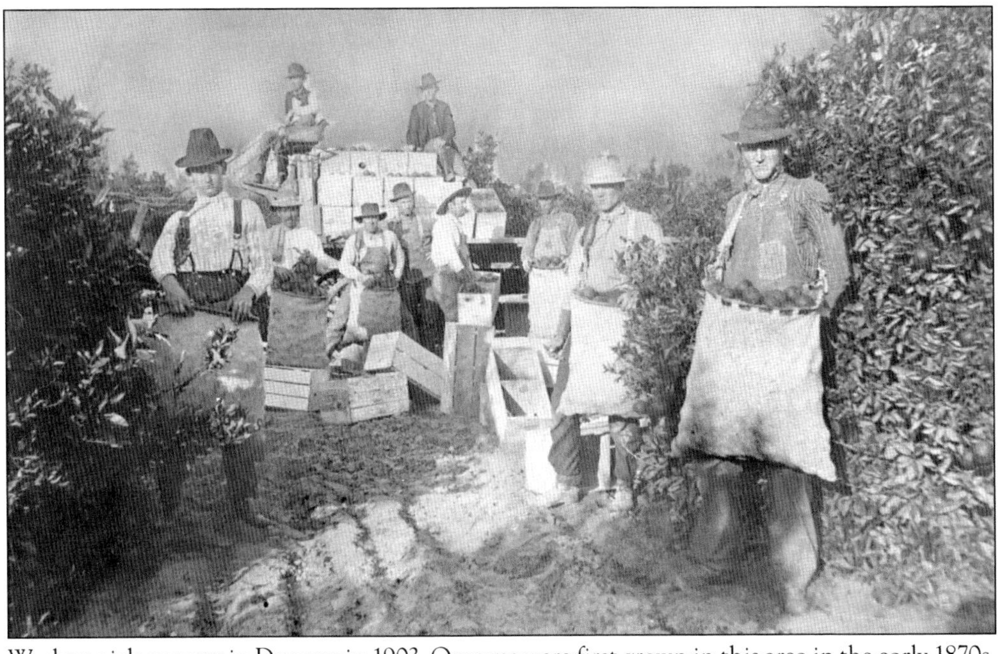

Workers pick oranges in Downey in 1903. Oranges were first grown in this area in the early 1870s. Naval oranges were planted in the 1880s. Valencia oranges were so successful that Downey soon became a citrus center. Other crops were corn, castor beans, barley, potatoes, sugar beets, and English walnuts. In 1879, the Downey depot shipped 7,941,825 pounds in produce. By 1890, North Downey was covered in citrus orchards.

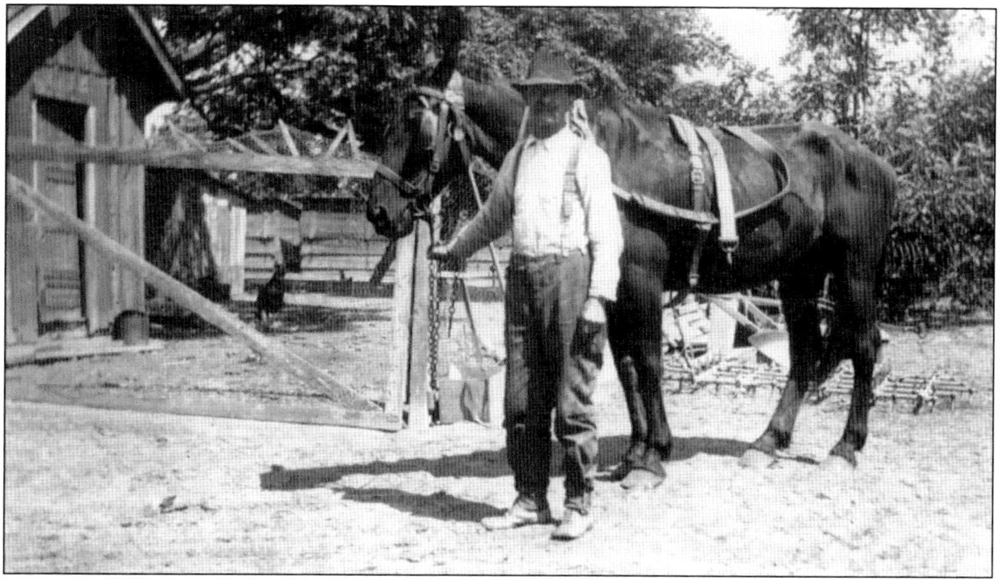

In 1852, the Mayes family trekked by wagon from Hopkinsville, Kentucky, to Lexington, California (today's El Monte). Robert H. Mayes soon married Mahalia Moffett of Arkansas. In 1864, when John Downey and James McFarland subdivided Rancho Santa Gertrudes, Robert Mayes bought property on Florence Avenue between Sanford-Bridge Road and Lakewood Boulevard. Robert S. Mayes, son of Robert Henry Mayes, is pictured here on his ranch on Florence Avenue. Robert S. Mayes attended the Southern Pacific College on Fourth and New Streets. He was later a director for the Downey Cooperative Creamery, and raised three daughters, Mabel, Agnes, and Burnice.

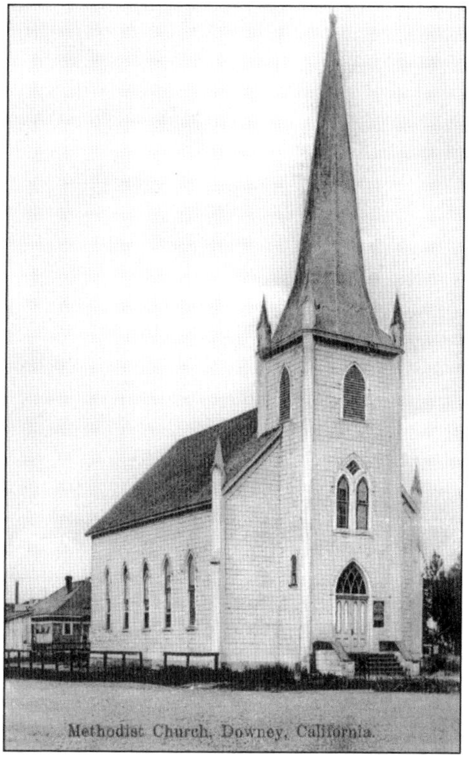

The First Methodist Church of Downey stood on the west side of College Avenue (Paramount Boulevard) near Orange and Alameda Streets. In April 1869, Reverend J. C. Ardis founded the Los Nietos Collegiate Institute—the beginnings of College Settlement. Located on the southeast corner near Orange Street, it was one of the first Protestant Colleges in Southern California. W. H. Steel donated land for the church, and parish members donated labor to complete the building in December 1877. The 110-foot steeple was topped with a massive golden hand, whose forefinger pointed toward the heavens.

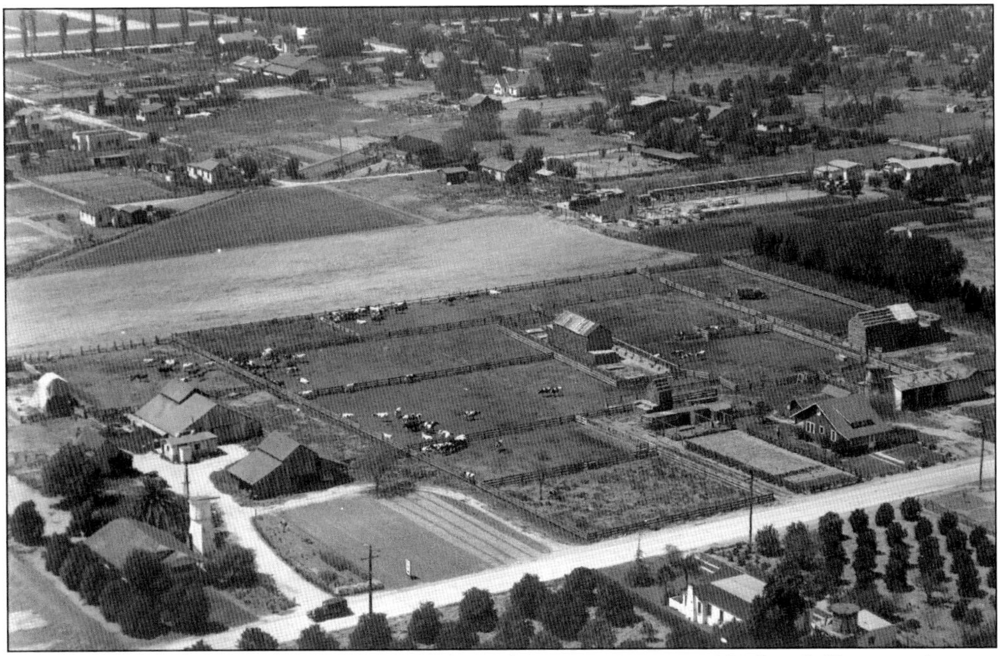

College Settlement is pictured in 1929, with Neal Moore's Dairy at 1033 South Downey Avenue and Donavan Street. The view looks northwest towards Paramount Boulevard (palm trees) and Orange Street. In the upper right, a large bare oak tree stands at the corner of Orange Street before Orizaba Avenue. In 1929, Orizaba Street (south) stopped and turned right to Conrad Street toward the north end of St. Raymond's Church at Paramount and Quoit Street. The area in the upper right of the picture was the center of College Settlement.

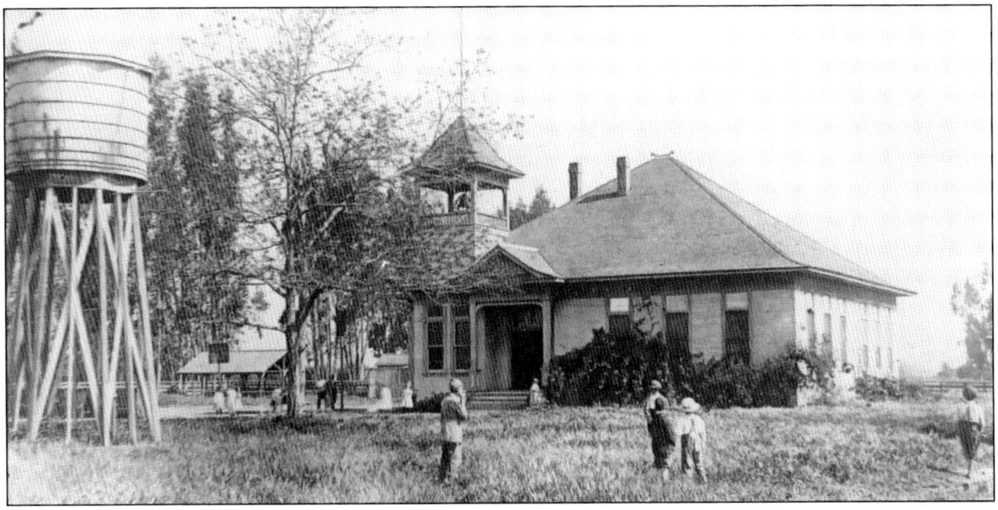

Alameda in 1869 was part of the southern section of the Silver School District. The original school met in a cabin on the southwest corner of John Dolland's property near Imperial Highway. The school was called Sandridge School until strong Santa Ana winds blew it down. On December 28, 1877, a new school was built on land secured by William Steel. In 1919, this second building was lost in a fire, and a brick building replaced it. The Alameda School had only two teachers until 1921. E. W. Ward served as the principal from 1923 to 1929. By 1937, the school employed six teachers, including Lynn Pace, Ethel Donaldson, and Elsie Vrooman.

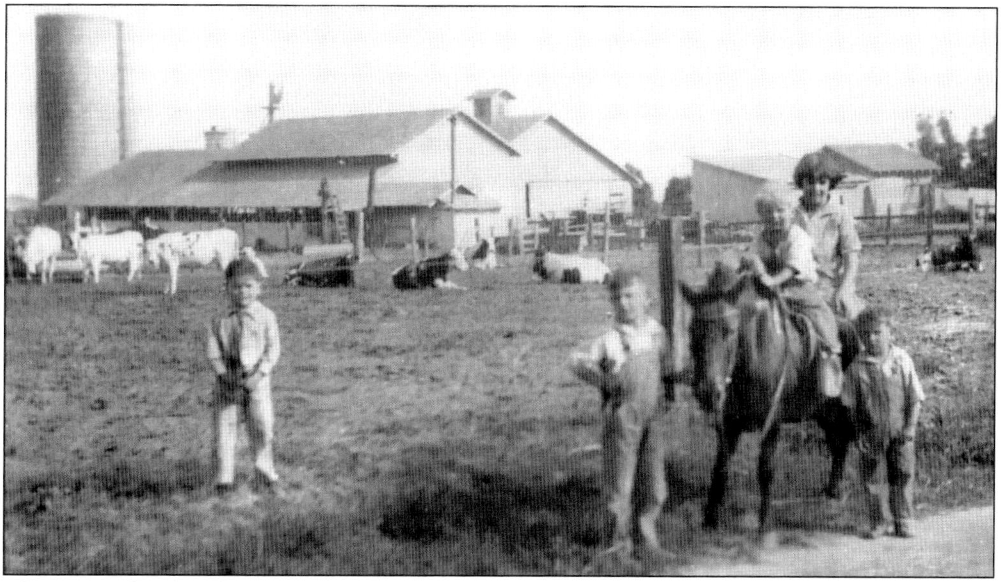

The Mussachia family farm near Lakewood and Stewart and Gray Road covered over 40 acres. Vultee Aircraft purchased that land and the historic old homestead was moved just west to Stewart and Gray Road. The Mussachias arrived in 1885. Son Tony Mussachia and his wife Anna had four children: Frank, Carl, Anthony, and Anne Marie. All of the kids went to Downey High. Tony himself graduated from Old River School in 1906.

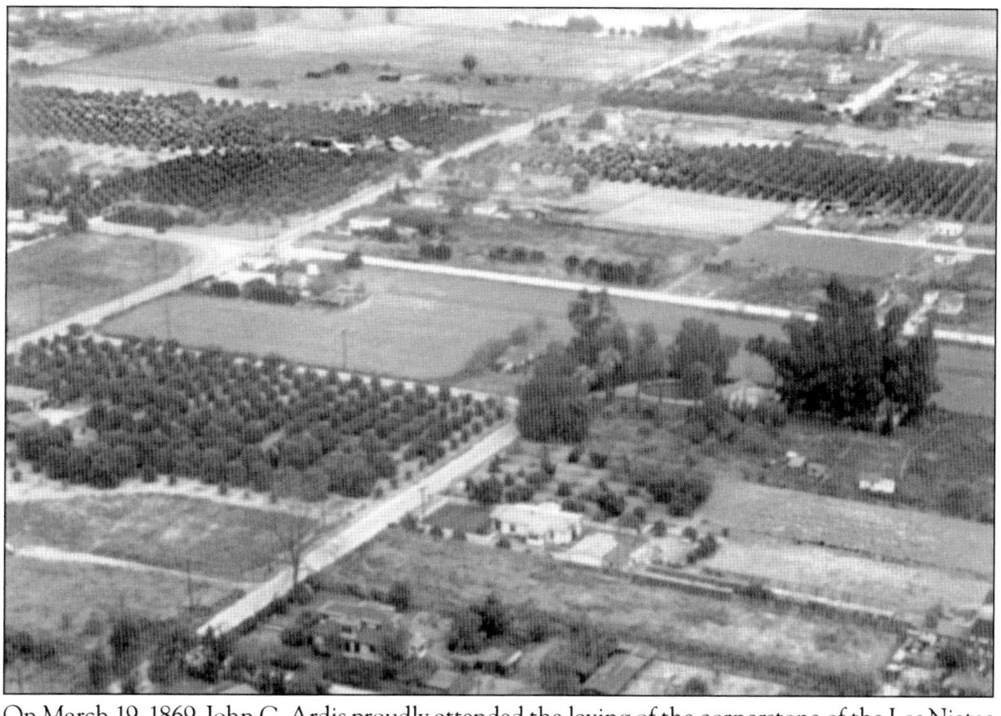

On March 19, 1869, John C. Ardis proudly attended the laying of the cornerstone of the Los Nietos Collegiate Institute on Alameda Street east of Paramount Boulevard. Orange Street runs up the center of the picture, curving left into Caladre Avenue. At the top left of this 1941 photograph is Downey Avenue crossing Alameda Street.

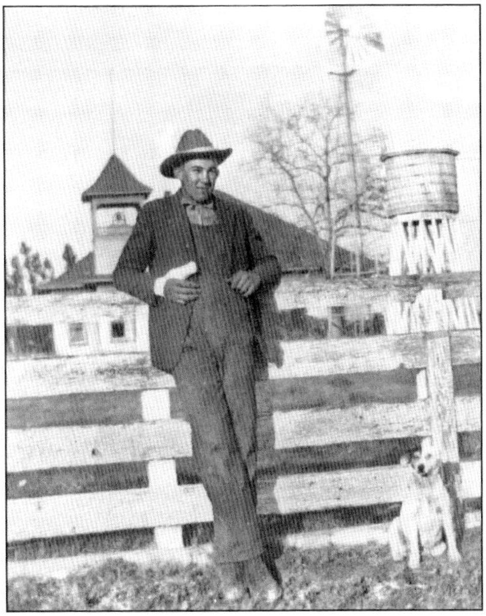

Ernest "Pete" Bohme is seen in 1918 in front of the old Alameda School. A lifelong Downey resident, Pete was the son of Frank Bohme, who came to Downey in 1891 from Ventura. Pete's older brothers were Frank, William, and Joseph. The family lived where Rio Hondo Country Club is today, near old River School Road. The Bohme family farmed until the housing boom hit after World War II. Born on August 18, 1903, Pete died on March 9, 1997, in his native Downey.

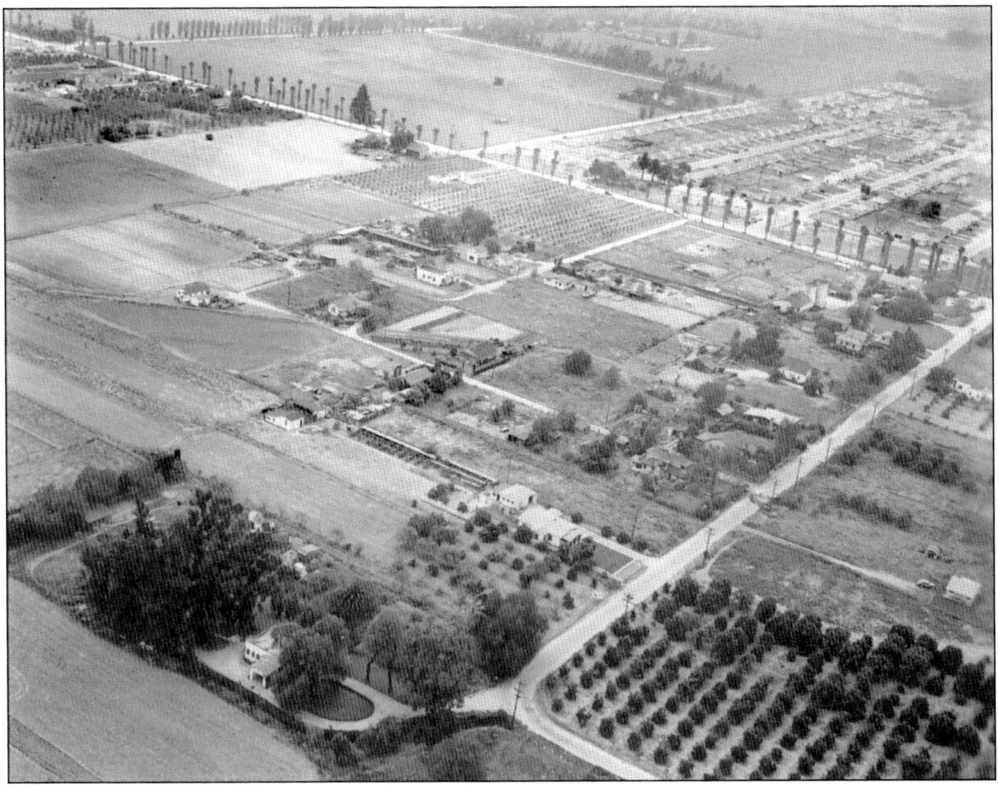

This 1941 aerial view of College Settlement, taken from above the intersection of Downey Avenue and Alameda Street, shows Orange Street curving from Caladre Street at the bottom right, ending up at palm-studded Paramount Boulevard. Conrad Street and Quill Drive are visible, and in the center of the picture Orizaba Street, a dirt road, connects Orange Street with Imperial Highway and Imperial School. Within 20 years, the area would be covered with new homes.

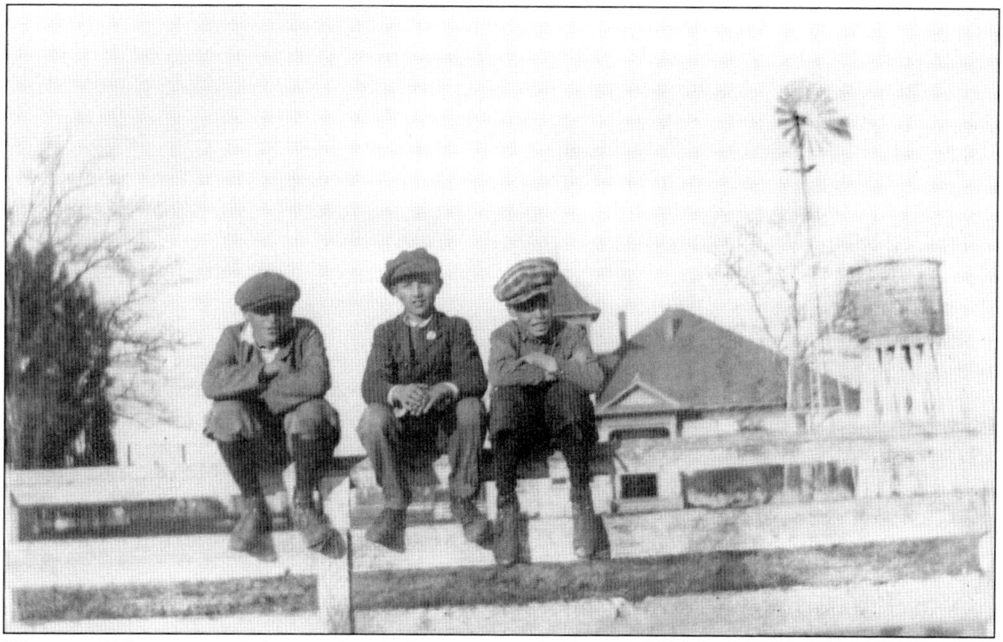

This c. 1915 picture of three school chums was taken outside the old Alameda School. The unidentified boys were friends of Frances Parke Barnes, who grew up west of the school near Alameda and Caladre Streets and graduated from Alameda School in 1915. Her father, Sydney Latimer Parke (1853–1936), homesteaded in College Settlement.

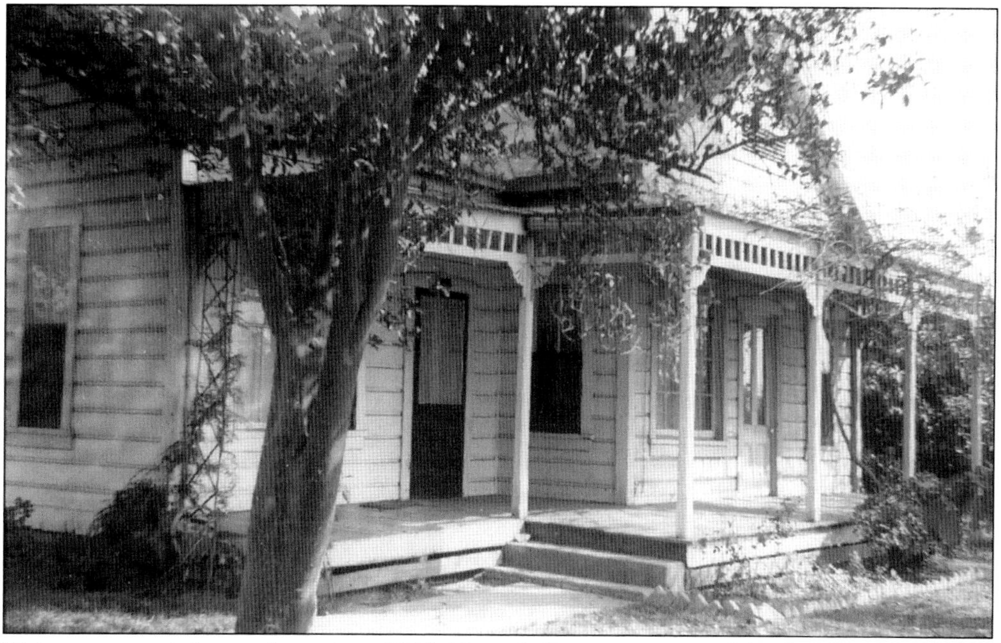

This cottage style home, formerly at 8045 Alameda Street, was typical for the area surrounding College Settlement. In many cases, rooms were rented to students and teachers. Frank E. Adams opened up a two story general merchandise building in 1869, allowing the use of the top floor by local fraternal organizations. Future stationmaster J. K. Banks had an apothecary, and Edward Barnett ran the village blacksmith shop.

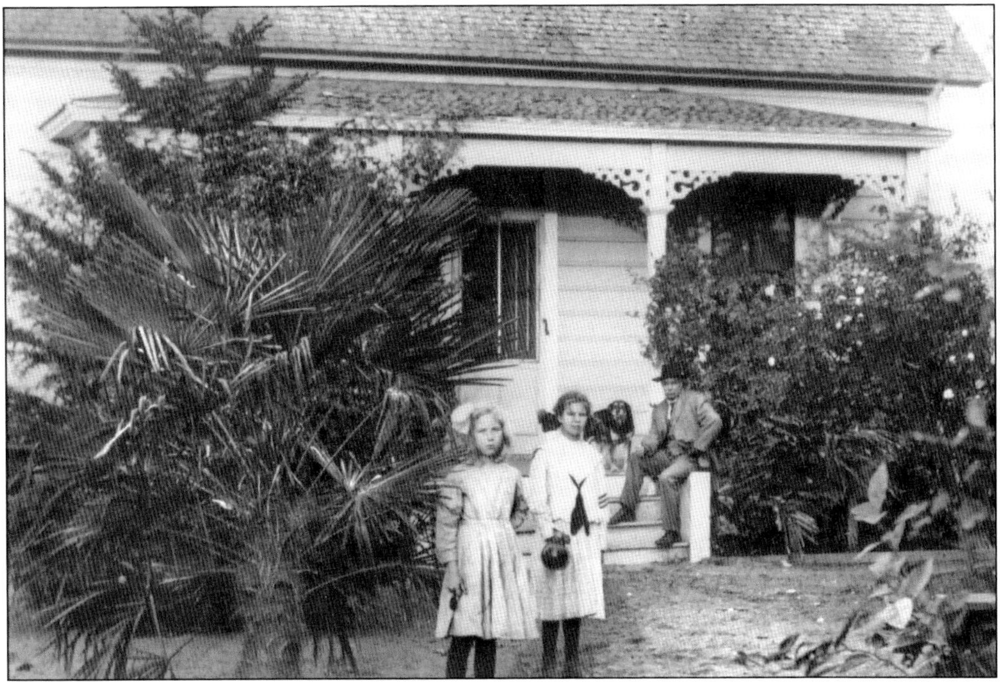

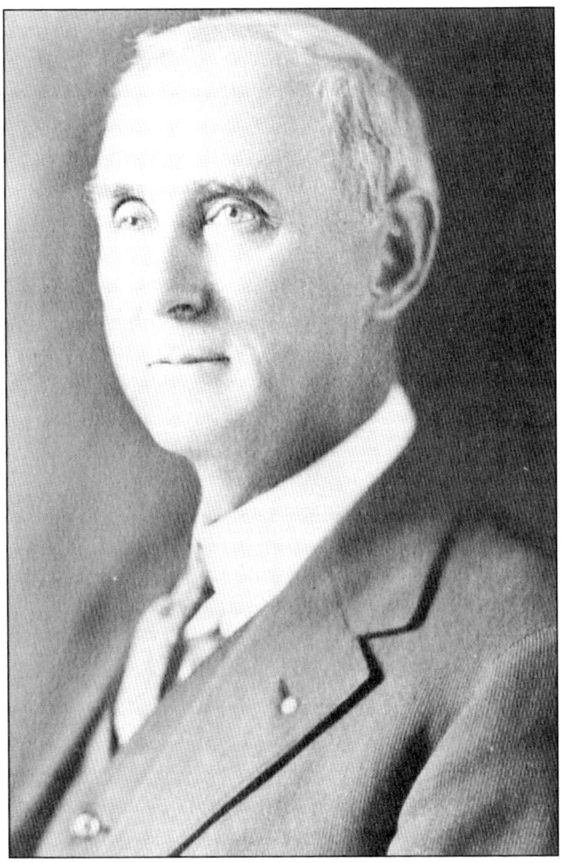

The photograph above shows the College Settlement area near today's Paramount Boulevard and Alameda Street. Paramount was called College Avenue from the late 1800s to the early 1900s. The Parke family home on Alameda Street was right in the center of the settlement on Alameda Street, west of Caladre Avenue.

Julius H. Ardis arrived in College Settlement via covered wagon at the age of four in 1867. Educated in Downey, Ardis also graduated from Emory University in Georgia with a law degree. A devout methodist, Ardis was the son of Rev. John C. Ardis, founder of College Settlement.

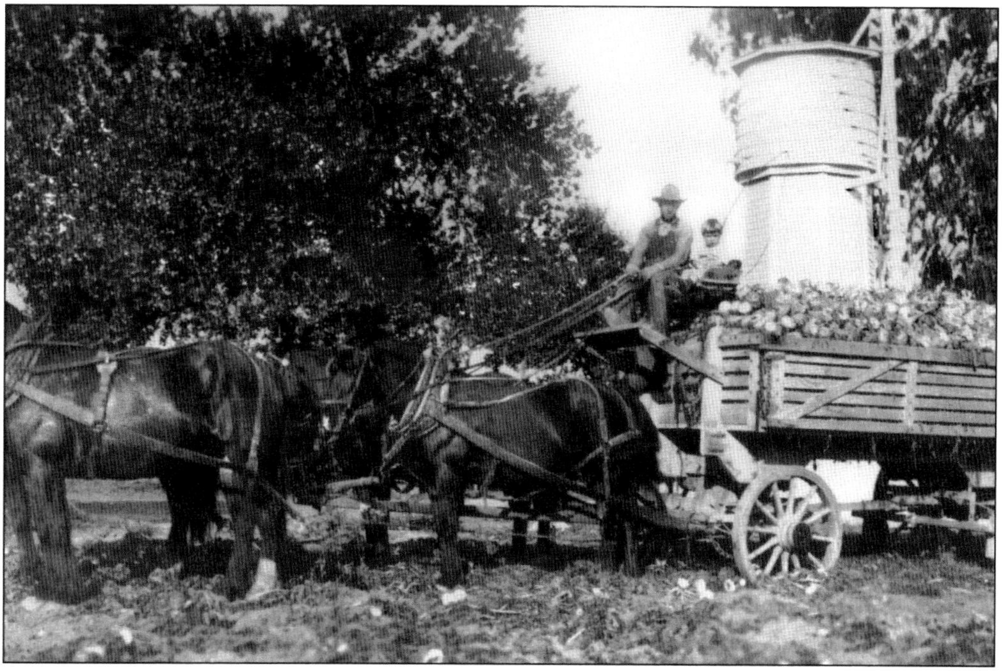

This undated photograph shows a farmer and his son in Downey with a wagon load of sugar beets. South Downey and Norwalk had some of the largest sugar beet farms in Southern California from 1890 to 1910. Thousands of tons of sugar beets were hauled to local train depots for shipment and later processing.

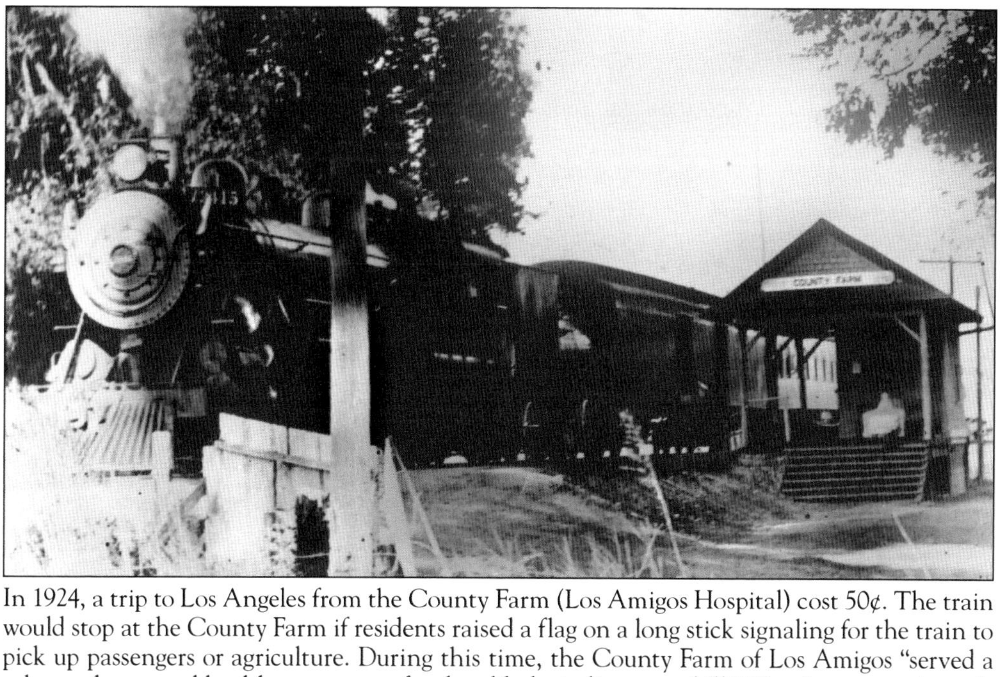

In 1924, a trip to Los Angeles from the County Farm (Los Amigos Hospital) cost 50¢. The train would stop at the County Farm if residents raised a flag on a long stick signaling for the train to pick up passengers or agriculture. During this time, the County Farm of Los Amigos "served a role as a home and health care center for the elderly, indigent, and ill." The farm went through supervisors at about one per year until 1915 when William Harrian stepped in and renamed the facility, "Rancho Los Amigos."

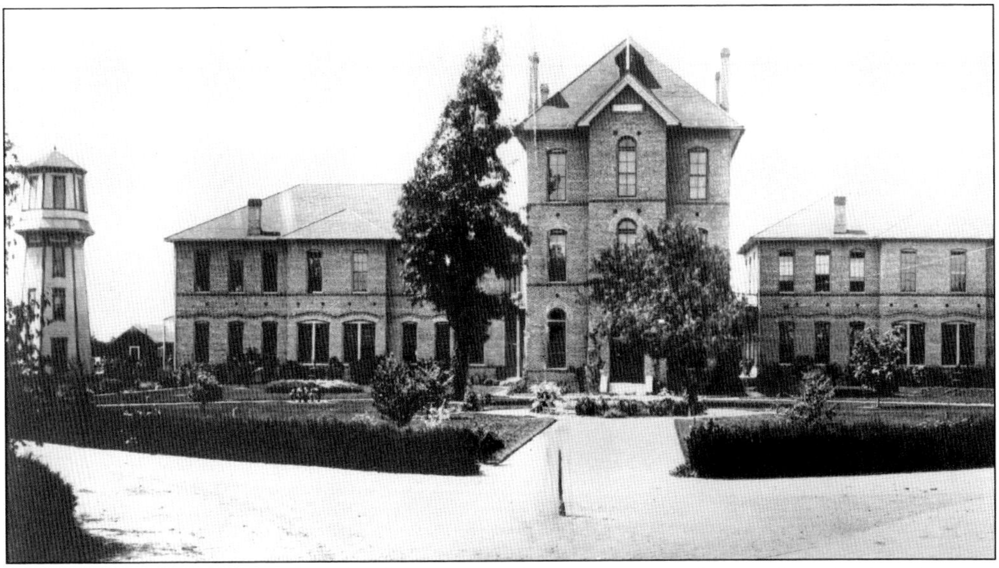

This c. 1906 photograph depicts the three-story Administration Building at Rancho Los Amigos. Years later, Superintendent Harriman's office was at the northeast corner of the first floor; the second floor was for general offices and accounting. The water tower on the left was demolished in 1913 to make way for the construction of Ward 30. A plaque in front of the Administration Building dates to 1889.

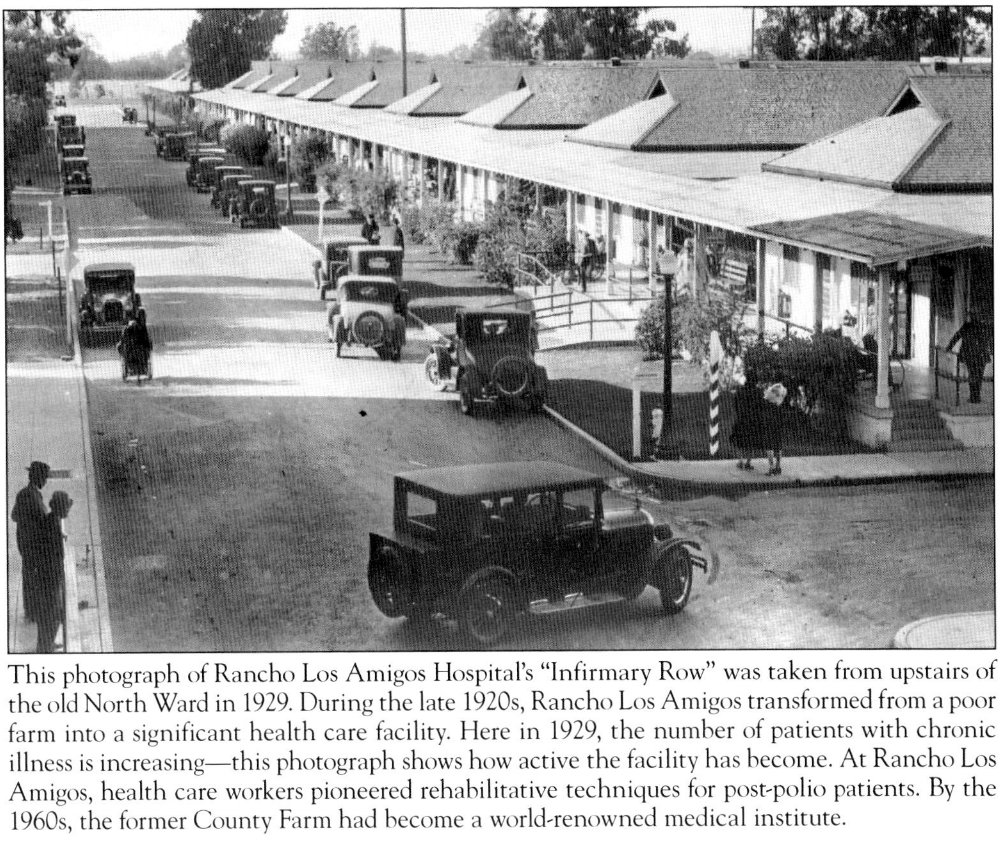

This photograph of Rancho Los Amigos Hospital's "Infirmary Row" was taken from upstairs of the old North Ward in 1929. During the late 1920s, Rancho Los Amigos transformed from a poor farm into a significant health care facility. Here in 1929, the number of patients with chronic illness is increasing—this photograph shows how active the facility has become. At Rancho Los Amigos, health care workers pioneered rehabilitative techniques for post-polio patients. By the 1960s, the former County Farm had become a world-renowned medical institute.

Two

Early Businesses, Homes, and Pioneers

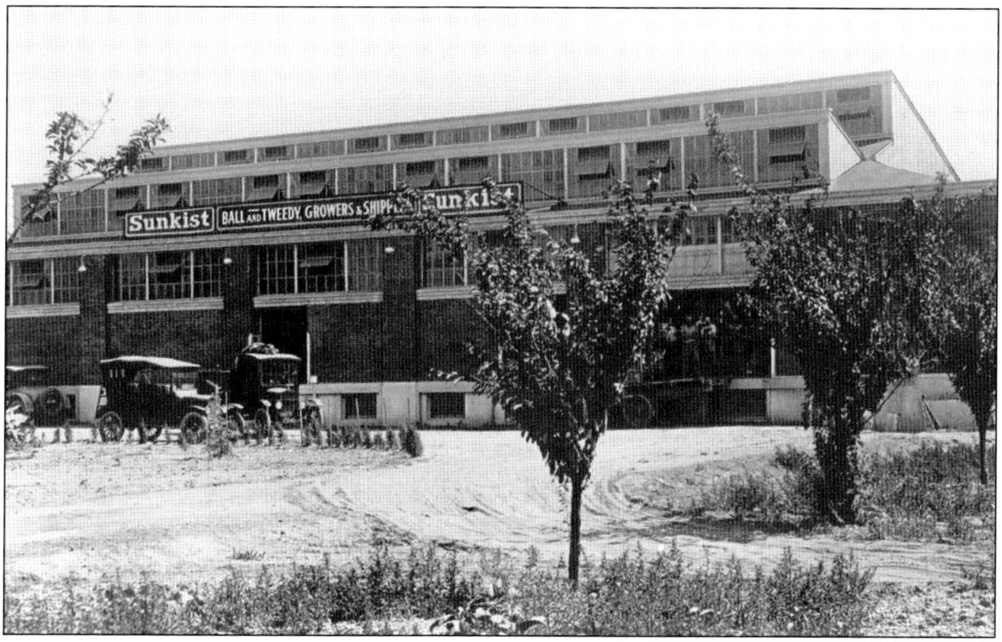

Citrus growers George Washington Tweedy and Albert L. Ball began packing fruit in 1895, using the old Southern Pacific Depot as their packing plant. In 1898 they relocated to the corner of what is now Firestone Boulevard and Dolan Street. In 1904, they moved west of the Downey depot until spring 1922. The Ball and Tweedy Sunkist Packing Plant's last home, shown here, was constructed for $50,000 and torn down in 1964. The plant's original members were J. J. Tweedy, A. L. Ball, W. F. Ball, James K. Tweedy, and Maurice A. Tweedy.

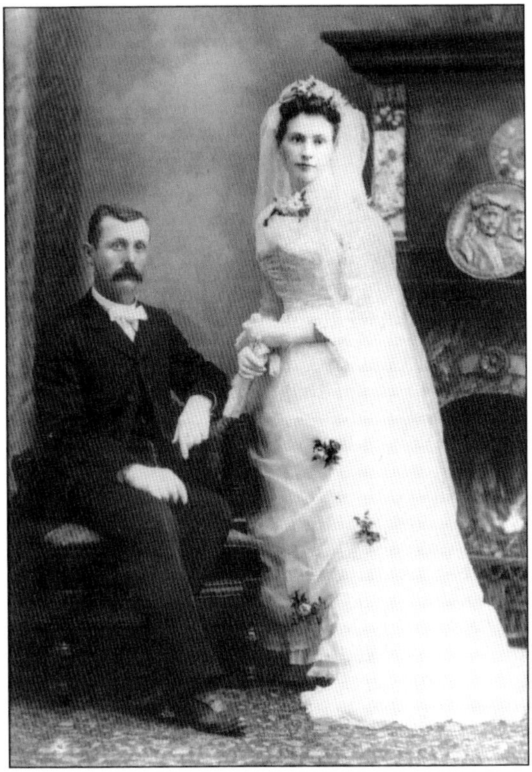

Shown here on their 1884 wedding day are Albert L. Ball and his wife Birdella M. Leffler. Albert came to California from Pennsylvania and Birdella from Illinois. The home ranch was located where Maude Price Elementary and Gordon Griffiths Junior High stand today. They had several children, including Louis, Elizabeth, Wayne, and Adelaide. Louis Ball married Judge Rives's daughter Pauline and Elizabeth Ball married Edward Rives, James Rives's oldest son.

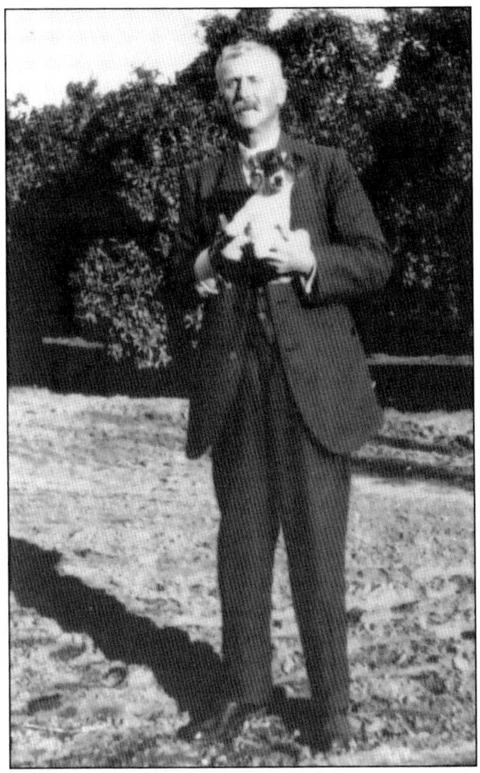

Albert Ball poses with his dog Caruso in front of the orange orchard near his Cherokee Drive ranch home. Ball completed the Spanish Colonial home in 1920. When Ball first settled in Southern California, he worked for a time at Alamitos Ranch, for the Anaheim Lighter Company, and for the Southern Pacific Railroad as a fireman and engineer. He became known for his citrus ranches, walnut groves, and the Ball and Tweedy Sunkist Packing House near the railroad tracks at Dolan Street.

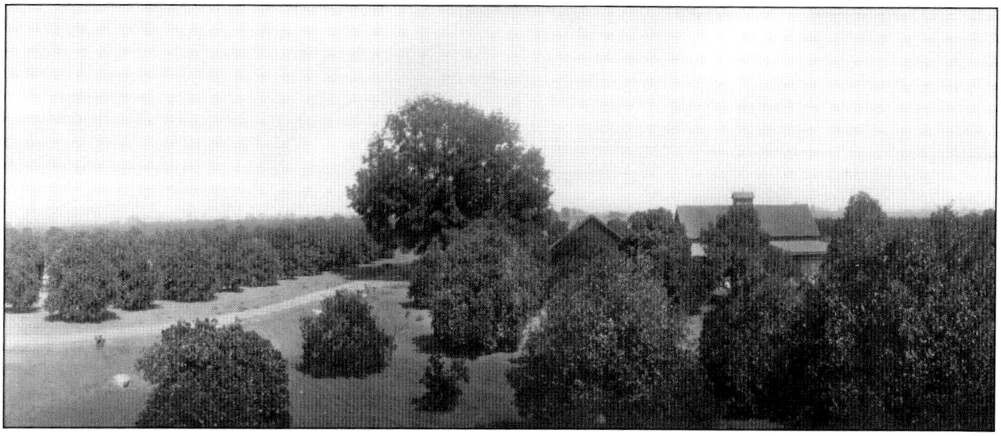

This picture was taken from an east-facing window upstairs at the Ball home on 380 Cherokee Drive in 1923. This view faces modern-day Lakewood Boulevard near Bellman Avenue. The citrus ranch on the left belongs to the Morgan Morago family. The Balls' stables are in the foreground. The east side of the Albert L. Ball house featured a solarium, seen here. Birdella Ball planted rows of Cherokee rose bushes on the lane leading to the home. On June 15, 1944, the home was sold to Dr. Richard Steere and his wife, who maintained the avocado groves. In 1956, the property was subdivided into Cherokee Estates.

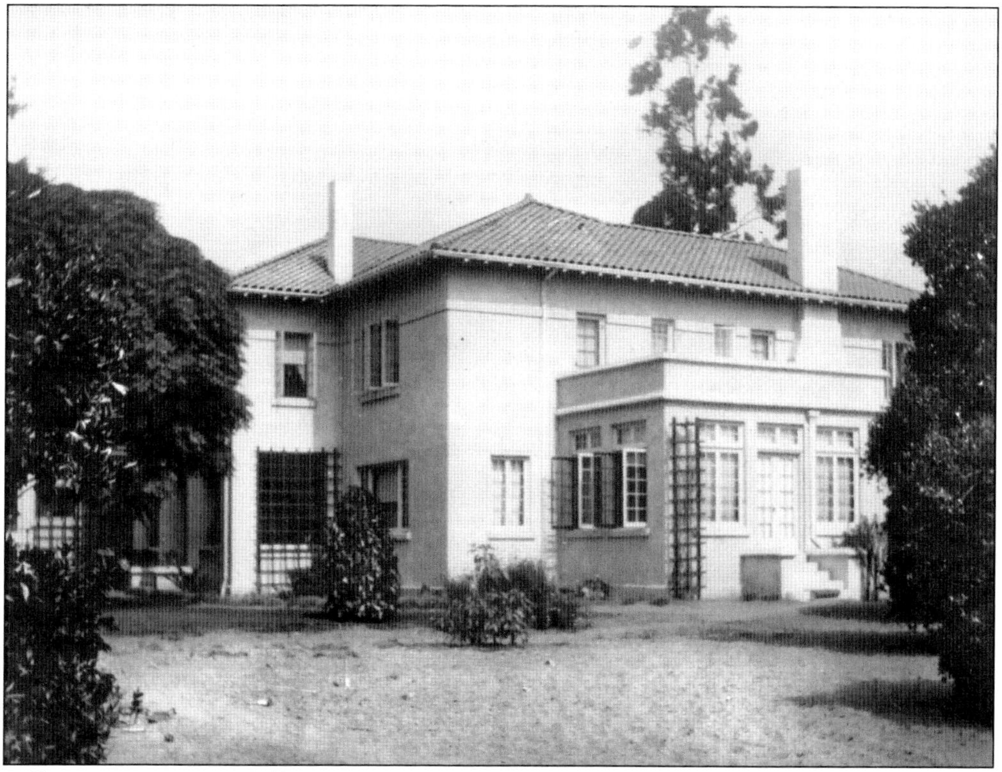

Ball's estate was surrounded by orange groves. The home was luxurious and the exterior had graceful columns over a covered arcade extending to a carport. Albert Ball was very active civically: he served as director of Arroyo Ditch and Water Company and director and vice-president of Los Nietos Valley Bank. He formed Ball and Tweedy (Packing) Company in 1895.

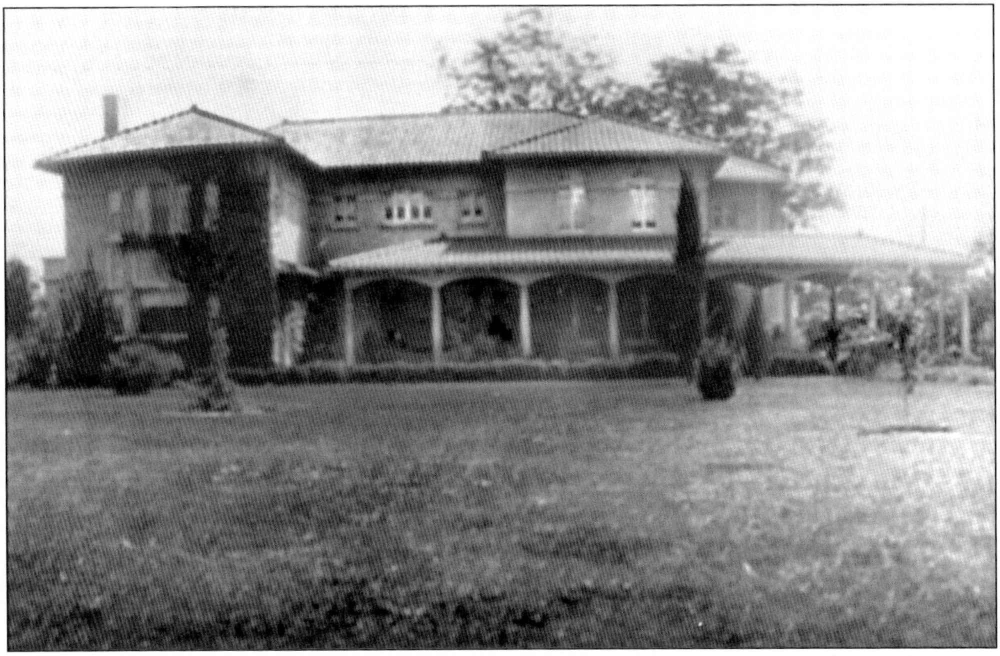

The Albert L. Ball home on Cherokee Drive is pictured in 1920 soon after completion. Designed by architect H. H. Whitely, the two-story home was surrounded by acres of orange groves. The inside was spacious and luxurious and the exterior had graceful columns over a covered arcade extending to a carport. The home was sold in 1944 to Dr. Richard Steere.

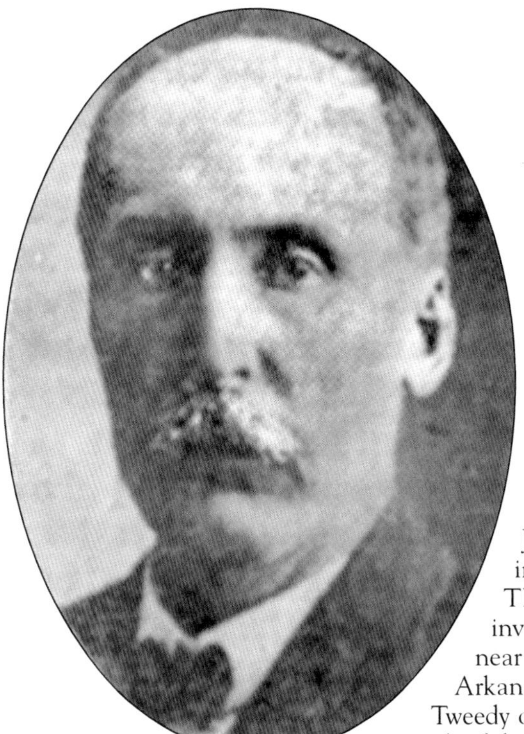

James Jackson Tweedy was Albert Ball's partner in the Ball & Tweedy Packing Plant business. The two were also good friends. Both were involved in citrus organizations and owned land near each other. Tweedy was born in Morrilton, Arkansas, on August 3, 1854, and his father Jackson Tweedy of Virginia died in 1855. Tweedy owned land north of the current Suva Street on Tweedy Lane.

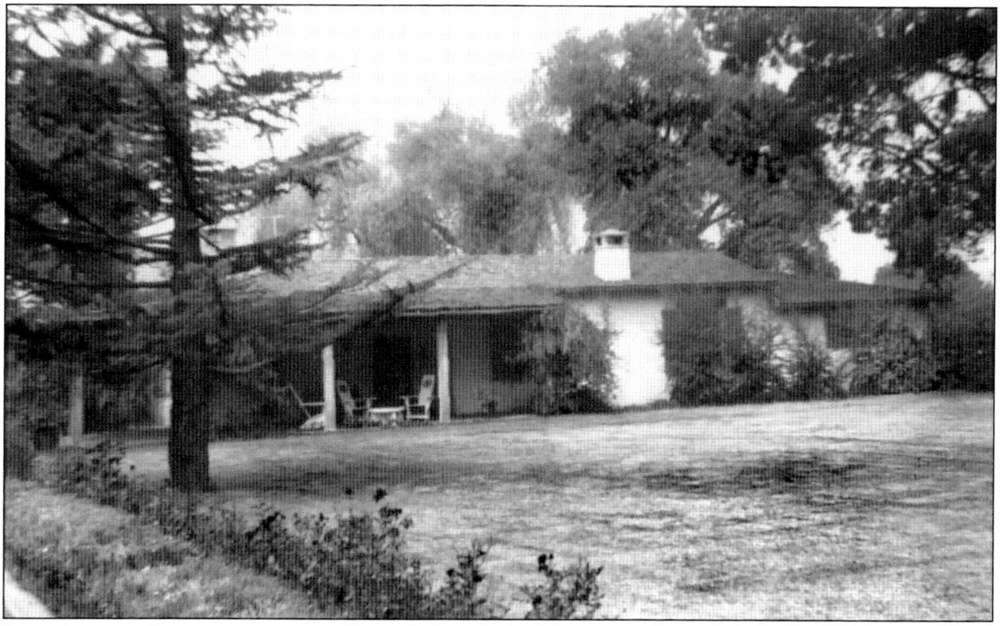

The home of James Jackson Tweedy on Tweedy Lane near Gallatin Road is pictured here. This 1925 "Early California Adobe" home was designed by architect Roland Coate. J. J. Tweedy is credited with planting some of the first Washington Naval oranges in the Downey area, soon followed by Albert Ball. James Tweedy was Robert Tweedy's nephew. Robert Tweedy owned much of current Cudahay and South Gate. James Tweedy married Eliza Sutton in October 1875 and settled in Downey in 1880.

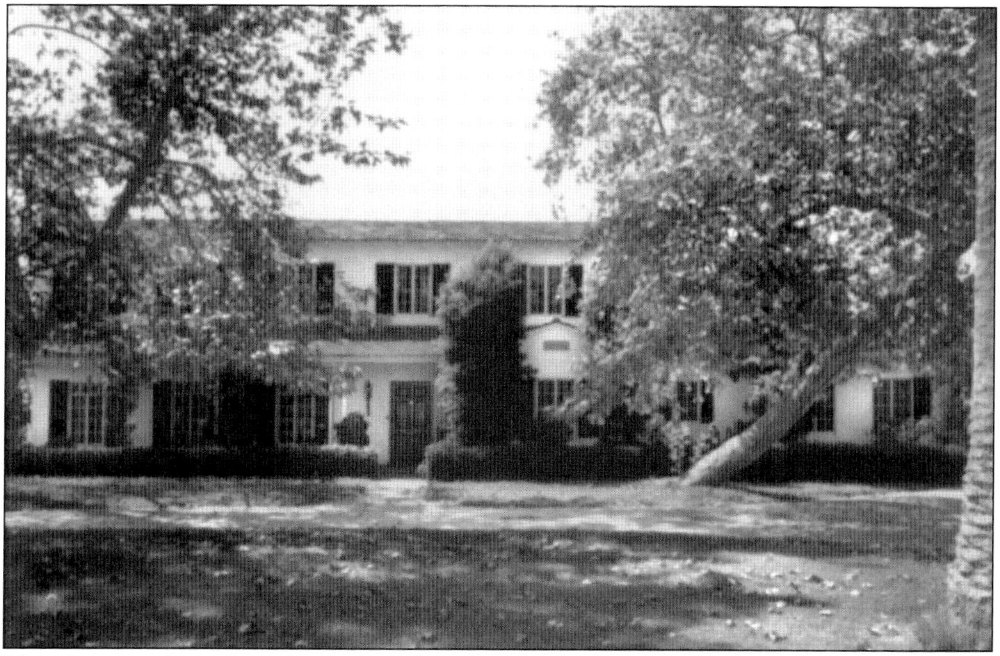

This photograph is of another Tweedy home near Suva Street in Downey. The original home burned down, and this one, (later owned by a Doctor Vracin), replaced it. A. J. Copass and his wife, Maude (James Tweedy's daughter), once owned these acres on Tweedy Lane.

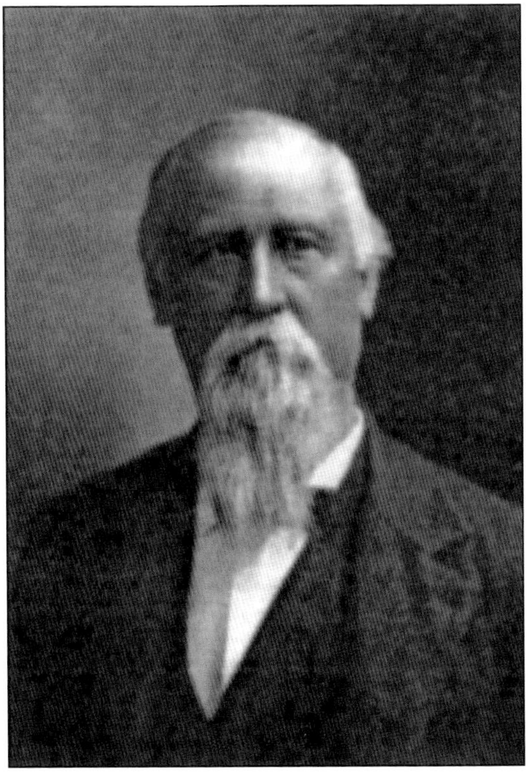

Arkansas-born George Washington Tweedy, left, was the son of Robert Tweedy, who arrived in Lexington (El Monte) in 1852. George Tweedy married Martha Nicholson of Texas on September 21, 1865, and in 1869 purchased 96 acres in what became Downey and modern day Pico Rivera. Tweedy cultivated walnuts and oranges and operated a dairy. George and Martha owned 234 acres west of Rivera and grew citrus. He was active in the Baptist Church and served for 12 years with the Rivera School District.

Below, standing in front of John Mitrovich's Depot, a general and liquor store, on the southwest corner of Crawford and Second Streets in downtown Downey is George Washington Tweedy (middle with white beard) with H. S. Redfield, a local jeweler, leading the horse. Mitrovich came to Downey from Boka, Yugoslavia, in 1875 and bought property from John Mcgarvin in 1876. Mitrovich was also called "Nick" and "Giovanni."

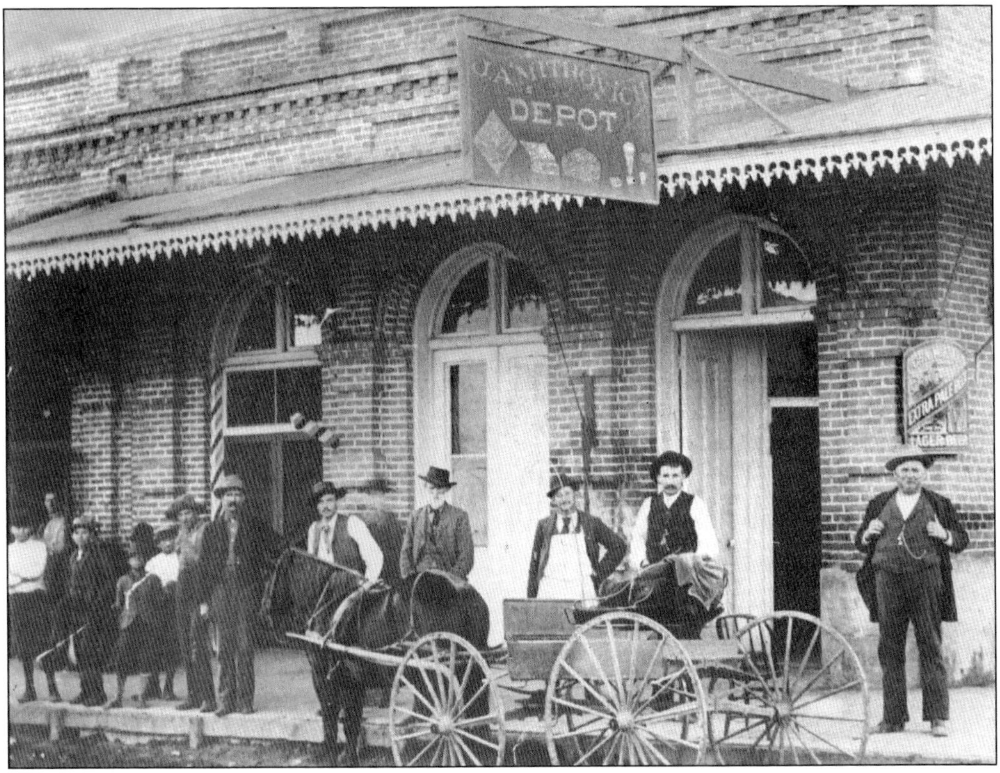

Gallatin Settlement was centered at Florence Avenue and Tweedy Lane. Before the late 1930s, this was called Telegraph Jaboneria Road on maps. Because of James Tweedy's ranch near Tweedy and Gallatin, and other Tweedy land holdings, locals knew it as Tweedy Lane. Palm trees were planted after 1900, and this photograph is one of the earliest of these trees, which still grow today. Also on Tweed Lane was Albert and Birdella Ball's orange ranch, which in 1930 sprawled across 107 acres.

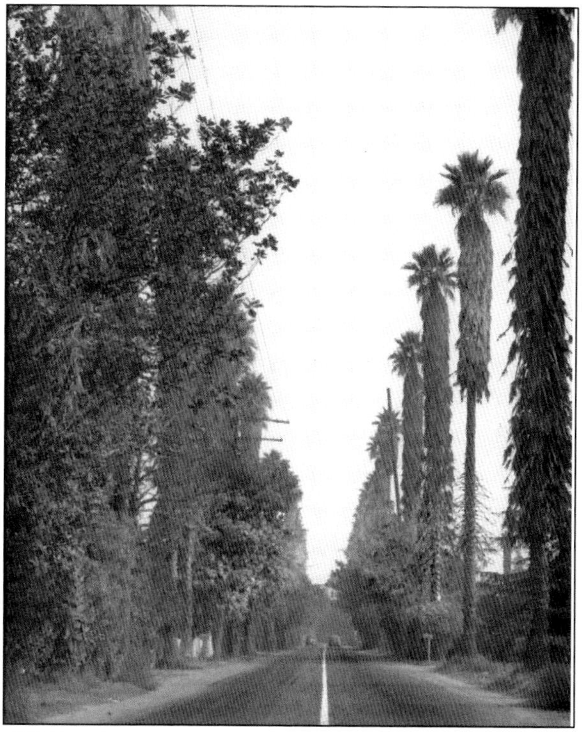

Ball and Tweedy citrus crate labels included the provocative Egyptian, shown below, along with labels named Defiance, Condor, El Oso, and Tanager with dynamic and colorful images. By 1876, oranges thrived in the Downey–Los Nietos area, along with peaches, apples, pears, and apricots.

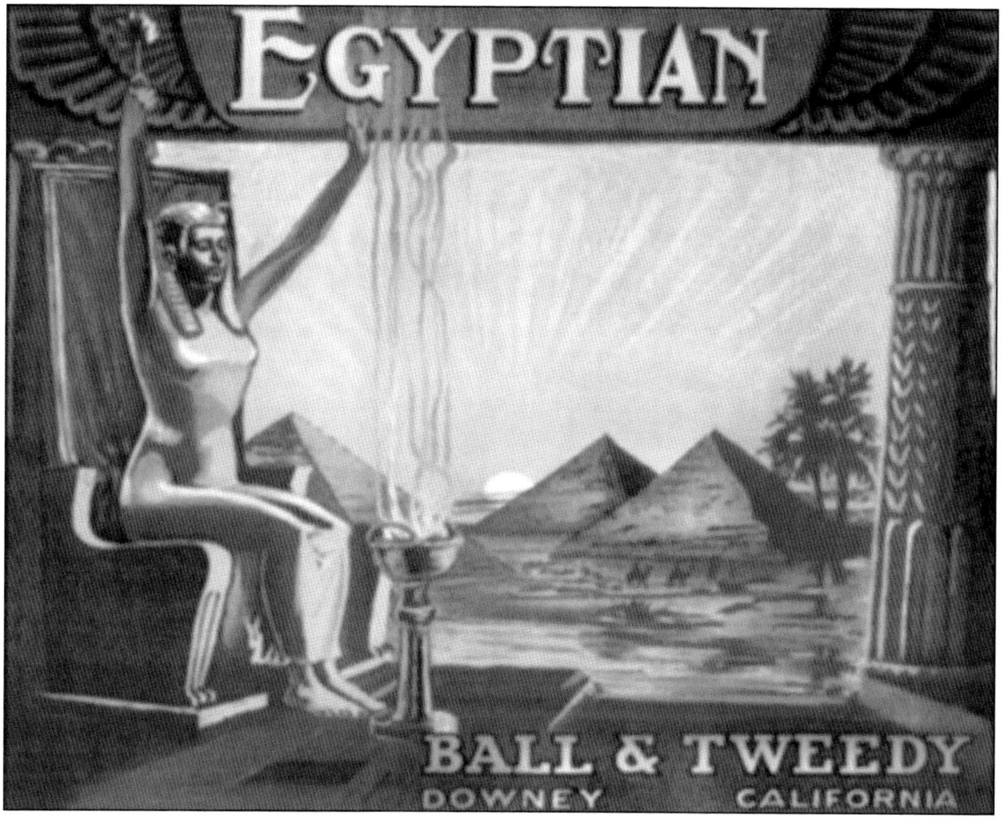

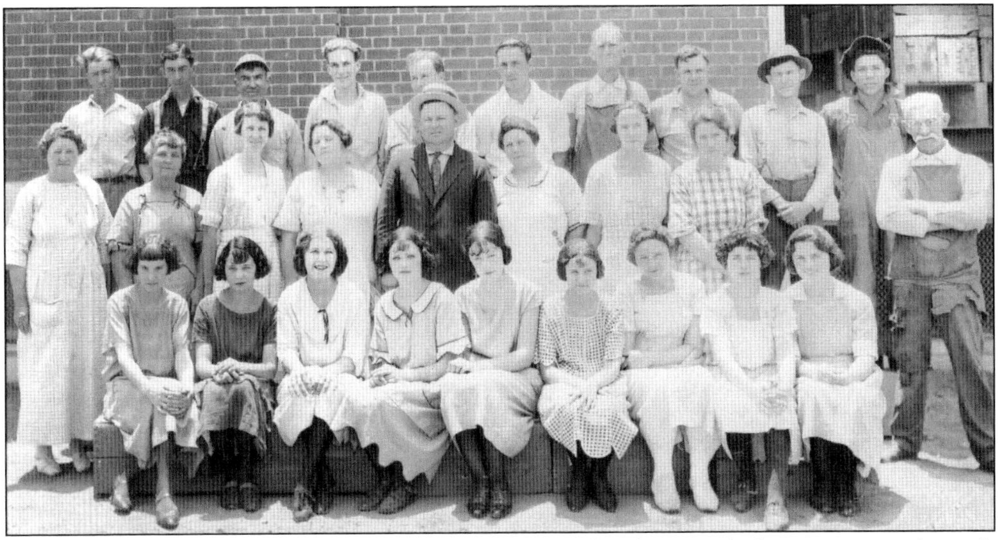

Maurice Tweedy, center, was the youngest son of J. J. Tweedy, who owned a large citrus ranch north of Suva Street. Many Downey youths worked at the plant, particularly at harvest time. Ball and Tweedy were members of an orange growers' exchange established in 1893 to the fight wind, insects, unfair middleman pricing, and particularly the frost, which had almost ruined the citrus industry in years past. Maurice Tweedy, born in Downey in August 1888, died in November 1942.

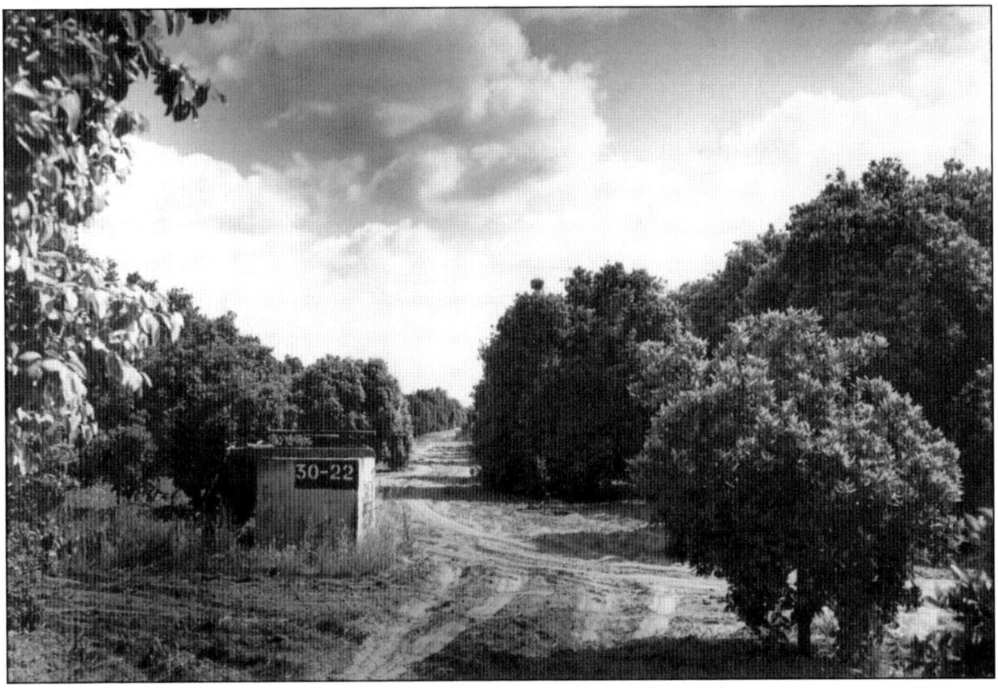

The Red Barn Ranch, formerly the Paxton Ranch, was located on Telegraph Road near Passons Road north of the current I-5 Freeway. Frank Garland purchased the citrus ranch in 1943. Concrete stand-pipes were used for irrigation and water from deep wells and nearby streams was pumped from underground pipes into these stand-pipes. A valve would be opened to allow water to flow out under pressure and fill the citrus orchards, walnut groves, or other crops. This is Garland's Valencia orange grove near the border of Rivera and Downey.

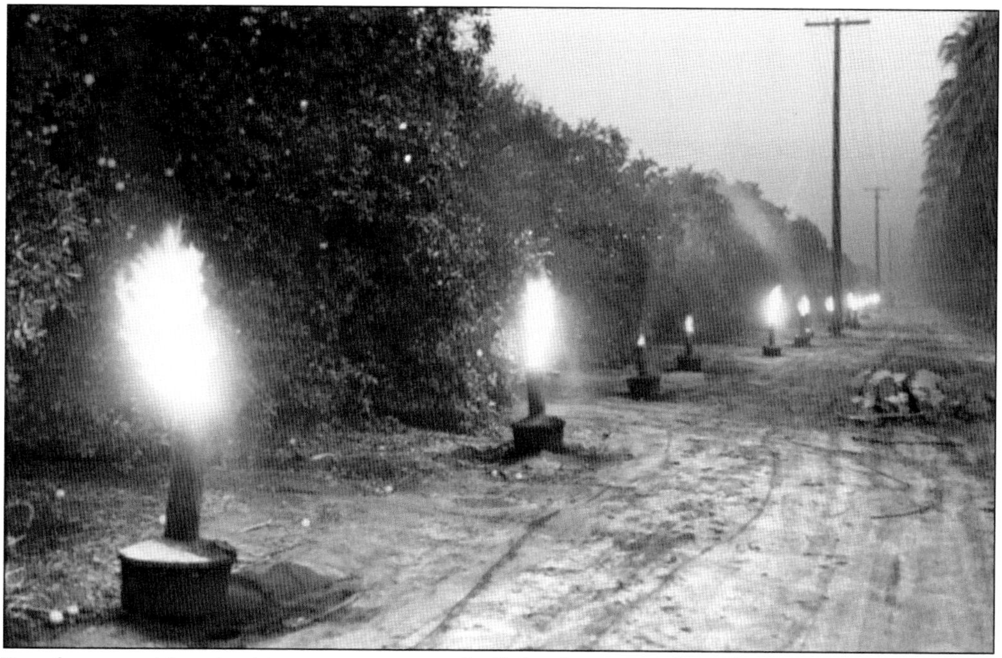

Smudge pots ablaze in this citrus grove ward off the dangerous frost that can destroy an entire citrus orchard. Maintaining orange trees was labor intensive, requiring regular fertilizing, irrigation, pruning, staking limbs, harvesting, and fumigating for bugs. During the cold weather, families would tune in to the radio for the local Fruit Frost Report. If there was a freeze and smudge pots were needed, ranch boys were excused from high school to help out.

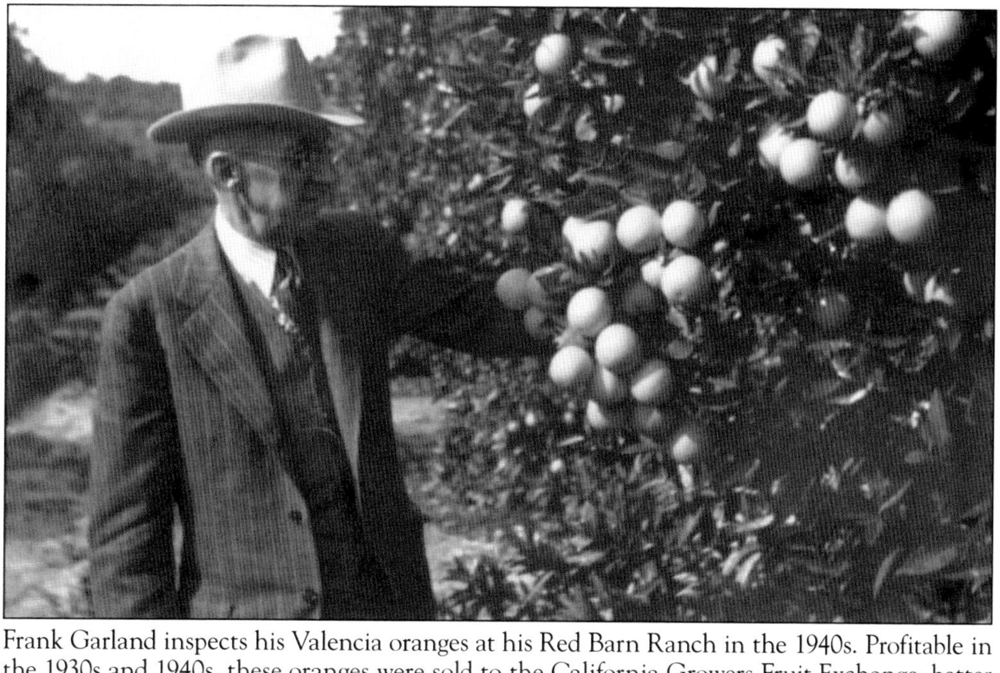

Frank Garland inspects his Valencia oranges at his Red Barn Ranch in the 1940s. Profitable in the 1930s and 1940s, these oranges were sold to the California Growers Fruit Exchange, better known as Sunkist. Most were processed into frozen juice concentrate. After a 1948 freeze damaged many trees, ranchers pulled them out and subdivided properties for homes.

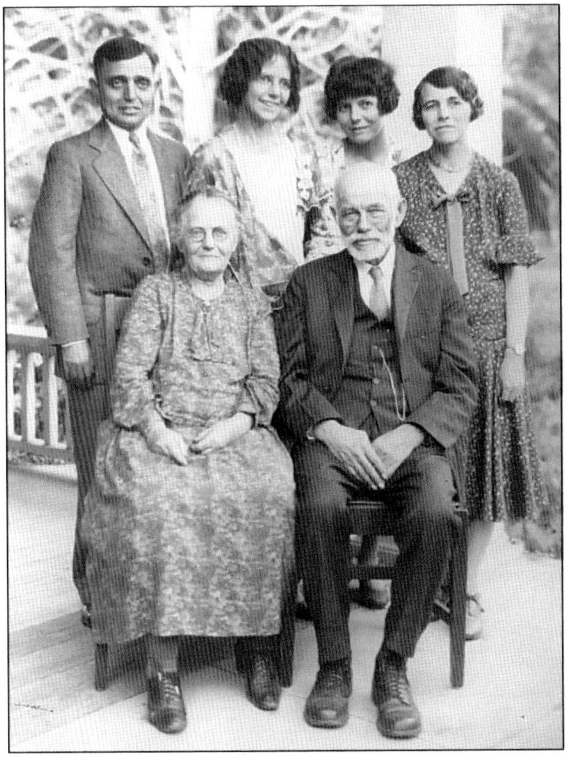

Leonard Rupert Paxton, wife Stella, and family are depicted in the early 1930s on their front porch surrounded by orange groves. The ranch was located south of Anaheim-Telegraph Road between Downey and Sanford Bridge Road (True Street) and Passons Road. The Paxton ranch was a portion of the Ireland Tract of the Rancho Santa Gertrudes Tract of Land.

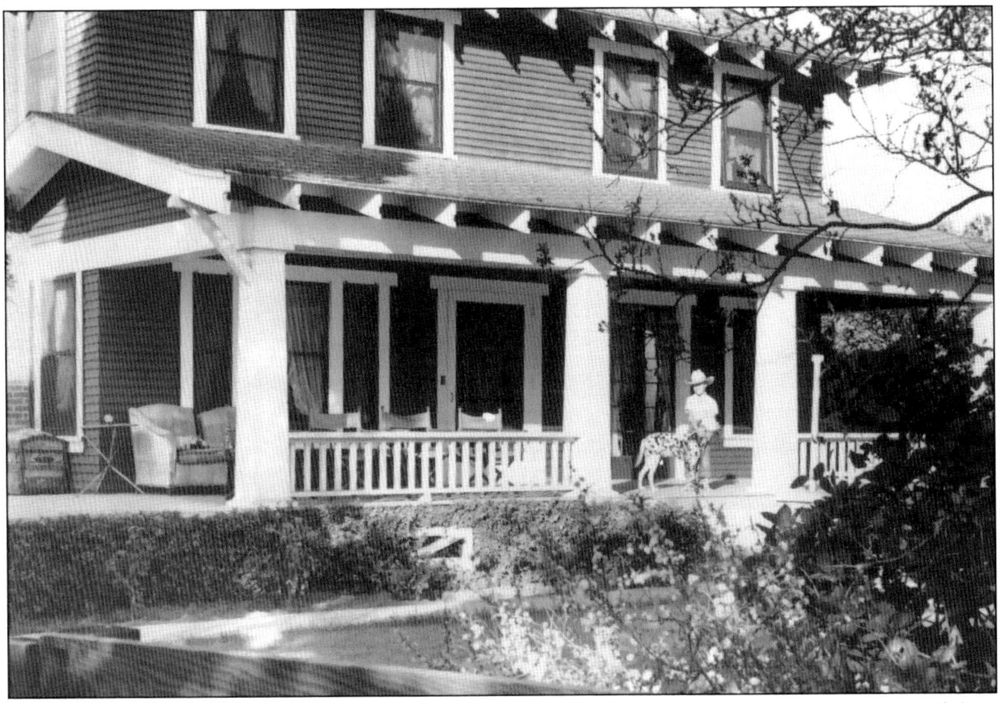

The Red Barn Ranch was 14 acres of oranges. Frank Garland and Margaret Swain raised four children after purchasing the ranch in 1943. The children attended Gallatin School. First through third grades were taught by Edith Unsworth, and fourth through sixth grades by Maude Price.

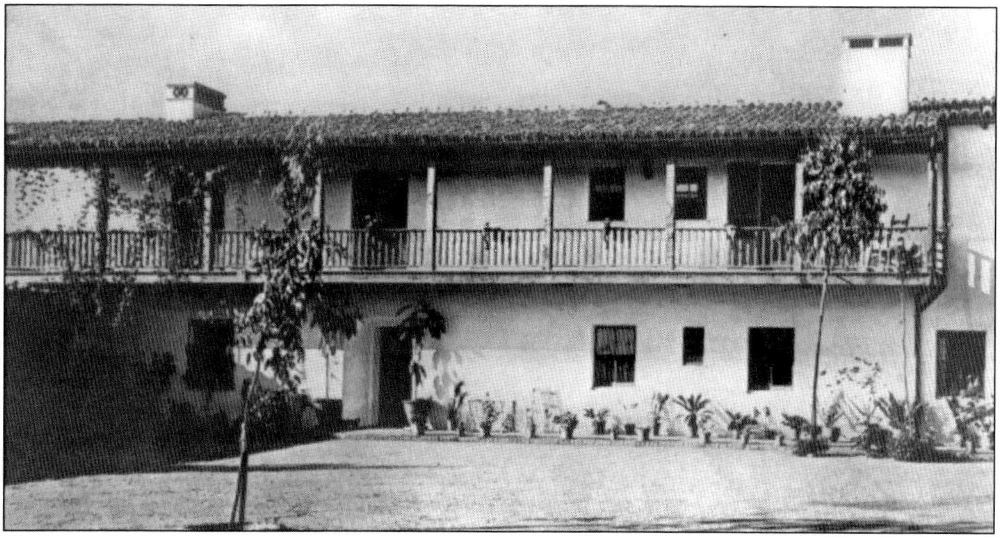

This is the home of Alexander Parley Johnson and his wife Geline Gates "Gypsy" Richardson. Like J. J. Tweedy's home, this house was designed by Pasadena architect Roland A. Coate in the Monterey genre design, combining formal elements in a relaxed country style, and built in 1926 and 1927 at 7749 Florence Avenue. Raised in Riverside where his father grew Valencia oranges, Parley invested in oil wells and real estate. Gypsy Johnson preserved their lavish home and donated it to the Downey Assistance League.

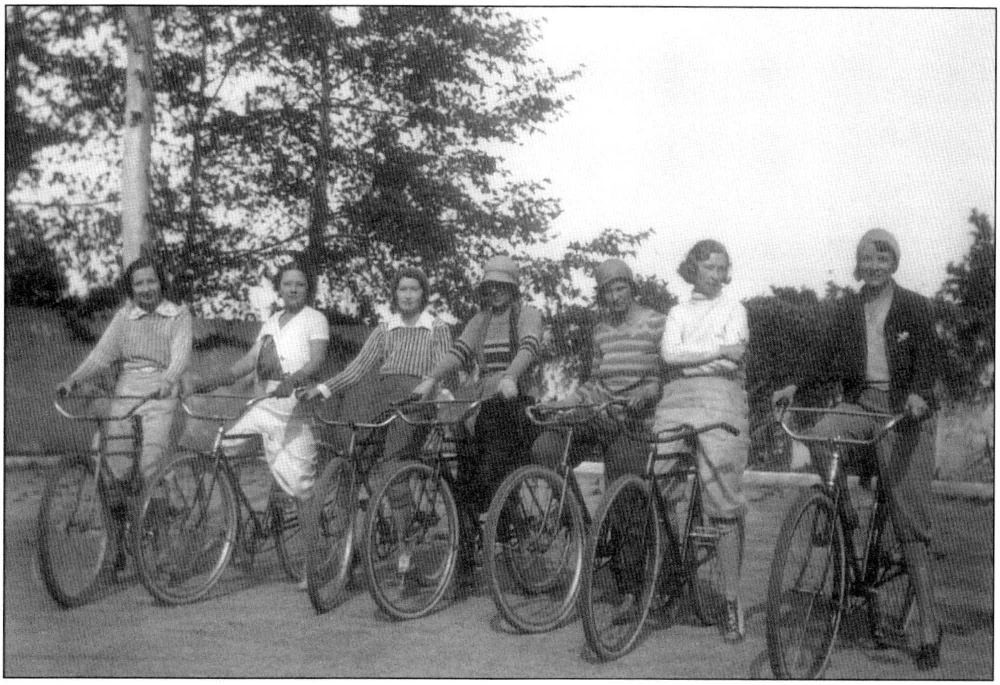

The Club of Eight Tuesday Bridge Club straddles bicycles in Gypsy Johnson's driveway during the late 1920s. One of the eight is absent, but among the women pictured are Ann Gittings, Lillian Burke, Dara Feather (YMCA house), Mable Tweedy, Ruth Ball, Edna Feather, and Gypsy Johnson. On bicycle rides, the club's path commonly took them from Casa De Parley Johnson to Jim Tweedy's place on 9117 Tweedy Lane and back.

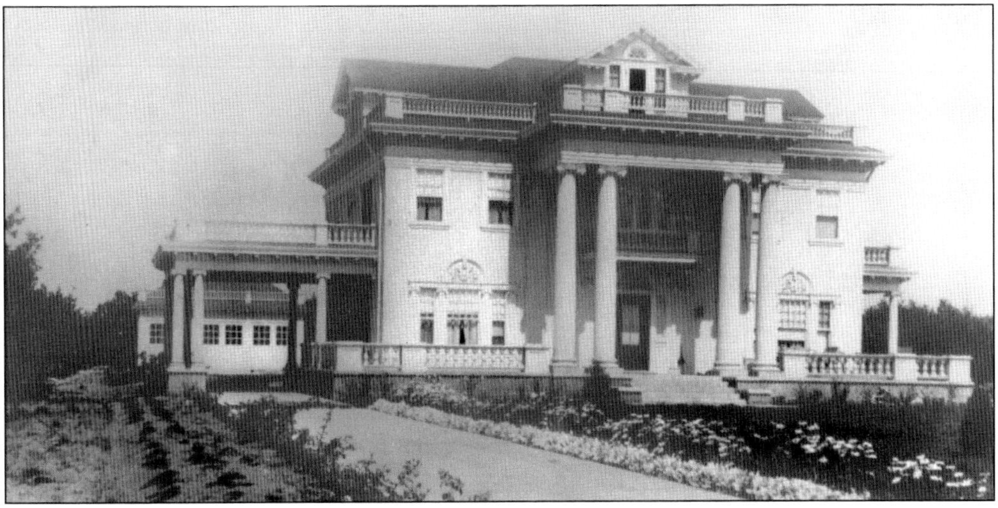

Finished in 1913, the stately Rives Mansion graces Paramount and Third Streets in Downey. The Rives Home was begun by John Buckles in 1911 on 75 acres surrounded by walnut and orange groves. Judge James C. Rives was a Superior Court judge for 16 years. Born in Georgia on January 4, 1864, Judge Rives and his family came to Downey when he was five years old. He worked as a printer for the *Los Angeles Times*, studied law, and in 1898 became district attorney for Los Angeles County. In 1907 he was elected to the Superior Court, on which he served until his death on January 18, 1924.

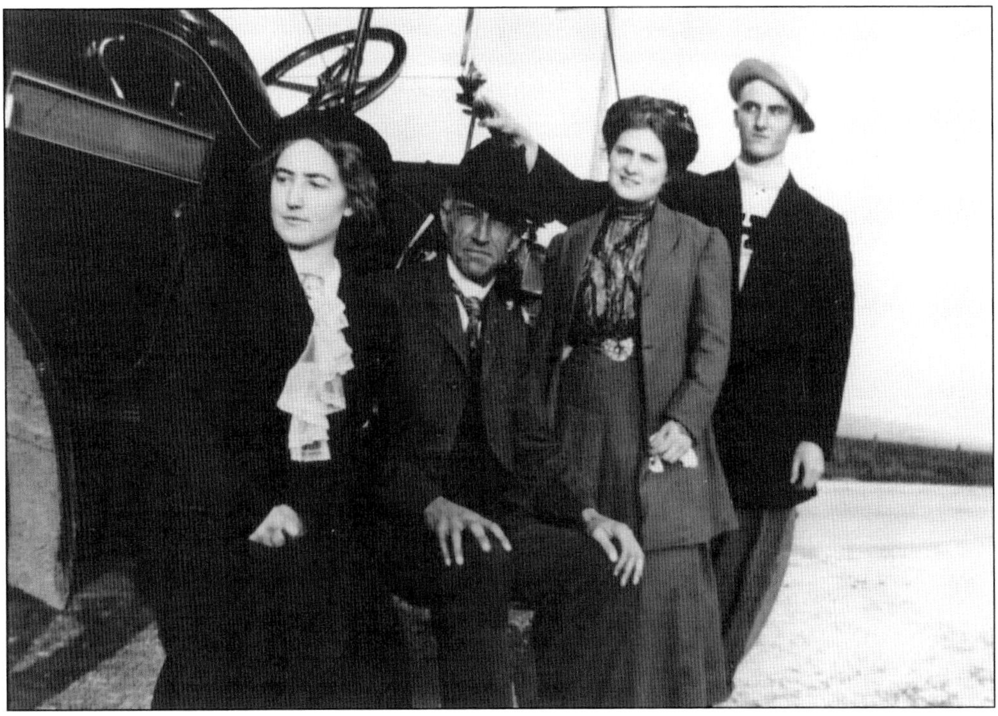

In 1883, young James Rives was publisher of the *Downey Review*. He married Mary Lee Crowell, daughter of another pioneering Downey family, and the couple raised four children. Edward Rives, James's oldest son, graduated from USC Law School in 1914. Shown here in 1915 from left to right are Mary Lee Rives, Judge James C. Rives, Ethel Rives, and Edward Rives.

The six Downey businessmen shown here in 1884 are, from left to right, (first row) James W. McKellar, Dan McKellar, and Rueben Arey; (second row) Pleasant Brown, James C. Rives, and Riley Manning.

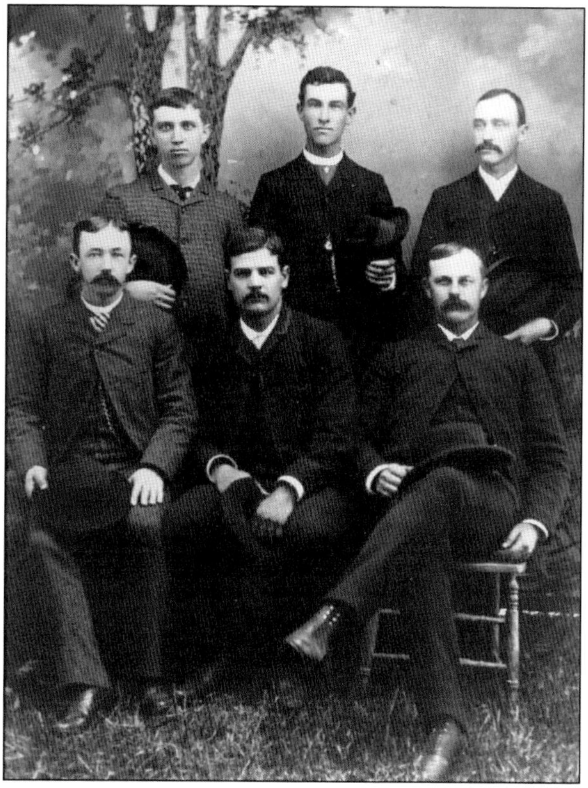

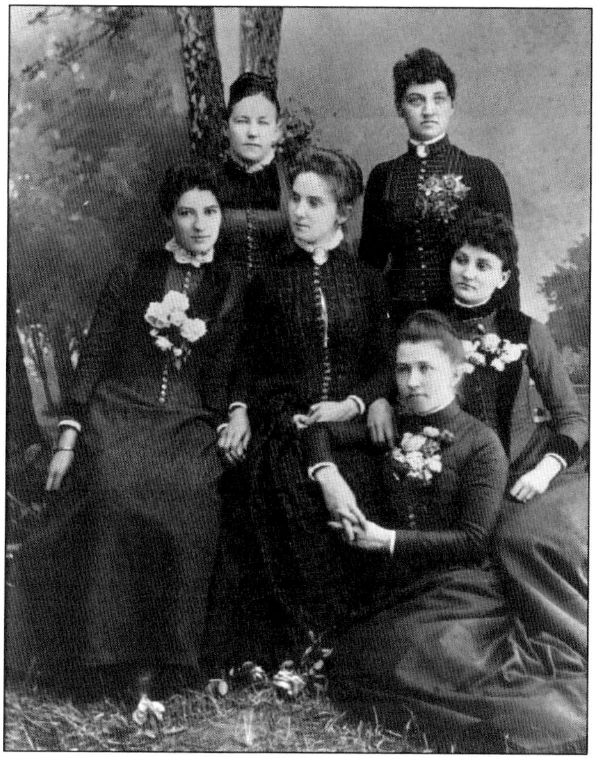

The Downey women pictured here in 1884 are Lee Crowell Rives, Josie McKellar Magee, Judie McKellar, Edna Burdick Stewart, Madge Darlington, and Lottie Davis McKellar. Lee Crowell Rives married future judge James C. Rives on September 4, 1889. Josie and Judie McKellar grew up in Gallatin Settlement, attended school in Downey, and later taught school in Downey.

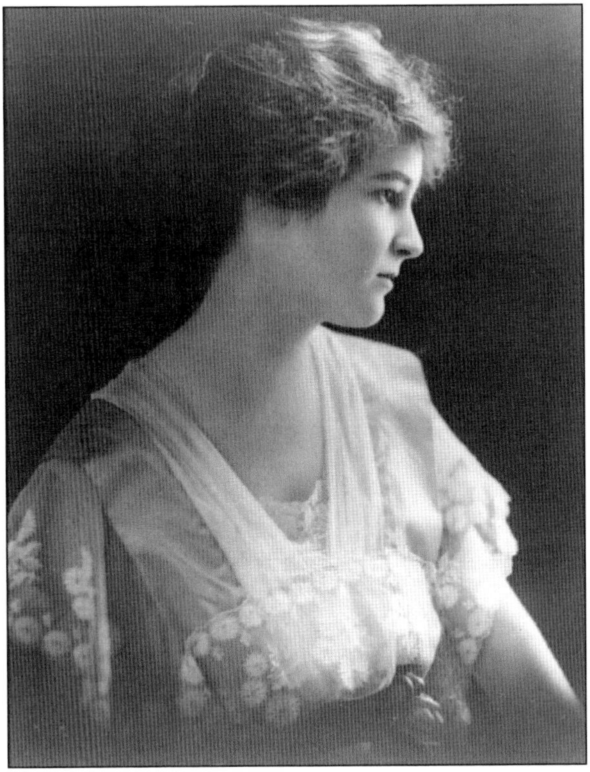

Pauline Rives (1898–1980) was James C. and Mary Lee Crowell Rives's only daughter. She grew up with three brothers: Edward, Robert, and Lawrence. Pauline loved horses. She lived in the mansion on Paramount Boulevard and Third Street. She attended Downey schools, graduating from Downey High School in 1916 as senior class president. Pauline married Louis K. Ball on February 6, 1922, and they had a son, Albert Louis Ball II.

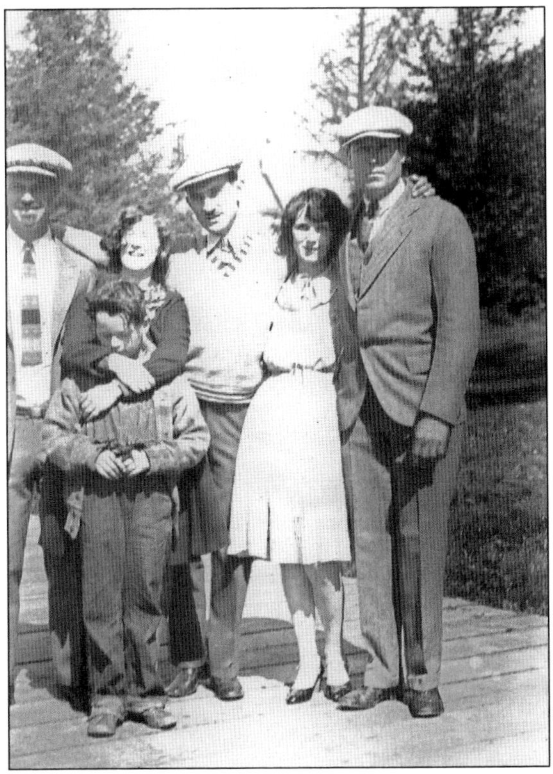

This rare photograph, taken in the 1920s, depicts, from left to right, Louis K. Ball, his wife Pauline Rives Ball, Wayne T. Sachs (from Sachs and Sons Ford), Ruth D. Ball, and her husband Wayne K. Ball. Wayne Ball Jr. is in front of his aunt Pauline. Wayne Ball and Wayne Sachs were good friends who loved to hunt. The Sachs and Sons car dealership on Downey Avenue northeast of Fifth Street displayed hunting trophies inside.

The 1884 photograph at right depicts Dr. W. C. Smith, Judge East, Judge J. W. Buster, and saloon keeper J. A. Mitrovich.

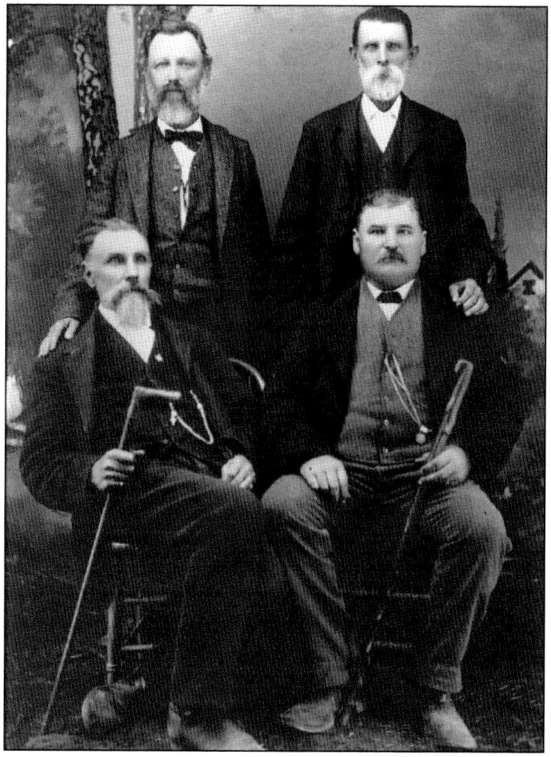

The Downey Cooperative Creamery, below, was begun in 1899 near the railroad on Downey Avenue. The Creamery was a popular early morning meeting place. Downey pioneer rancher Robert Mayes is pictured third from left. The creamery handled an average of 10,000 pounds of milk daily and made about 700 pounds of butter daily. John Bartlett was president, T. E. Haas vice president, and Robert Mayes was on the board of directors.

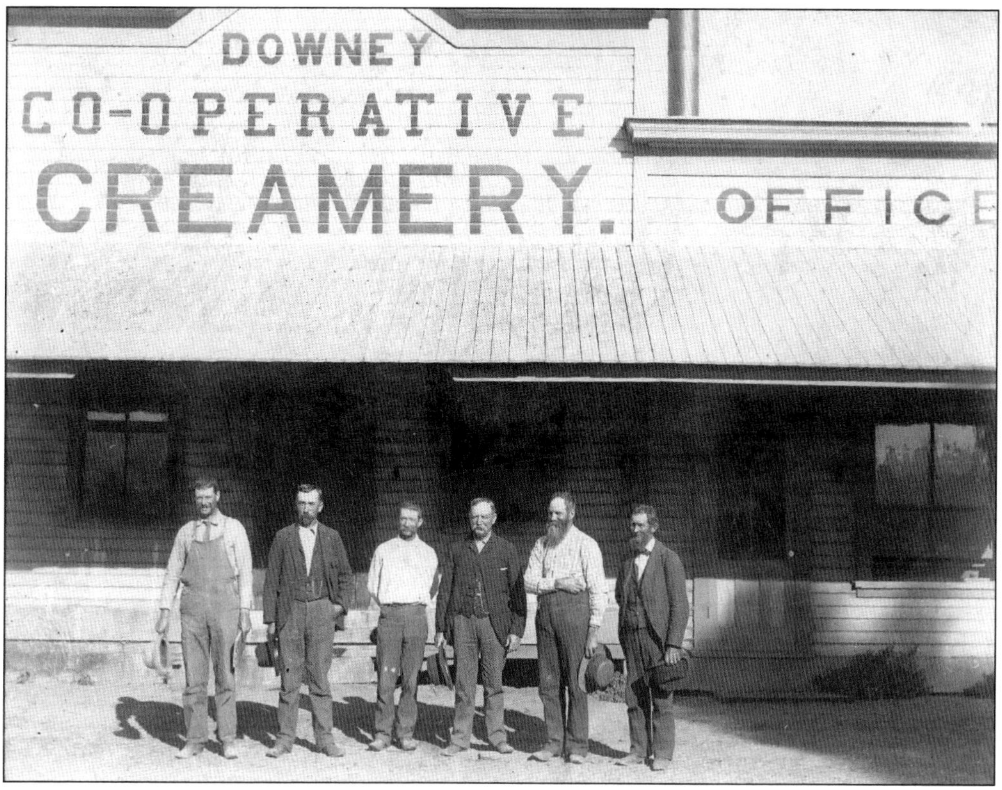

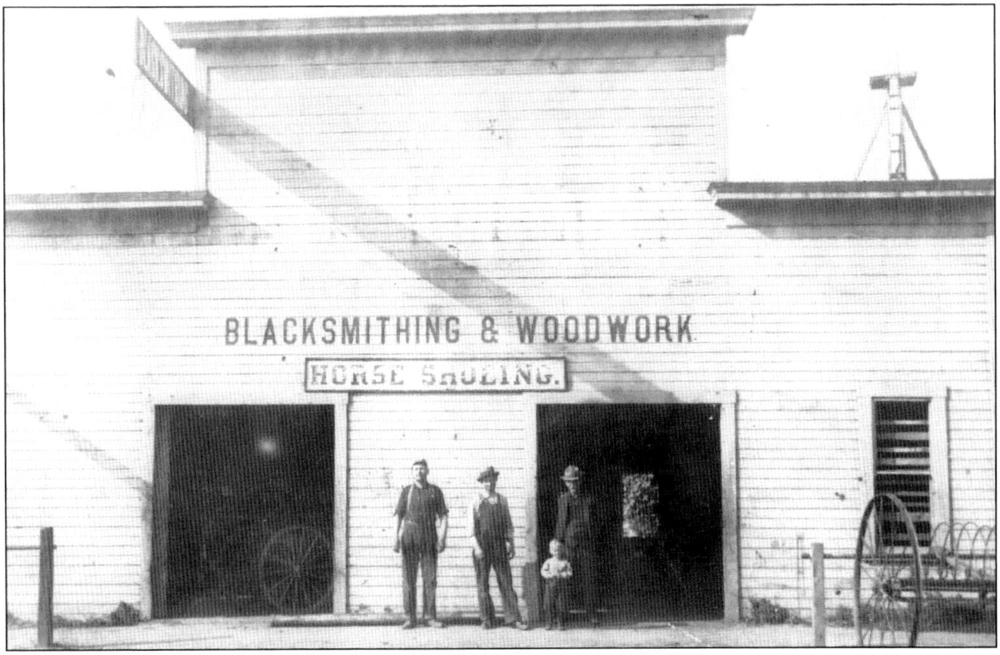

This 1910 photograph shows Joseph H. McCullough's blacksmith shop on Firestone Boulevard. McCullough was born January 23, 1859, in Tarrington, Canada. He worked for the Townsley Blacksmith shop on east Second Street in Downey before he opened a wagon and buggy business. He sold out in 1921 to R. O. Pollard and turned to real estate. In June 1894, he married Julia Ardis, a clerk at the Strine Brothers' store, and they raised two children, Ardis McCullough and Katherine McCullough Cooper.

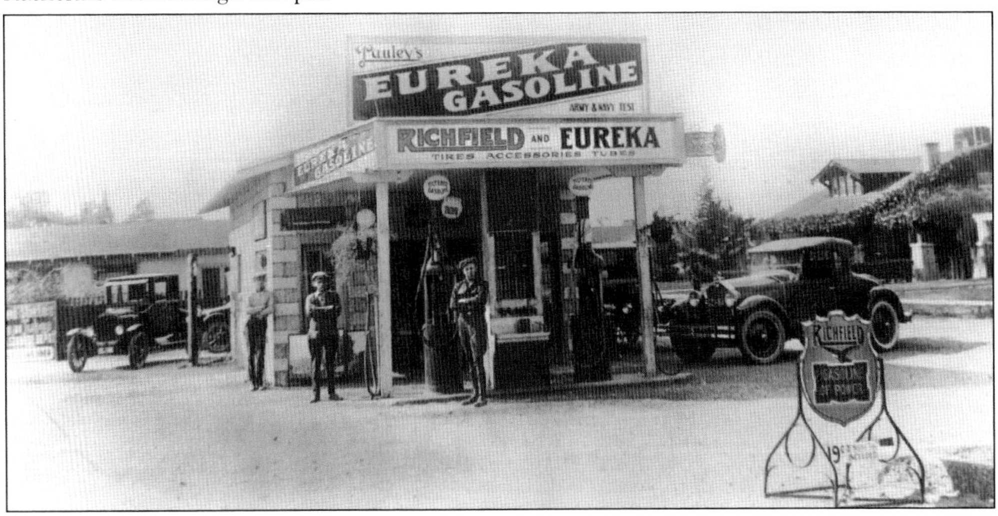

The Newbold and Speaker filling station was located on Crawford and New Streets. In April 1922, static electricity caused a truck unloading gasoline here to explode. The blast killed nine people, and more than twenty others were seriously burned. Some were injured when they came to help and a second explosion occurred. Our Lady of Perpetual Help Church was erected near the old station (the statue of Our Lady is on the tragedy's site). The fatalities included Leamon Pulley, Fred Bigby, Guy Reiman, and Harry Johnson. Burn victims included Haygood Ardis, James Stamps, Lawrence Manning, Frank Zamboni, Raymond Strine, George Clark, and L. E. Price.

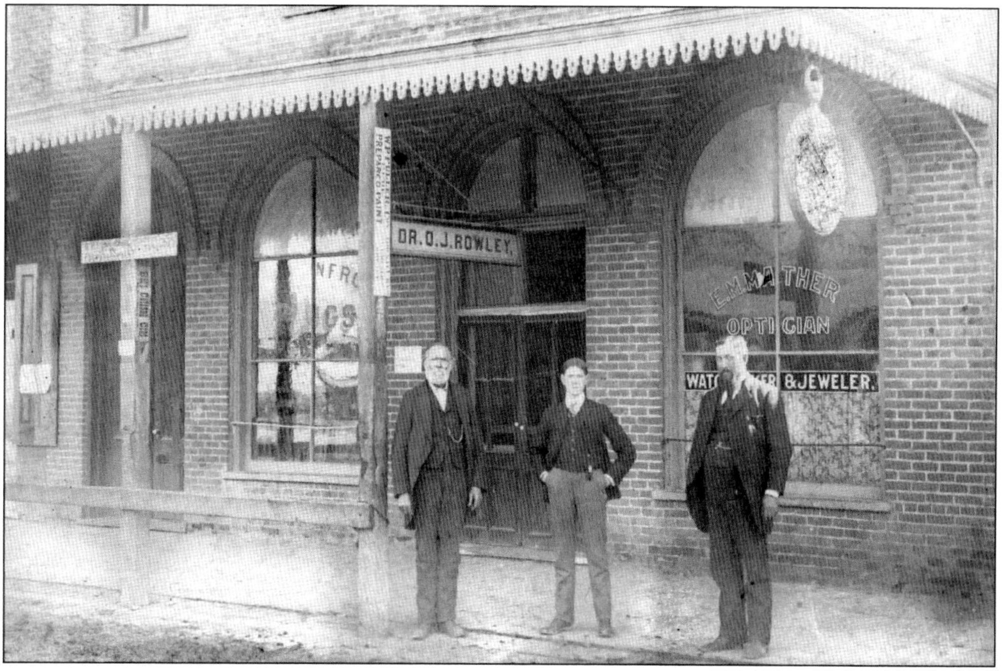

Depicted on Crawford Street (Downey Avenue) about 1900, from left to right, are Captain T. R. Renfro, optician Dr. Ed Mather, and Dr. Q. J. Rowley. In 1888, Renfro opened the drug store in this picture on the east side of Crawford Street between Firestone and Second Street. That same year, he also purchased a home on College Avenue. Dr. Rowley operated his medical practice in Renfro's drug store until 1907. Ed Mather had a jewelry shop inside.

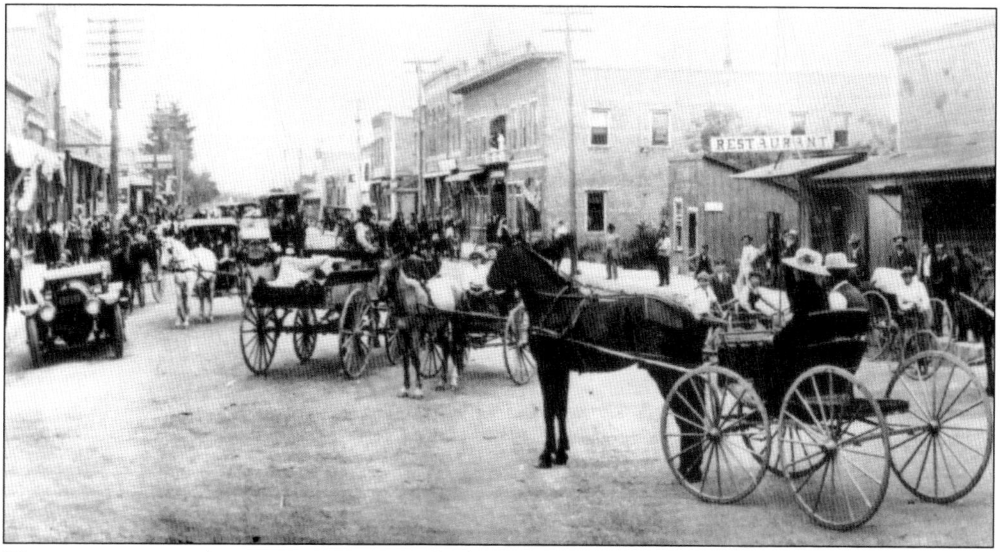

This picture was taken in 1911 on Crawford Street near First Street (Firestone Boulevard). In early 1911, Crawford Street and other roads in Downey were paved. This was a big event, and occasioned the taking of one of the best photographs of early Downey. Looking south down Crawford Street, this photograph captures Downey's early district shortly before World War I. On the near right is McKellar's Furniture Store. McKellar's first store was destroyed by fire in 1901, and this brick building replaced it.

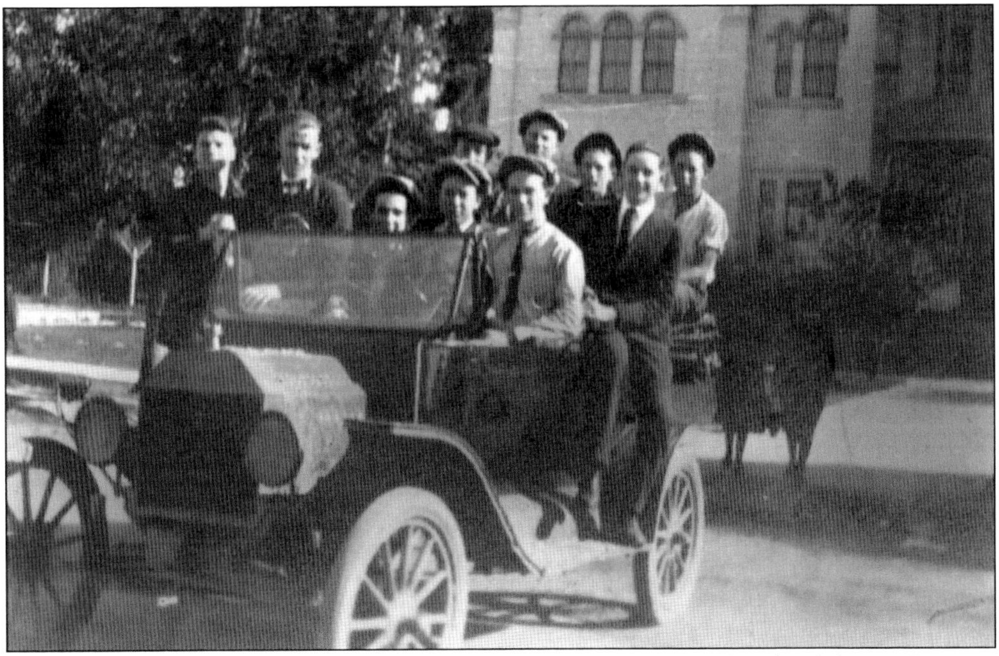

This *c.* 1919 picture shows a group of Downey High boys in a 1914 Ford. Behind them is Downey Union High School, previously known as Los Nietos Valley High School. High school classes began in the Downey Grammar School auditorium at Dolan and Second Streets. On December 9, 1905, the high school was dedicated and, in 1915, renamed Downey Union High School.

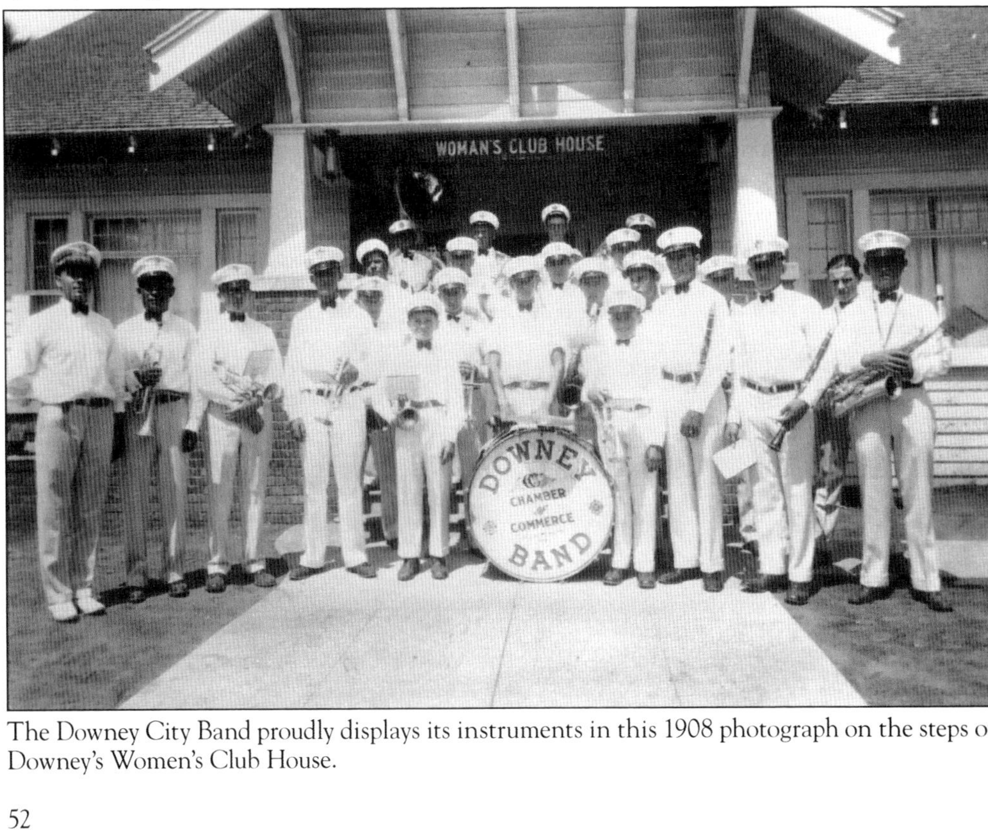

The Downey City Band proudly displays its instruments in this 1908 photograph on the steps of Downey's Women's Club House.

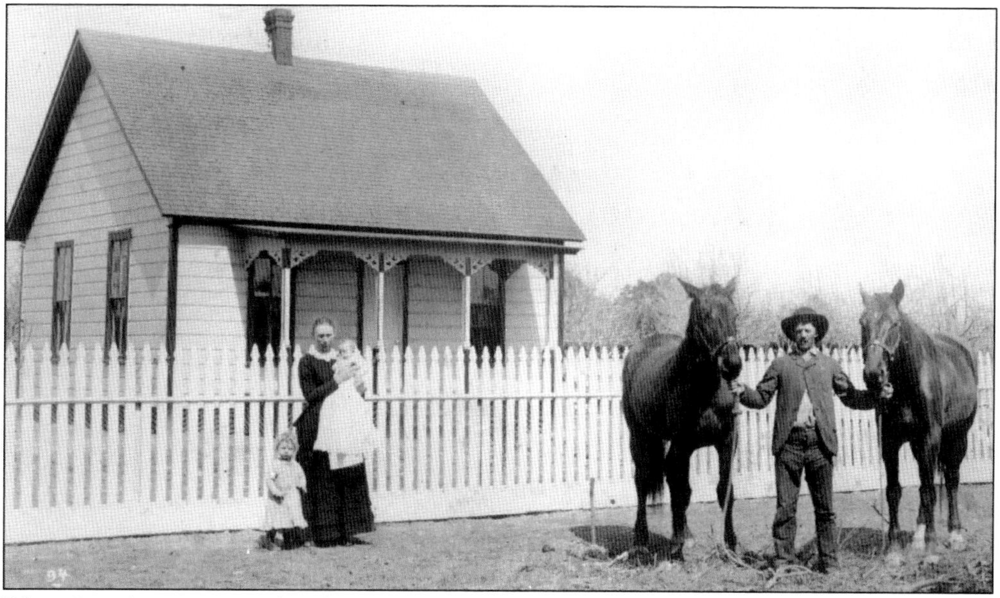

Edwin P. and Nannie Maude Adams Dismukes built their home in 1897 near the northwest corner of Firestone and Paramount Boulevards. Nannie's father was Rev. Samuel M. Adams, a Mississippi native who arrived in Downey in 1874. A Southern Methodist minister, Adams was one of the Los Nietos Collegiate Institute's first teachers. Edwin P. Dismukes was born in Tennessee in June 1858. His father, George E. Dismukes, brought his family to Downey in 1874.

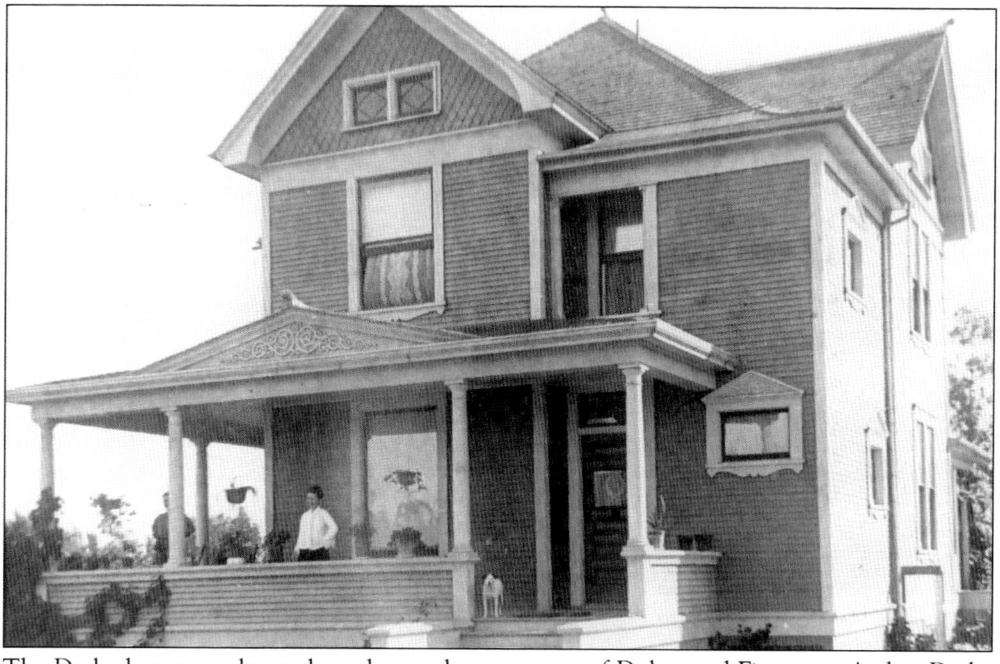

The Darby home was located on the southwest corner of Dolan and Firestone. Arthur Darby worked over the years for the Downey water works, Home Telephone Company, as an insurance agent, and as vice-president of the Los Nietos Valley Bank. His father, hotelkeeper John Howell Darby, came to Downey in 1888. As a young man, Arthur Darby started his business career while bookkeeping for the Smith, Darby, and Nolan grocery store partly owned by his father.

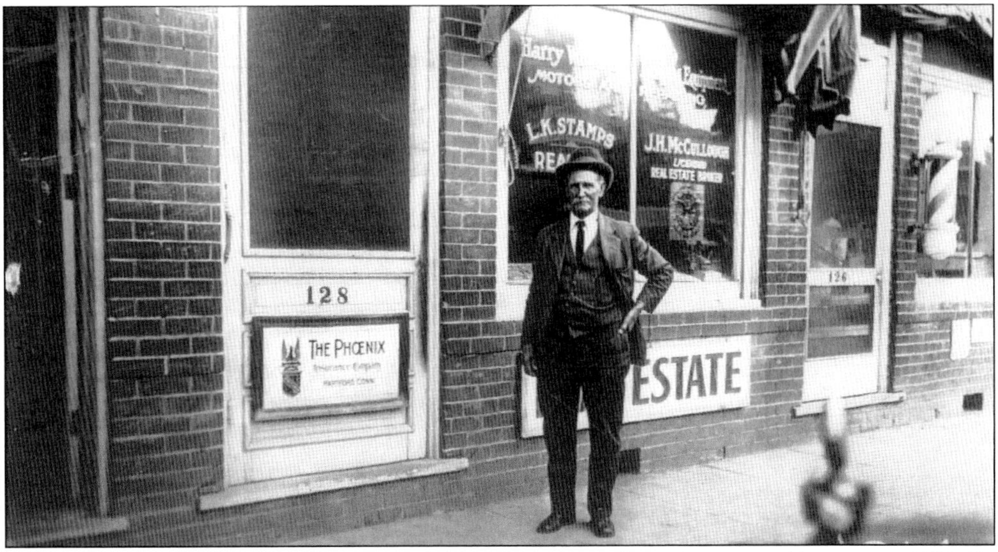

A former lumber man, Lucius K. Stamps came from Lewisville, Arkansas, to Downey in 1892. By 1898, Stamps had purchased acreage in the Downey area and raised a family with his wife Eleanor Sanders. When Lucius retired from farming, he opened this real estate office and became partners with Joe McCullough, the former blacksmith. This photograph was taken on Crawford Avenue in 1915. Stamps died in 1937 and his descendants include Downey's first mayor, James L. Stamps.

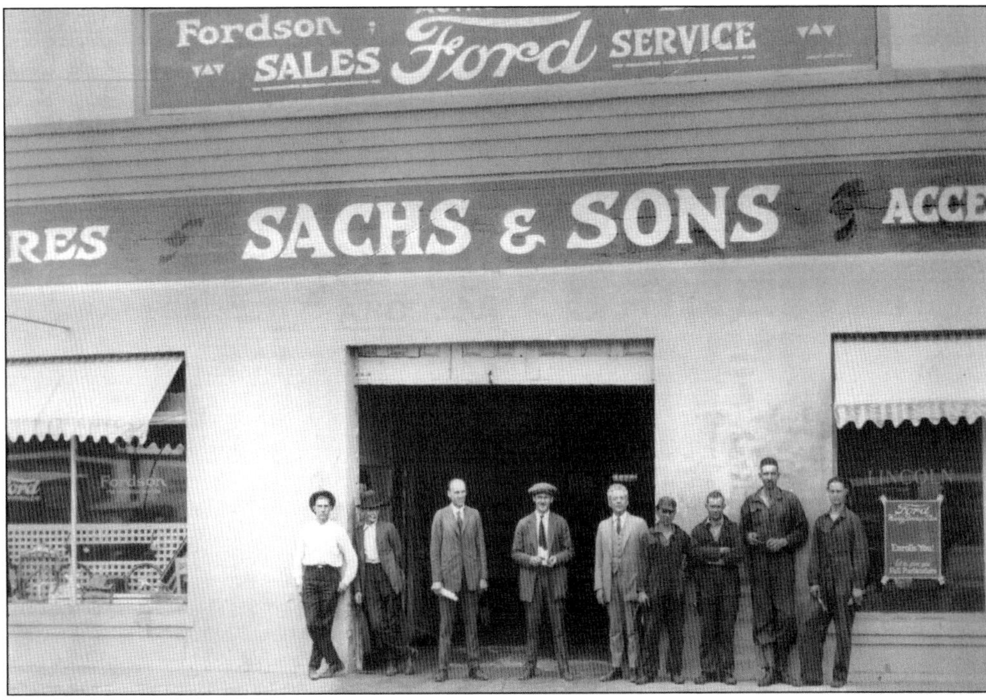

This photograph shows Sachs and Sons Ford dealership on Crawford Street around 1922. Second from the left is Leonard "Pop" Sachs. His son Wayne T. Sachs stands in the center of the doorway wearing a hat. Leonard and sons Ray and Wayne sold Fordson tractors, Ford cars and trucks, and Lincoln automobiles. In the 1940s, the dealership moved up to Downey Avenue, later becoming Sachs & Sons Lincoln Mercury.

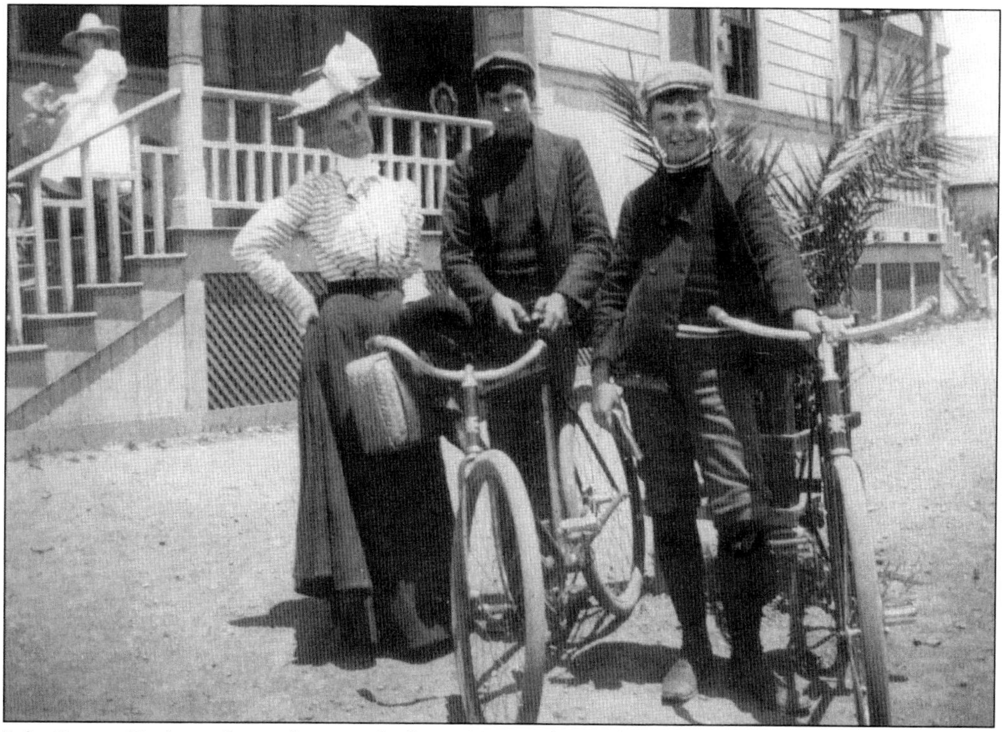

Julia Reavis Butler is shown here in the late 1890s with two boys on bicycles in a photograph that captures the country feel of early Downey.

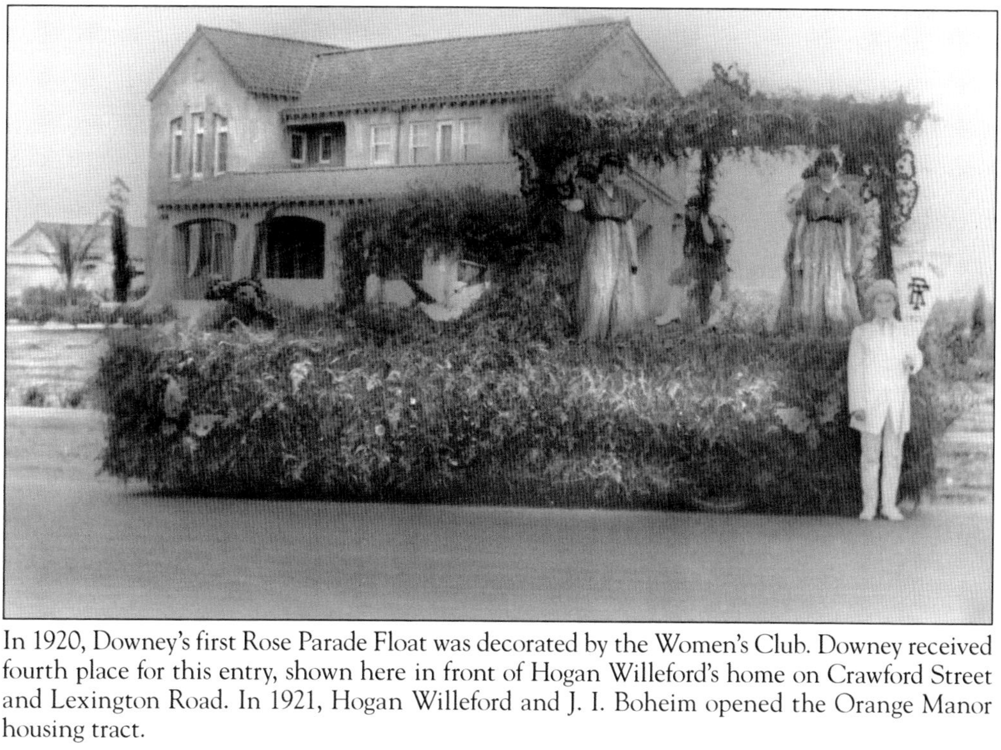

In 1920, Downey's first Rose Parade Float was decorated by the Women's Club. Downey received fourth place for this entry, shown here in front of Hogan Willeford's home on Crawford Street and Lexington Road. In 1921, Hogan Willeford and J. I. Boheim opened the Orange Manor housing tract.

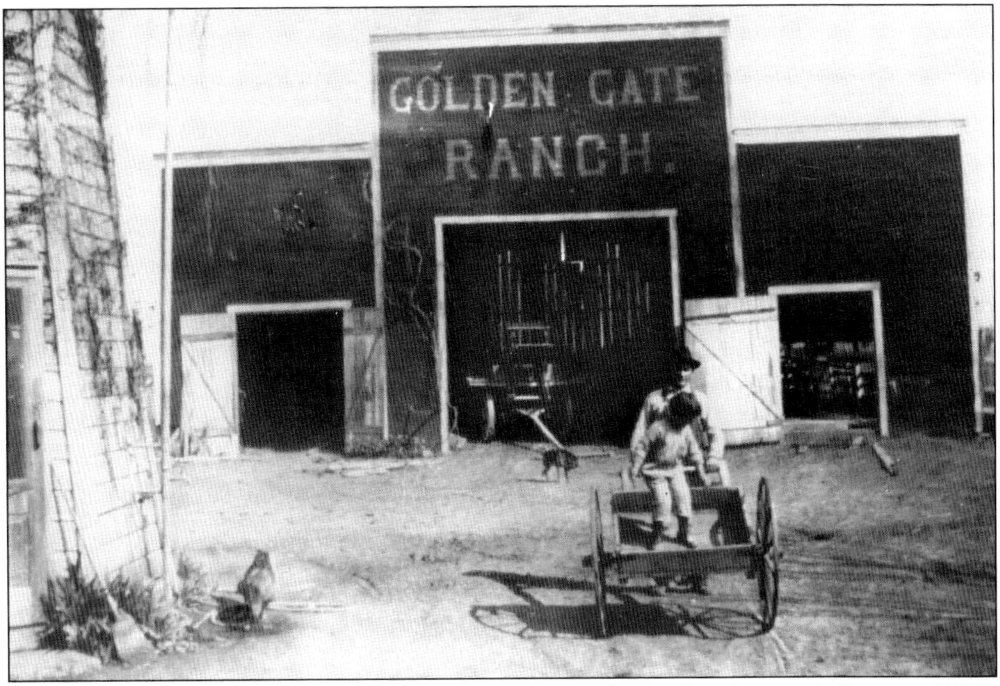

The Golden Gate Ranch was in the 9000 block of Foster Bridge Road in south Downey. Ed W. Lewis came from Nebraska in 1895, and his sons Joe and Bill bought 50 acres near Woodruff Avenue and Foster Bridge Road, where they farmed sugar beets and Klondike strawberries. Son Ed C. Lewis bought 25 acres on Foster Bridge Road and Ardis Street and opened Golden Gate Ranch, raising alfalfa, sugar beets, corn, and walnuts.

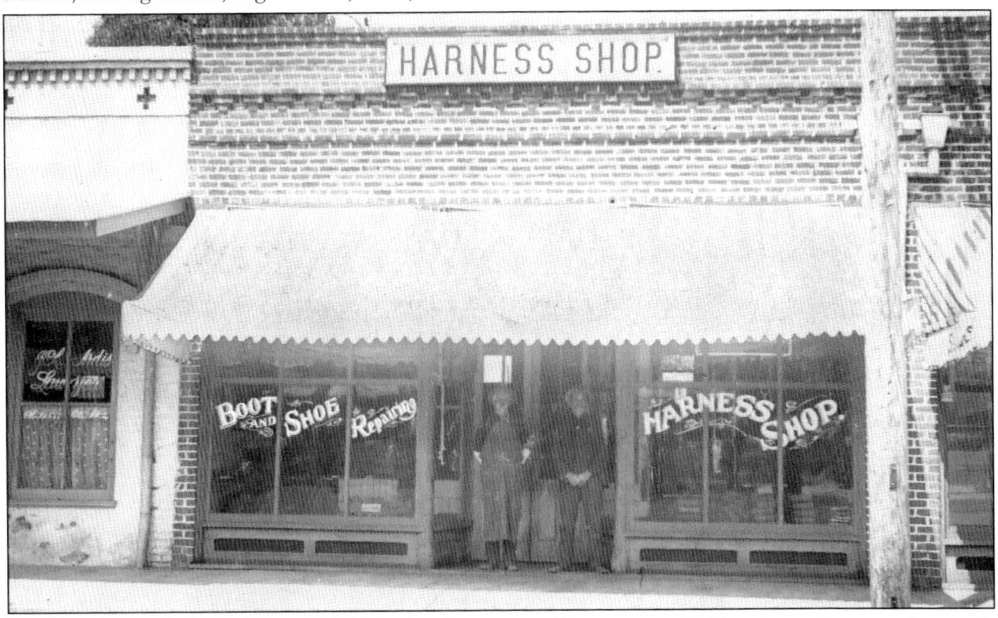

William Weirbach Sr., a native of Boyle Heights, visited Downey in 1887 and was impressed enough to move his business to this shop. Weirbach became Downey's first cobbler and charter member of the Downey Board of Trade, whose vision was to "arouse and concentrate public opinion on all matters of general importance to the town of Downey and vicinity."

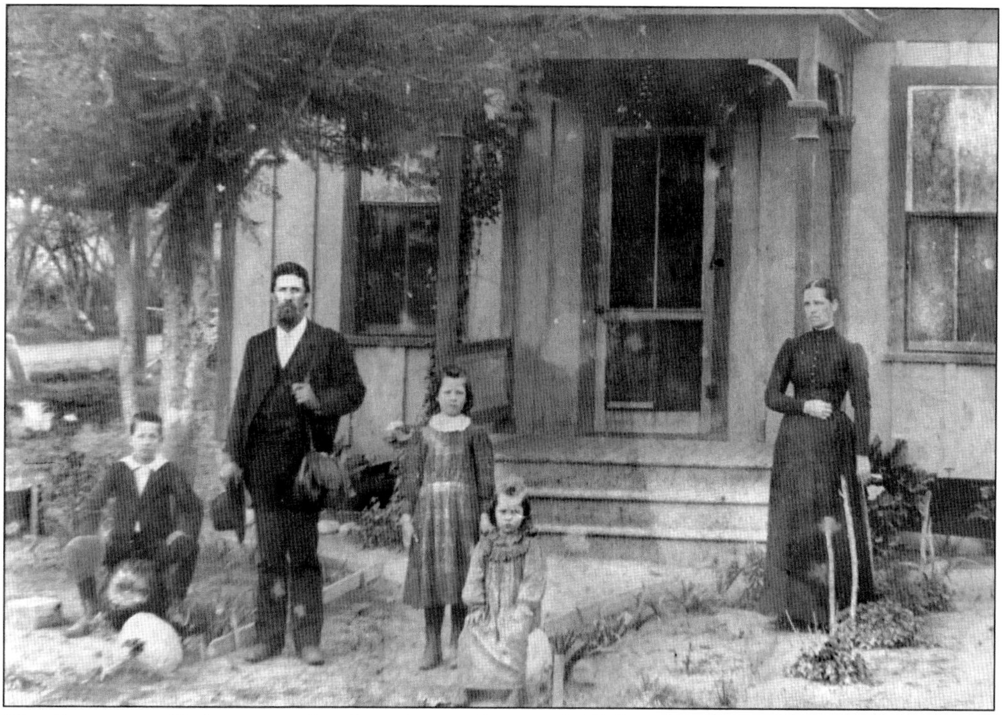

The Benjamin Witherspoon family is depicted around 1895 at their home built in 1889. Shown here from left to right are Lester Witherspoon, Benjamin Witherspoon, Della Witherspoon, Zora Witherspoon, and Maniza Witherspoon (pregnant with child). Benjamin Witherspoon was Downey's deputy sheriff for 39 years. The Witherspoon home was on the northeast corner of Paramount and Firestone Boulevards.

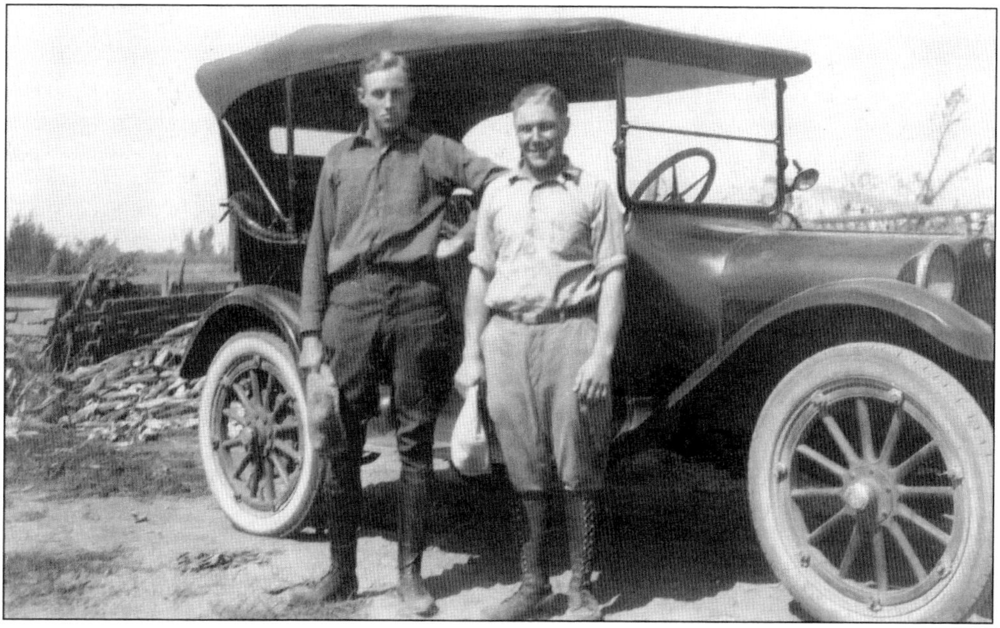

Willie Stevenson and friend Foster Bruce pose near the Stevenson Ranch on Washburn Crossing Road. The Stevenson family ran a citrus orchard in Downey.

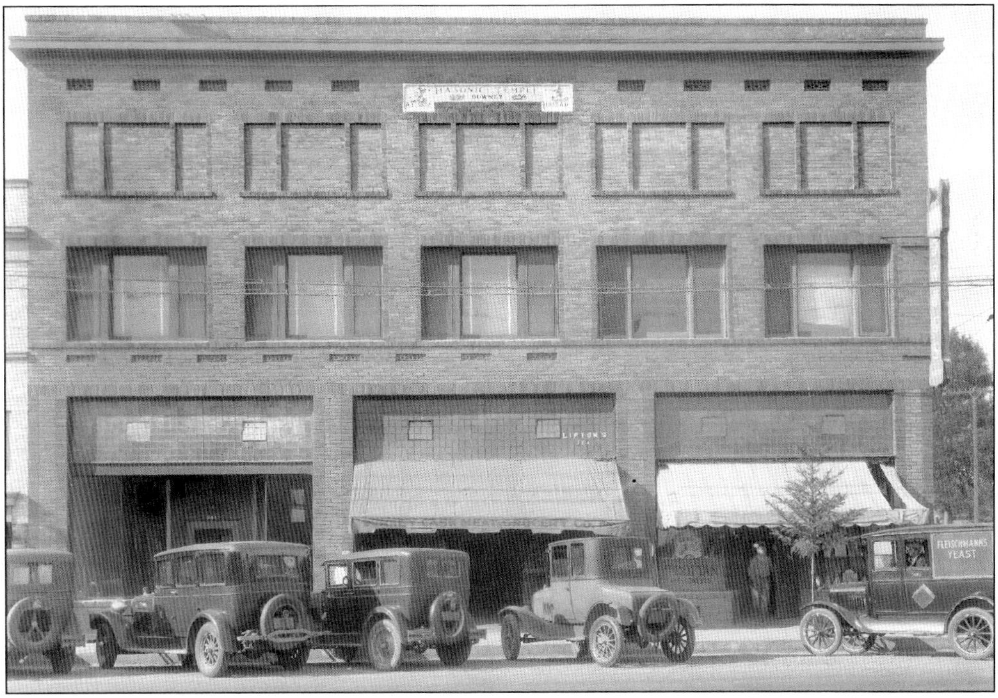

Downey Masonic Temple is depicted here in the 1920s at Third and Crawford Streets. The cornerstone was laid "in true and ancient form" on November 13, 1922, for the "new" Downey Masonic Temple. On August 1, 1871, local Masons met at Rev. Spurlock's home to discuss a future lodge. The first lodge meeting was held in the Mercantile House of Frank E. Adams at College Settlement. Gov. John Downey presented the lodge with a set of silver officer jewels at its first official meeting.

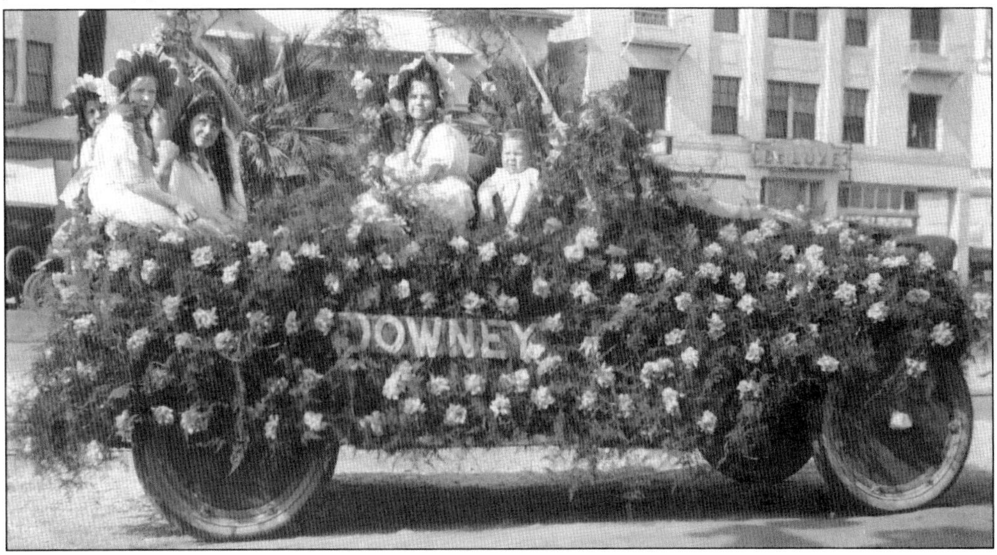

On January 1, 1921, the City of Downey received a prize for a float entered in Pasadena's Tournament of Roses Parade. Inside of the flowery were Mida Edmonson, Dorothy Dismukes, Muriel Nyers, Edna Clare Vam Matre, and Jenevieve Holman. The award winning float was sponsored by the Downey Women's Club. Downey has had many prize winners since 1920 due to the hard work of the Downey Rose Float Association.

Seen here in 1910, barber Sid Moore operated a barbershop and delivery service in Downey on Crawford Street (Downey Avenue) at Second Street near Downey Heat and Power Company. He sold the barbershop in 1918 to R. L. Culley.

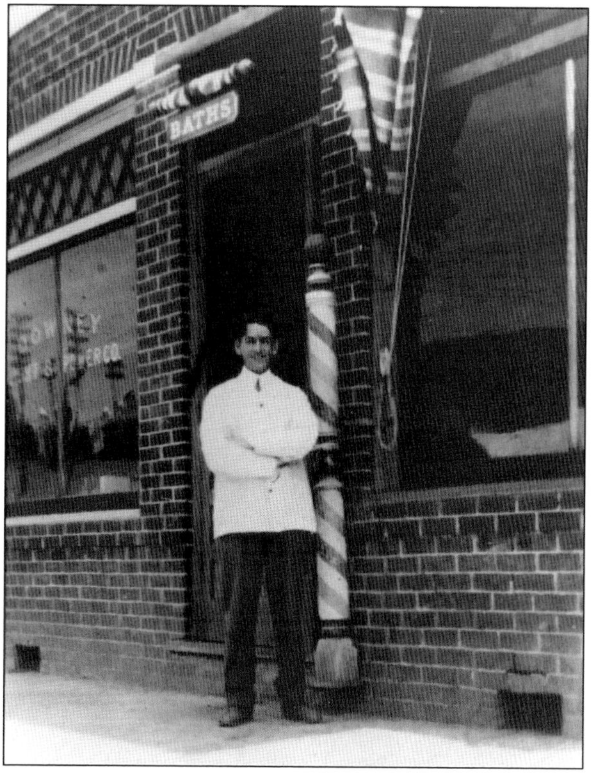

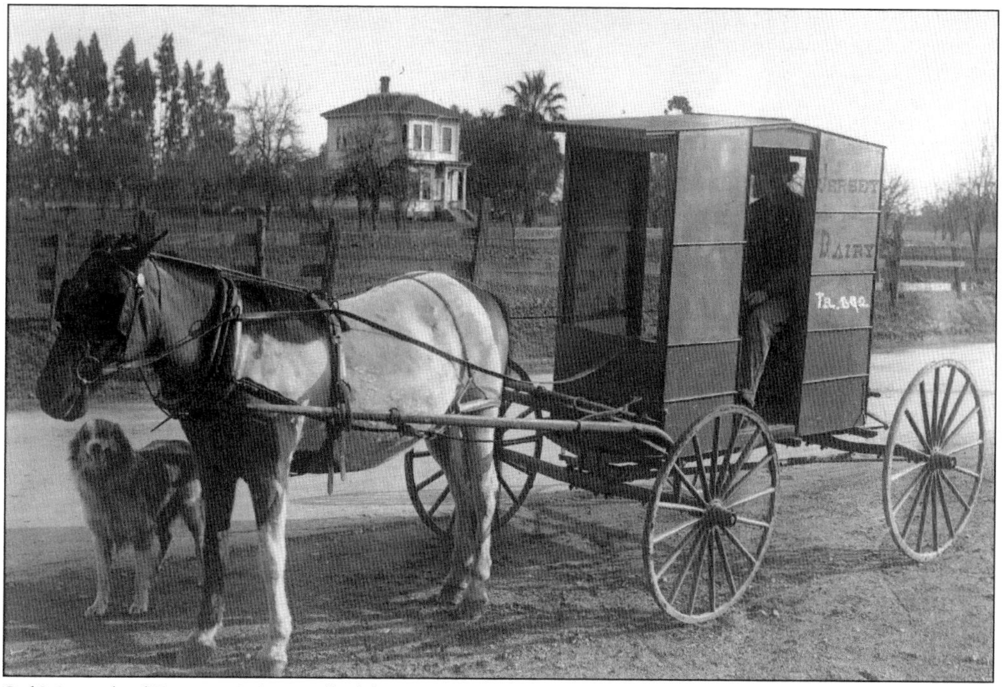

Sid Moore had Downey's first milk delivery service with "Doc" McCormic as driver. This photograph was taken looking from west to east on North Crawford Street (Downey Avenue) near Lexington Road in 1909. Lexington currently runs between Downey and Brookshire Avenues.

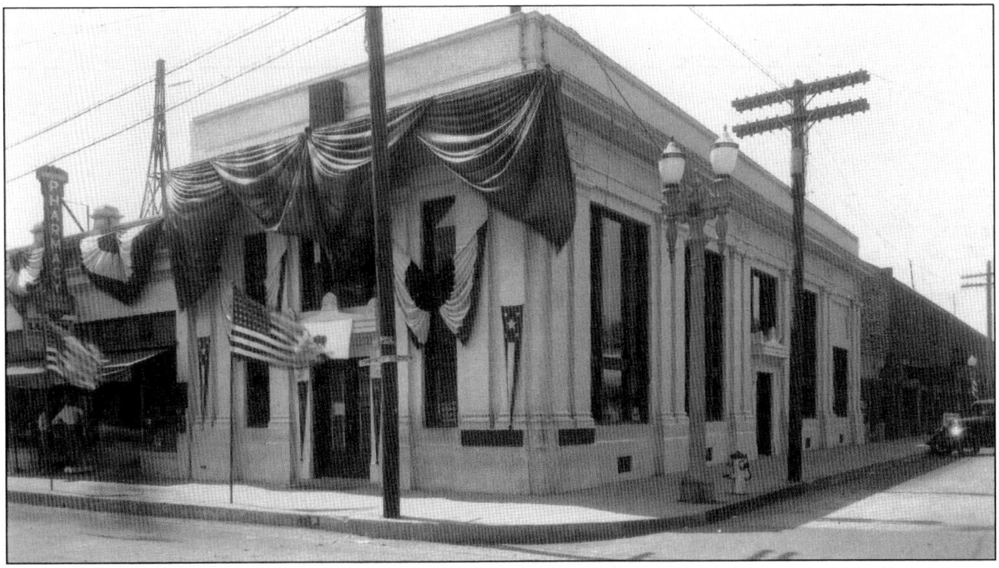

Located on the corner of Crawford and Second Street beside Preston's Pharmacy was Los Nietos Valley Bank. The bank's original owners, H. A. Scott and O. Mahome, opened its doors in 1887. Four years later, the bank was incorporated. The bank's officers included Dr. Rowley, A. L. Darby, John Rudd, C. R. Church, and Joseph Smith. Its board of directors included James C. Rives, Frank Burke, and Albert L. Ball—all pillars of the local community. Just after World War I the bank advertised a capital surplus of $93,750.

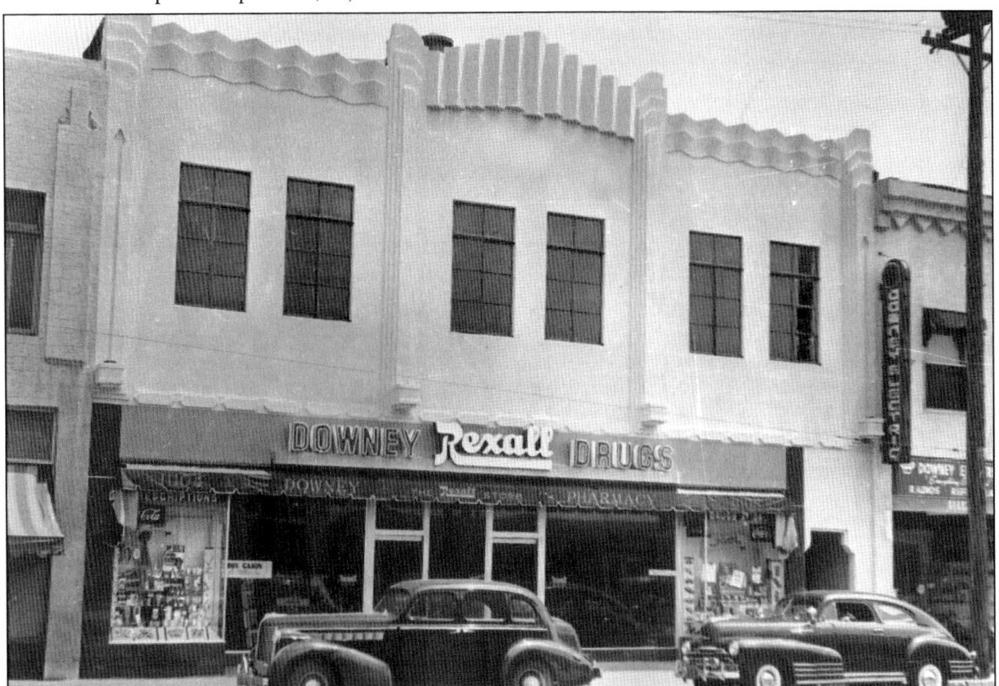

This picture shows Downey's Rexall Drugs in the 1940s. Rexall was located on 11104 Downey Avenue near the southeast corner at Second Street. With its beautiful art deco accents, Rexall Drugs survived until the Downey Avenue widening and redevelopment in the 1960s and 1970s.

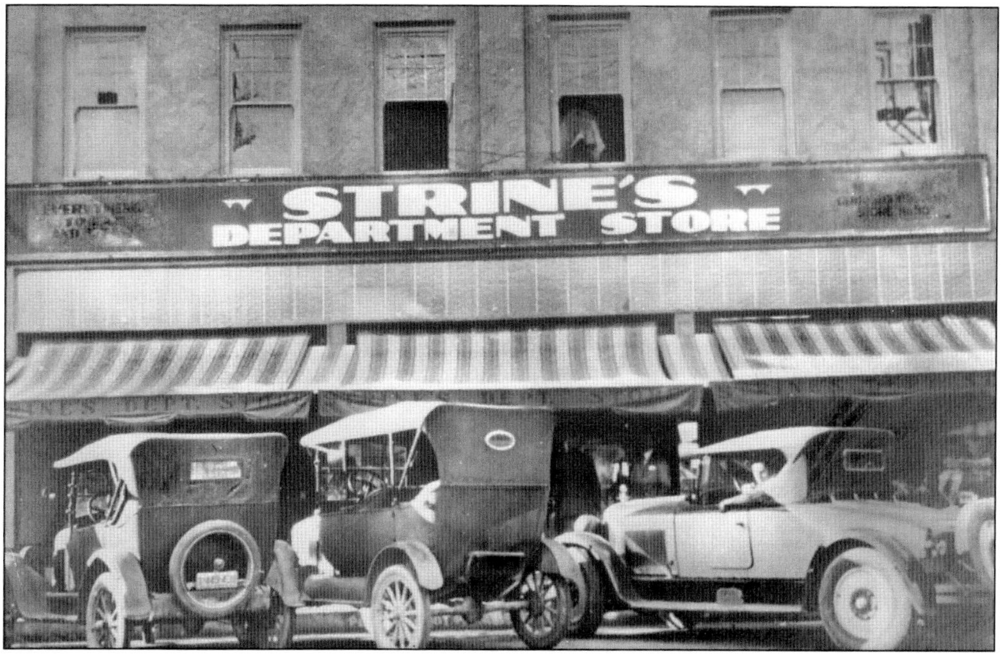

The Strine Brothers store is pictured here in 1925 on the west side of Downey Avenue, near the alley at Second Street. The Strine Brothers wagon delivered daily general merchandise and was a common sight each weekday delivering "hay, grain, and groceries" to the Downey area.

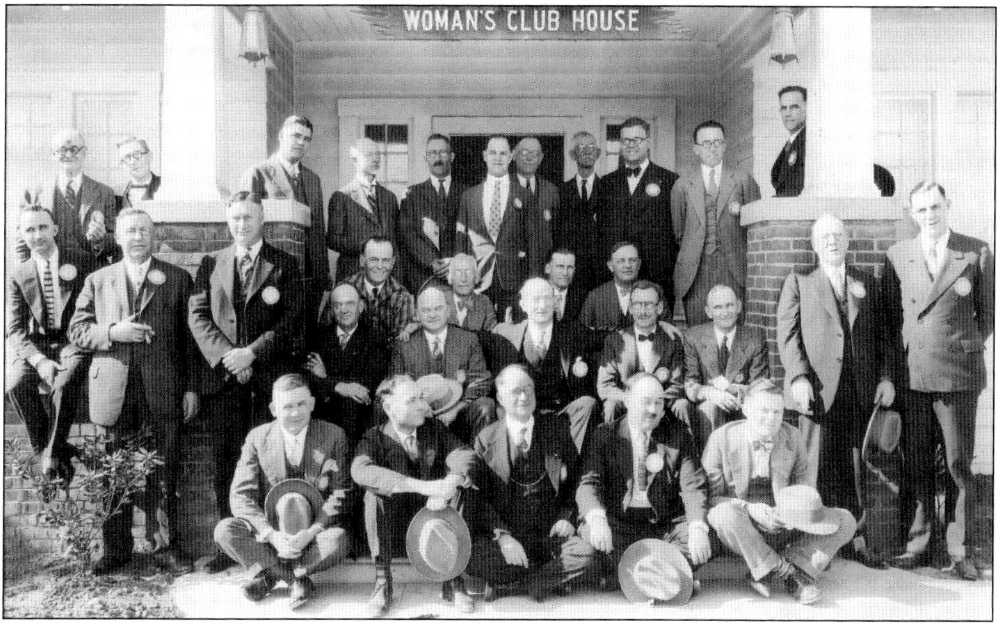

The Downey Rotary Club meets at the Women's Club House in 1930. The Women's Club of Downey purchased the land to build this house in 1901. Originally known as the "Friday Afternoon Club," and later the "Saturday Afternoon Club," the Women's Club of Downey used this as their meeting place for many years. The "Friday Afternoon Club" began in the home of Mrs. J. W. McKellar in December 1898. The Women's Club established a public library in 1901 under the determination of Josie McKellar.

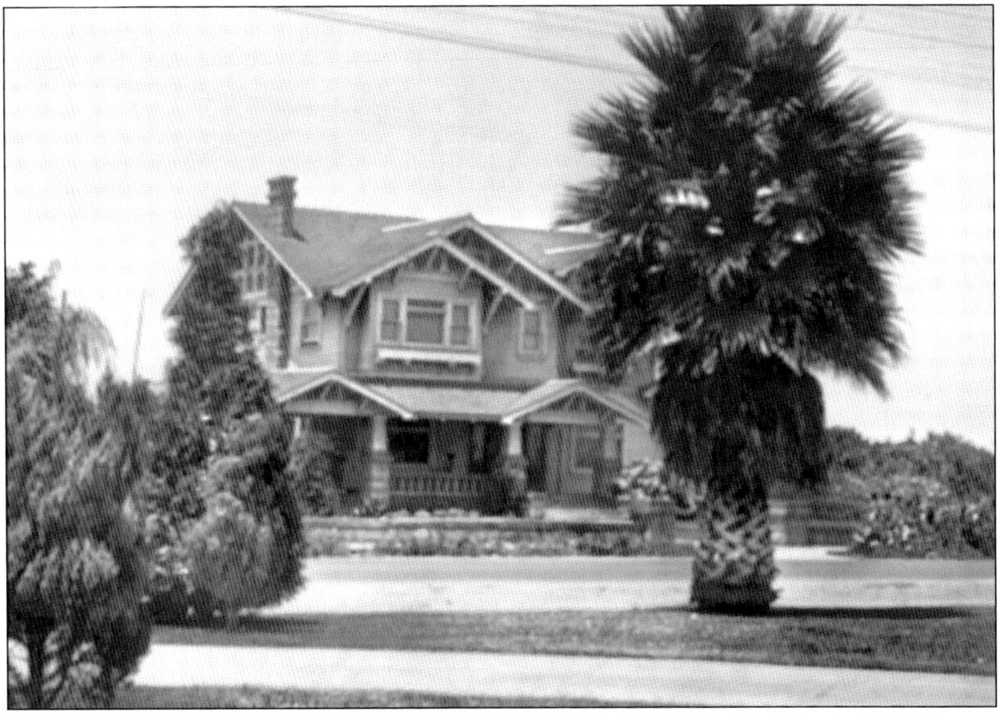

The Manning home was at 10451 Downey Avenue at Cherokee between the Villa Nova Apartments and Our Lady of Perpetual Help School. This Craftsman style home was a Downey landmark built in 1913 by T. R. Manning. "Riley" Manning came to Downey from Arkansas in 1871.

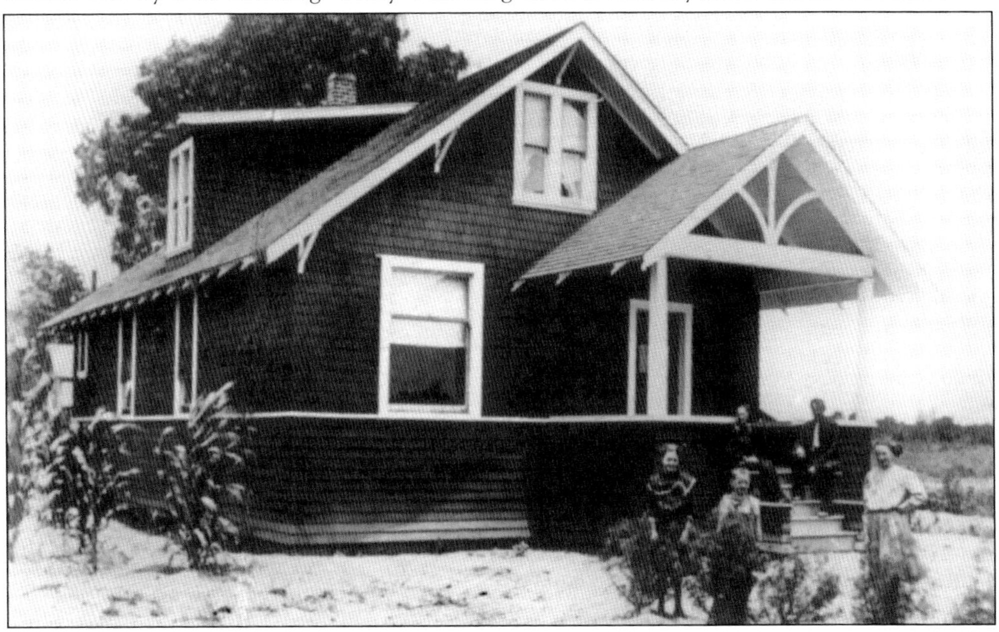

Orey Gifford and family moved into this home at 9635 N. Downey Avenue in 1909. During the years 1908 and 1909, electricity came to Downey and on March 15, 1908, J. H. Ardis remarked to a celebratory dinner crowd, " Nature has been kind to us, but we have been slow to develop its resources."

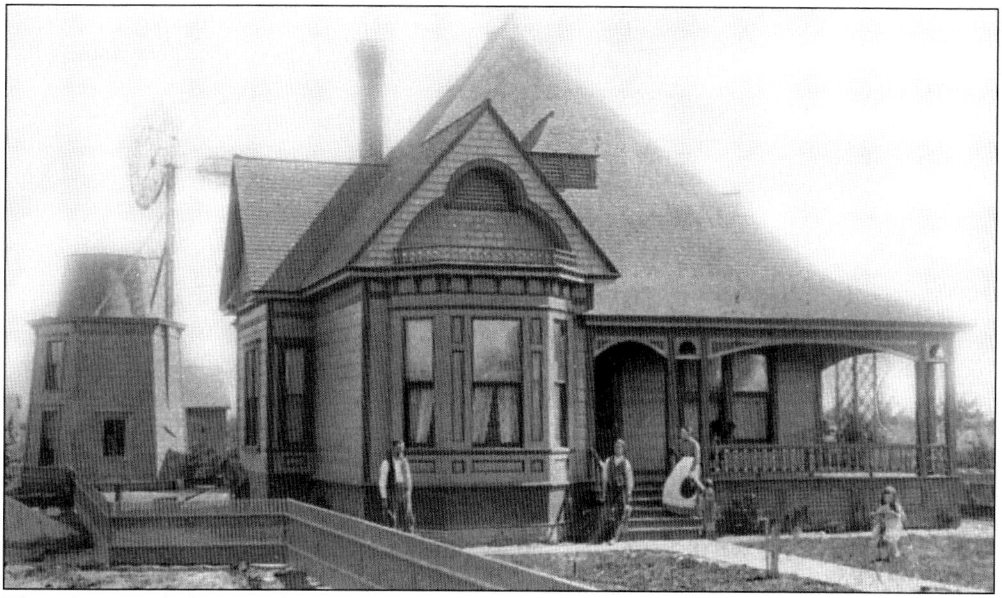

This photograph from Myda Hass Bartgis, who was born in this house, shows the J. E. Jenison home and ranch in Downey in the early 1890s. John Ewing Jenison, Roy Jenison, Susan Jenison, and Girlie Jenison are pictured here. By 1930 the Jenison Ranch was located in the lots between Florence Avenue south to Firestone Boulevard and Lakewood Boulevard to the west off Woodruff. On Woodruff south from Florence Avenue to Firestone Boulevard, much of the acreage on the west side belonged to J. E. Jenison and then son Roy Jenison, Roger Ball's grandfather.

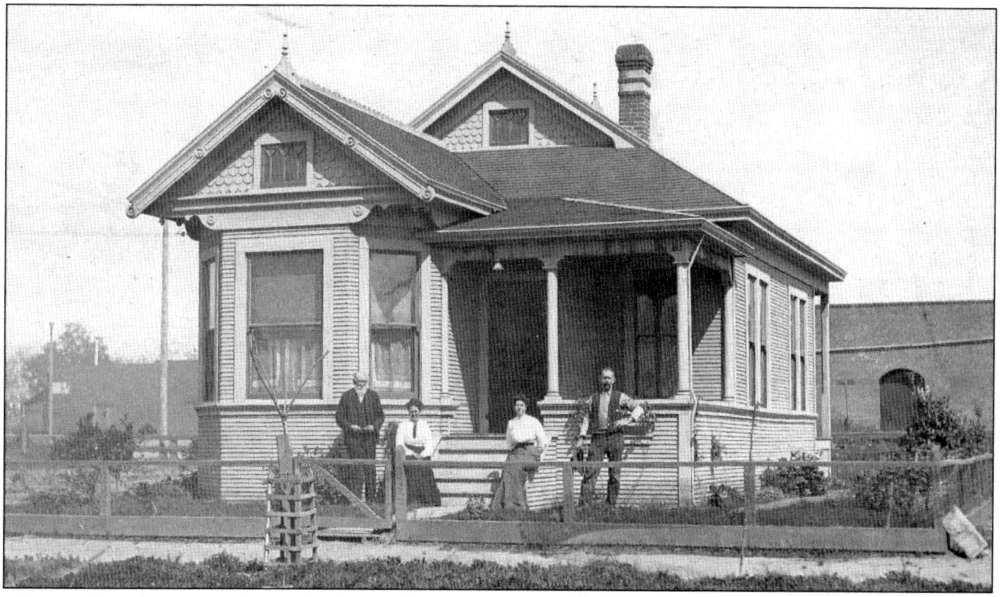

This undated picture shows William Harper, Mrs. William Harper, and Mr. and Mrs. Robert Harper at their home in north Downey. In 1876 William Harper married the daughter of Jacob Lower, Alpha Jane. The Harpers' first two children were daughter Clara and son Robert. William Harper purchased 20 acres in Downey near "Florence and Lexington" with 10 acres of alfalfa and 10 acres of oranges. The children attended the original Gallatin School on Florence Avenue and Tweedy Lane and their teacher was Josephine McKellar.

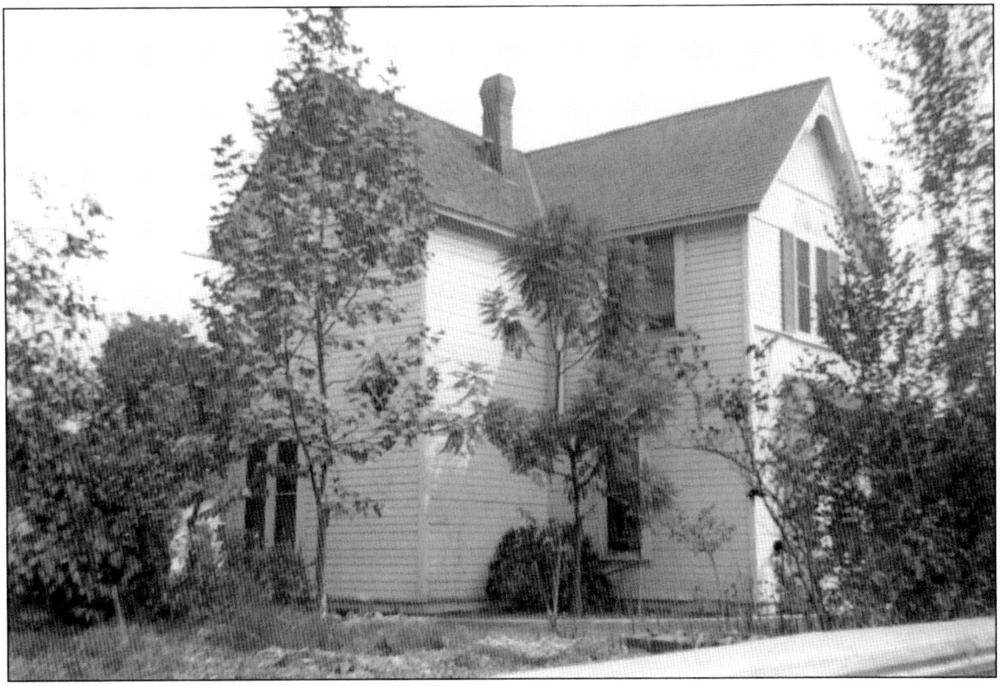

This photograph shows the home of Dr. Q. J. Rowley on the northeast corner of Third and La Reina. Local physician Rowley opened his office in T. R. Renfro's drug store in 1887 and stayed in Downey until 1907 when he moved to Los Angeles.

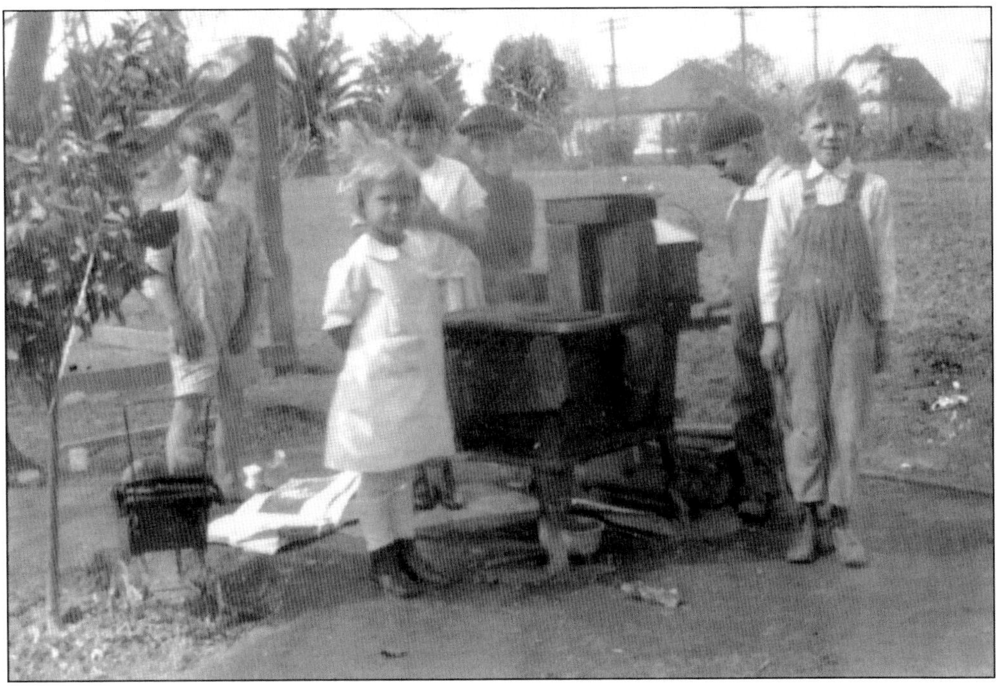

Kids are shown here at play in the neighborhood of Third Street and La Reina near the Wilson home, around 1917. The Wilsons lived across College Avenue (Paramount Boulevard) from the Rives Mansion near Second and Third Streets.

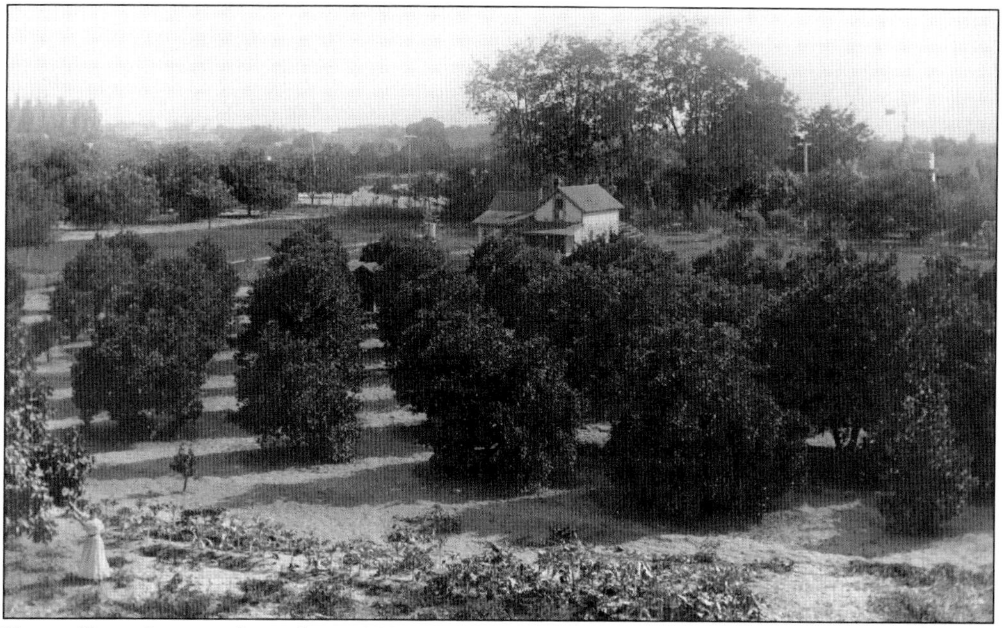

Here is Harry Jannison's ranch in 1908 next to Rupert Paxton's citrus ranch in northeast Downey located just south of Telegraph Road between Passons and True Streets. Notice the Paxton ranch windmill and locust trees in the background. This area was known as "Rivera" until Downey's borders became more precise.

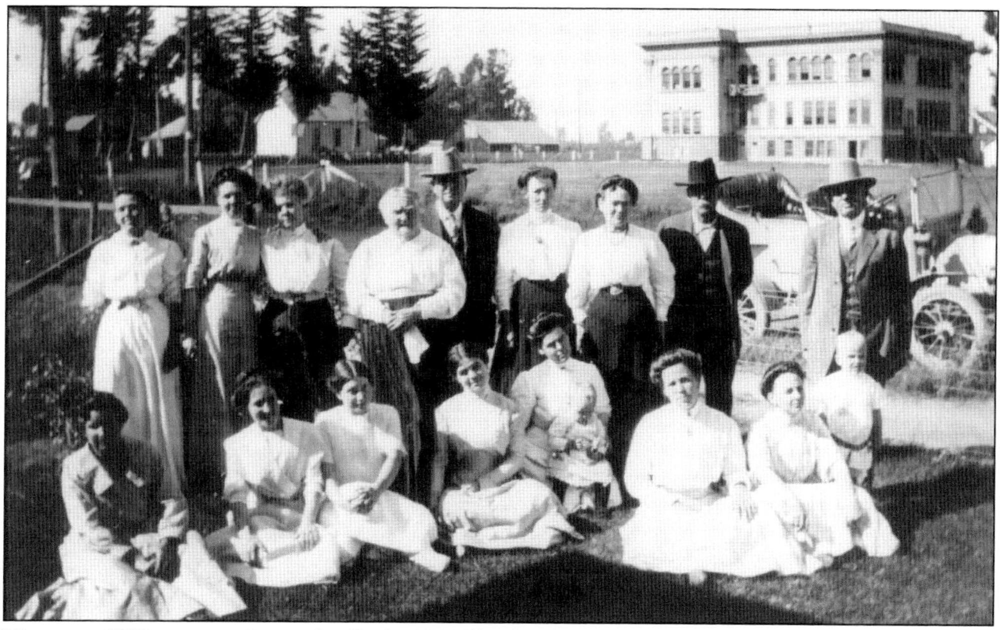

This pre–1920 picture shows the Rufus W. Ellis family at the home of Sarah and John Barnett on First Street (Firestone Boulevard). In the background is Downey Union High, seen from the side. Pictured are, from left to right (second row) Beth Ellis Triggs, Olive Ellis Taylor, Sarah Ellis Barnett, unknown woman, John Barnett, Maggie Ellis, Hanna Ellis, Jim Ellis, and Tom Ellis. Among those pictured in the first row are Bess Ellis and Jennie Ellis. Rufus W. Ellis came to California from Tennessee in 1873 and raised 10 children.

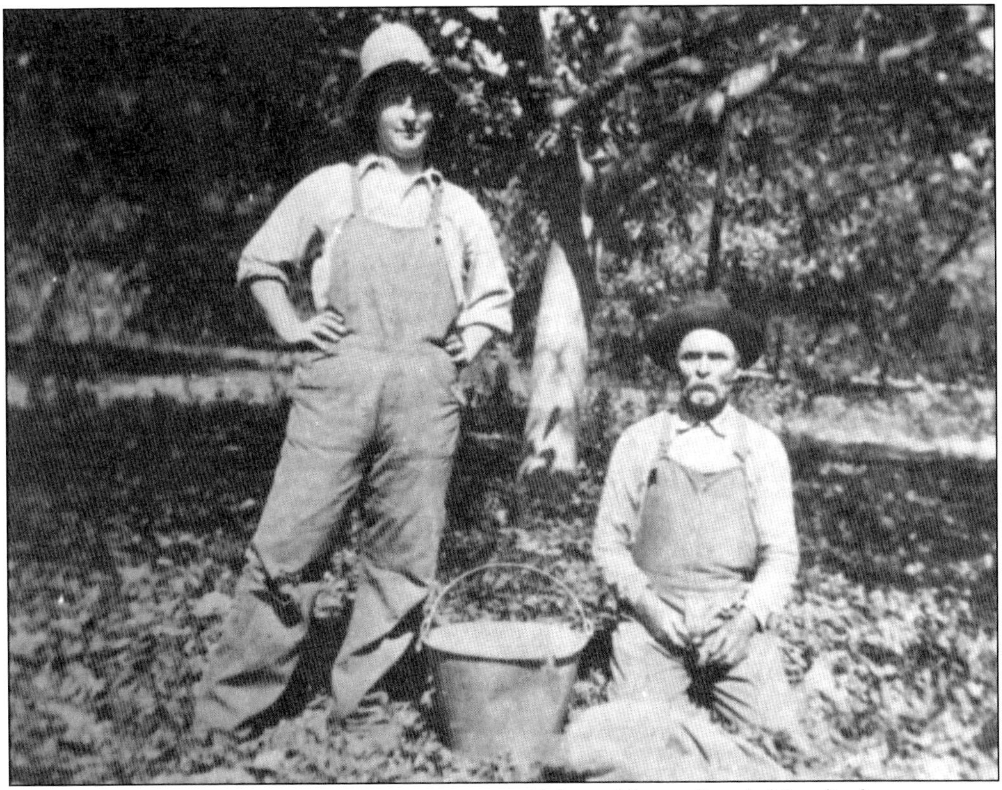

Eula and James Brookshire dig for potatoes in 1917 on the Brookshire ranch north of Cherokee at Brookshire Avenue, just south of 10th Street.

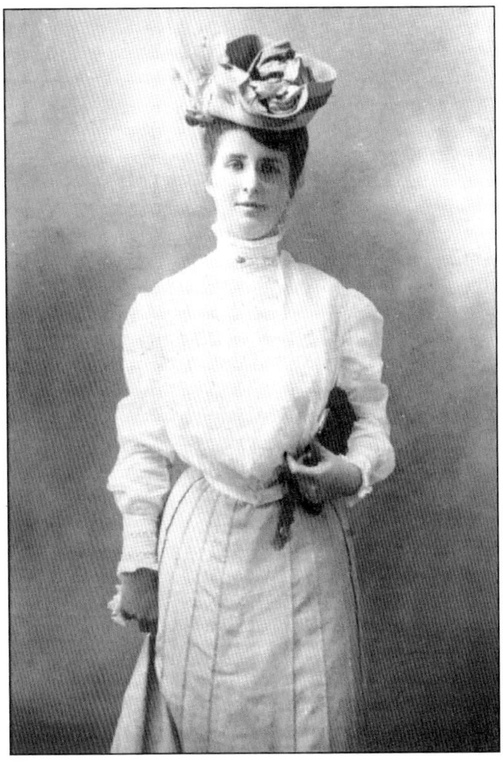

Eula Brookshire Rowe, daughter of James and Emma H. Brookshire, posed for this photograph around 1920. The Brookshire home was at 10336 Brookshire Avenue, known in other parts of Downey as Price Road, San Gabriel Boulevard, and Church Street. James Brookshire's daughter Margaret married William H. Morrow Sr. in 1866. Eula Brookshire opened a dressmaking shop on Downey Avenue in 1924 next to Miss Coke's Variety Store.

Clara Mayes was a daughter of Robert Henry Mayes who traveled by covered wagon to Downey in 1864 from Hopkinsville, Kentucky. Clara was his sixth of 10 children. She was born in 1868 in Downey and attended Gallatin School. She was the younger sister of Robert S. Mayes who owned property near Arrington Square at Florence Avenue and Lakewood Boulevard east to Downey–Sanford Bridge Road.

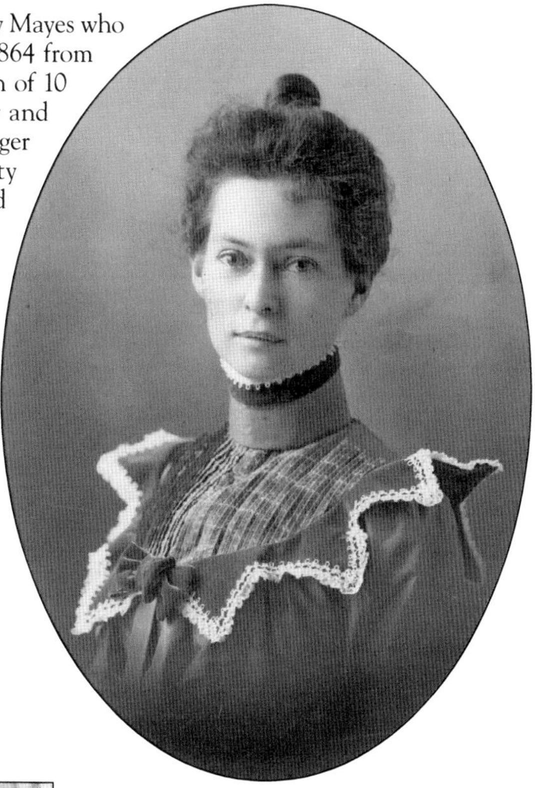

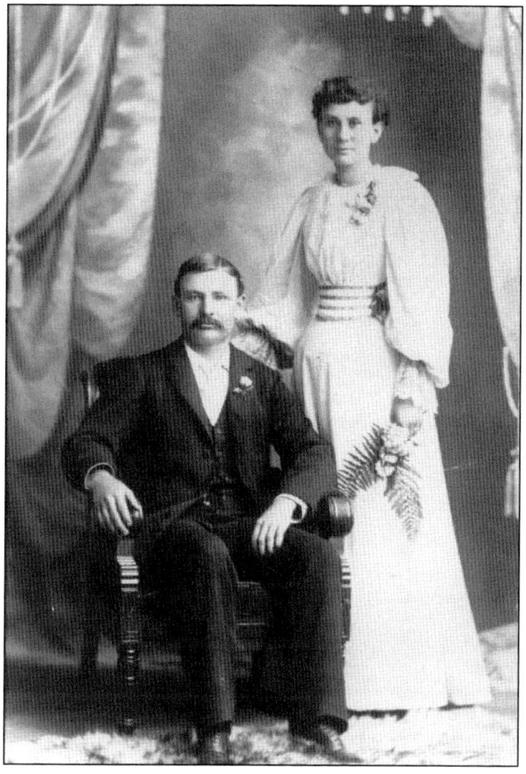

William H. Morrow Jr. and Alma Cecilia Gray on their wedding day, August 22, 1896. William Morrow Jr. was the third of nine children and was born on December 9, 1870 and died on November 5, 1942. He was the son of Margaret Brookshire and William Morrow Sr. William Morrow Jr. ran the large family ranch in north Downey. The Morrows were neighbors to the Brookshire family.

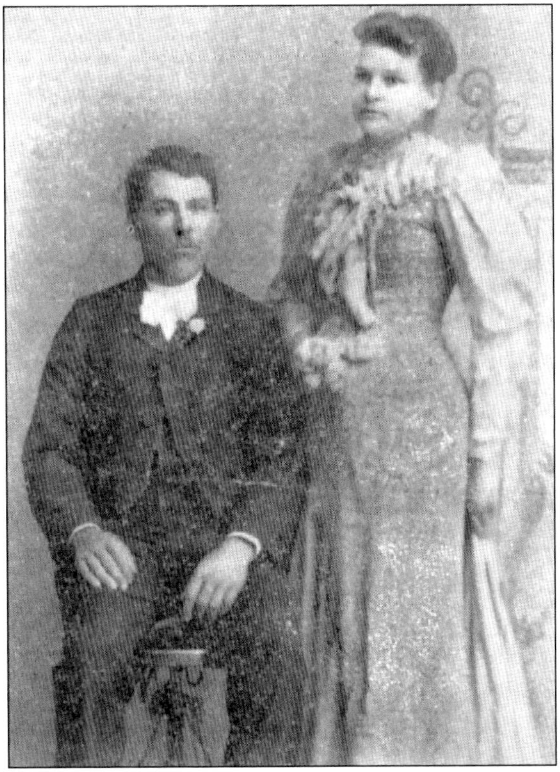

Frank Morrison and Easter Bangle Morrison were married on March 27, 1895, in their home on Bangle. Easter Morrison wrote *History of Downey and Vicinity* in 1939. Frank Morrison came to Downey in 1884 and Mrs. Morrison came to Downey in 1874, a few months after being born in Lafayette Springs, Mississippi. Soon after marrying, they purchased 10 acres near Dacosta and Mattock in Downey, and lived there for 57 years.

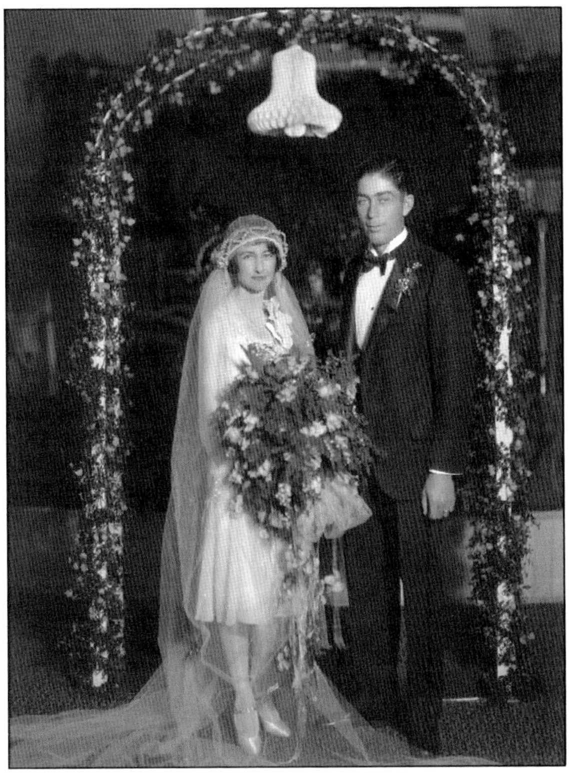

This is a photograph from the December 28, 1927, wedding of Walter Love and Burnice Mayes. Burnice was one of three daughters of Robert S. Mayes, son of Robert Henry Mayes, who purchased property in 1864 on what is now Florence Avenue between Sanford-Bridge Road and Lakewood Boulevard. Walter and Burnice Love began developing the old ranch property after World War II with homes, apartments, and commercial business.

Arthur Darby, son of John Howell Darby and Georgia Benbrook Smart, were married on May 12, 1901, in Downey. Arthur Darby was born in De Soto Parish, Louisiana, on September 24, 1877 (d. 1941), one of 10 children. A banker and insurance agent, Arthur was owner of the Downey Water Company and president of Home Telephone Company. Mrs. Georgia Darby was the daughter of Mr. and Mrs. Dave Smart who came to Downey from Missouri. Georgia Darby was born on May 5, 1878, in the first house built in Downey, at the corner of First Street (Firestone) and Dolan Avenue.

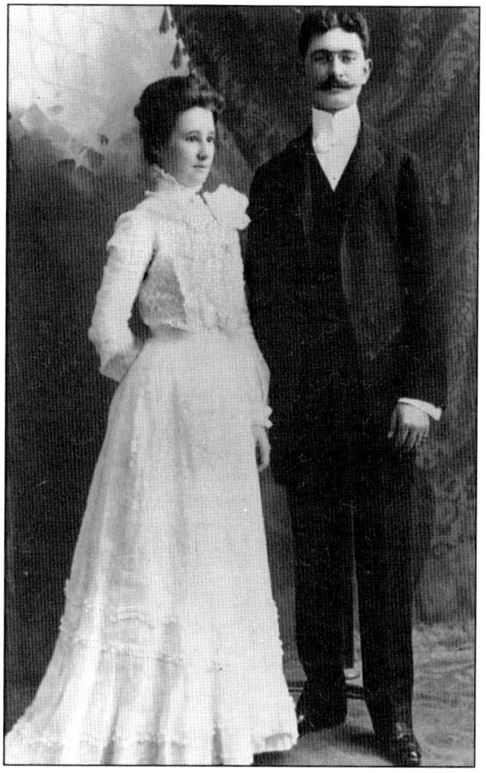

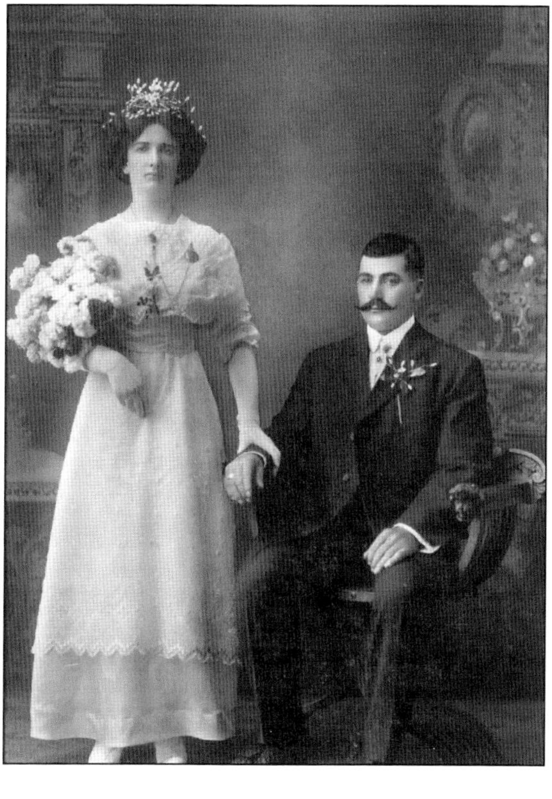

Francois Celestin Pellet and Agnes Crevolin Pellet on their wedding day in spring 1913. The Pellets owned a ranch at the northwest corner of Old River Schoolhouse Road and the railroad tracks just south of Rio Hondo Country Club. The Pellets' neighbors on the east were Frank Burke and James H. Wiley.

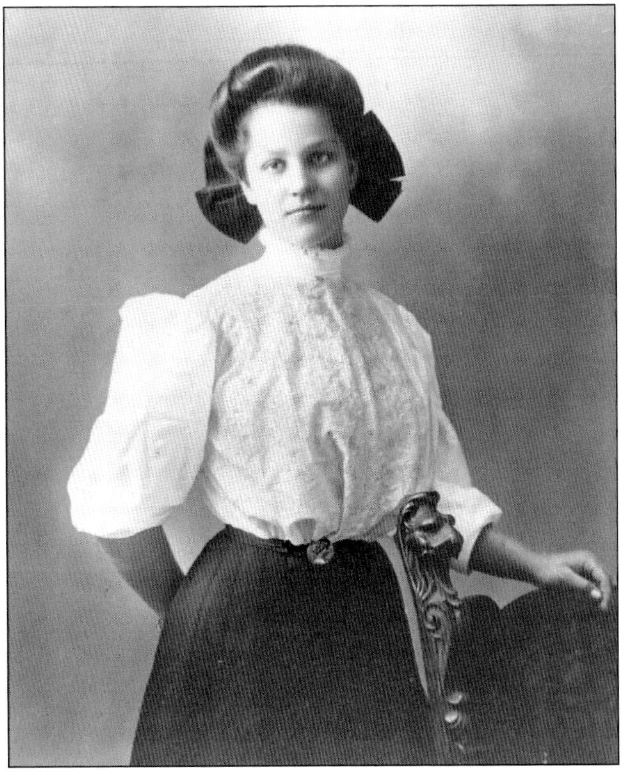

This picture of Zora Witherspoon was taken when she was 16 years old. She was married in 1911 at 20 years old to first husband Otto McComic. The Witherspoons, who lived at Paramount and Firestone Boulevard, were neighbors and friends to the Rives Family. Zora and her husband owned two gas stations in Downey, one at Third Street and Downey Avenue and another at Second and Paramount. Zora lived well into her 90s, and often reminisced of the "horse and buggy days" in early Downey.

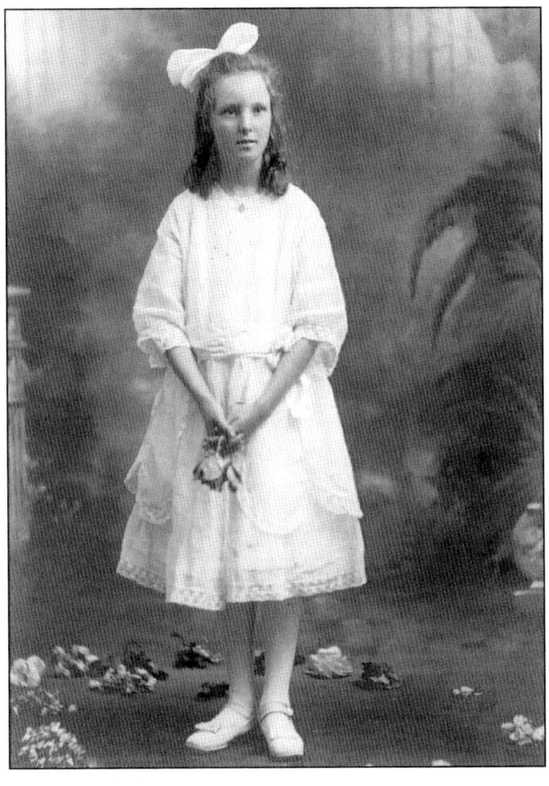

Seen here as a young girl, Lillian Stevenson grew up, lived, and worked with her family at their Washburn Crossing ranch in south Downey. By 1930 the Stevensons still owned 30 acres along Washburn Crossing Road between the current 605 Freeway and Cerritos Avenue (Lakewood Boulevard). This property is just east of former EMSCO Aircraft, now Downey Studios.

Born July 13, 1862, in Los Angeles, Mary Emily Foy was one of the most influential women in Los Angeles County history. At one time a teacher at Alameda School, Foy was an early spokesperson for Women's Suffrage and equal rights. She was Los Angeles County librarian from 1880 to 1884. (When the Los Angeles County Library was founded in 1872, women were not even permitted inside.) The mother of Downey pioneer Margaret Haas, Maude Adams Dismukes, was a student of Foy's at Alameda School. Mary Foy was also a delegate to the 1920 Democratic National Convention.

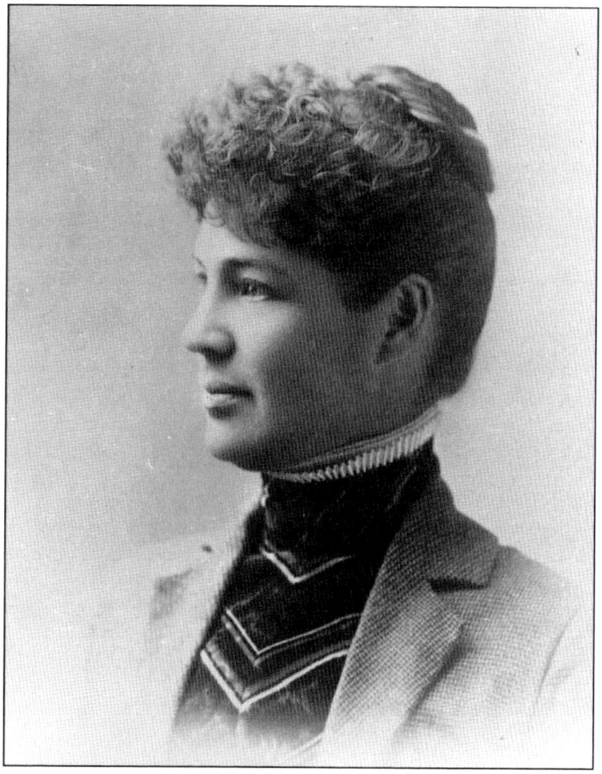

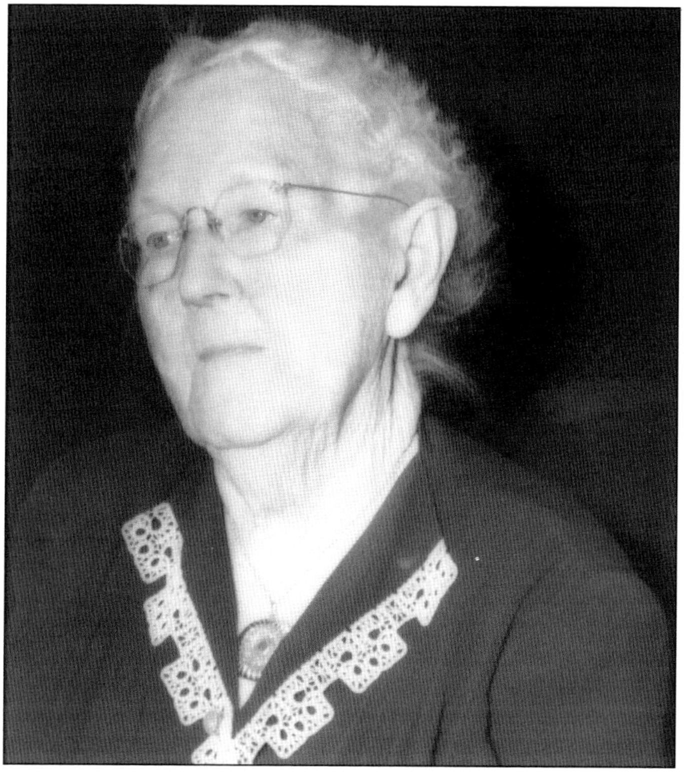

Early Downey pioneer Judith McKellar "Miss Judy" was born on November 4, 1855, in Kemper, Mississippi. She lived until February 3, 1961, passing at age 105. Her father was Daniel Henderson McKellar, who married Margaret McMahon in November 1842. Their union resulted in six children. Judith came west with her family by train to San Francisco, sailing to Redondo Beach, and then by Butterfield Stage to Gallatin Settlement. Miss McKellar later taught at Gallatin School, helped begin Downey Union High School, and was a founding member of the Women's Club in Downey.

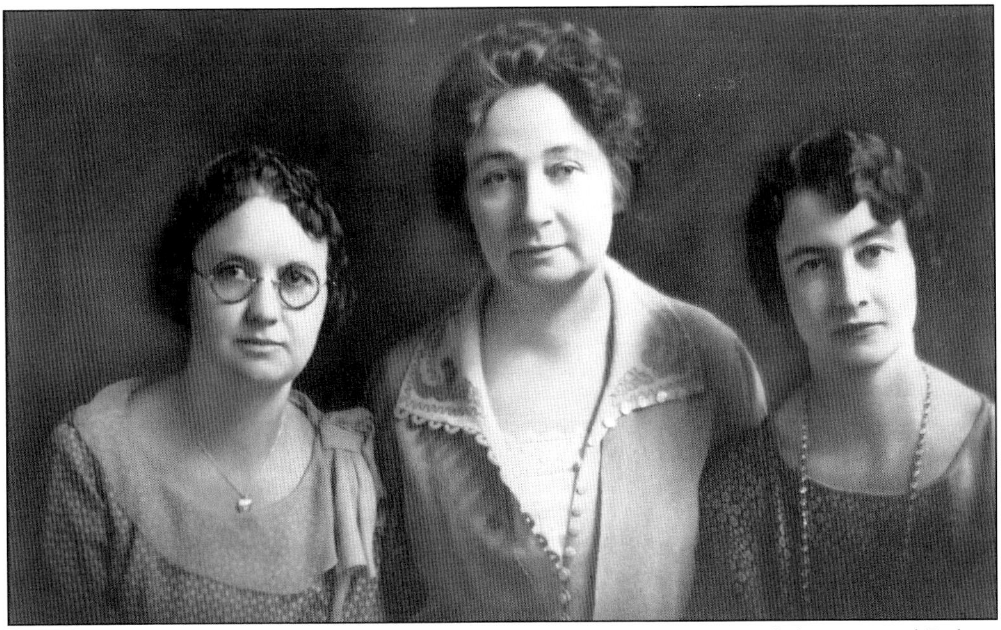

Agnes, Mabel, and Burnice Mayes. The Mayes girls were the daughters of Florence and Robert Mayes. Their grandfather, who came to Downey from Kentucky, was a Los Nietos Valley pioneer and Los Angeles County supervisor from 1868–1871. Agnes was the second daughter and died in 1945. Her oldest sister Mabel lived in their parents' home until her death. Burnice and husband Walter Love built just east of her parents on Florence Avenue.

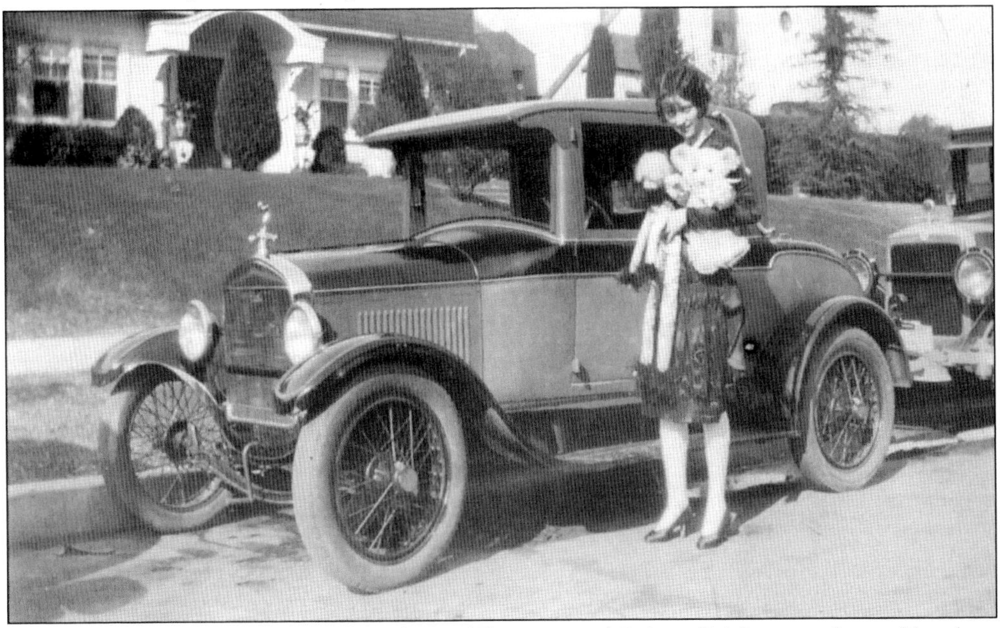

Burnice Elizabeth Mayes was the daughter of Florence and Robert S. Mayes, and granddaughter of Robert Henry Mayes. She married Walter Love and developed the family property northeast of Florence Avenue and Lakewood Boulevard. Burnice Mayes Love was a cousin to Estella Mayes Krueger. Krueger's Shoe Store on Second and Crawford (Downey Avenue) was owned by Estella Krueger and her husband.

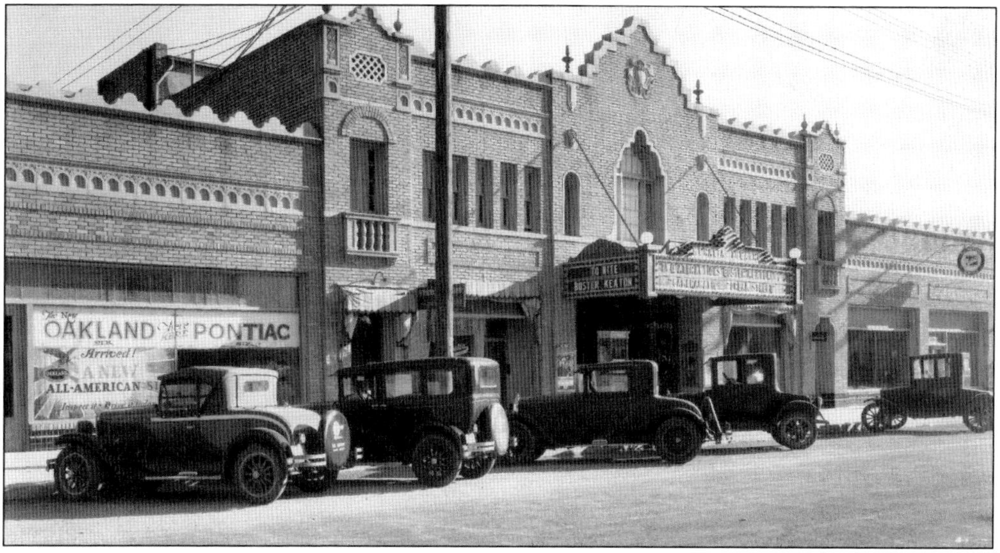

This photograph from 1929 shows the Meralta Theatre, which opened on November 24, 1924, on North Crawford Street (Downey Avenue), complete with a pipe organ played by Johnny Van Matre. Here in 1928, the Buster Keaton movie *The Cameraman* is playing. The local Pontiac and Buick dealers flanked the Meralta on each side, with a small door leading to the office of dentist C. J. Hanley.

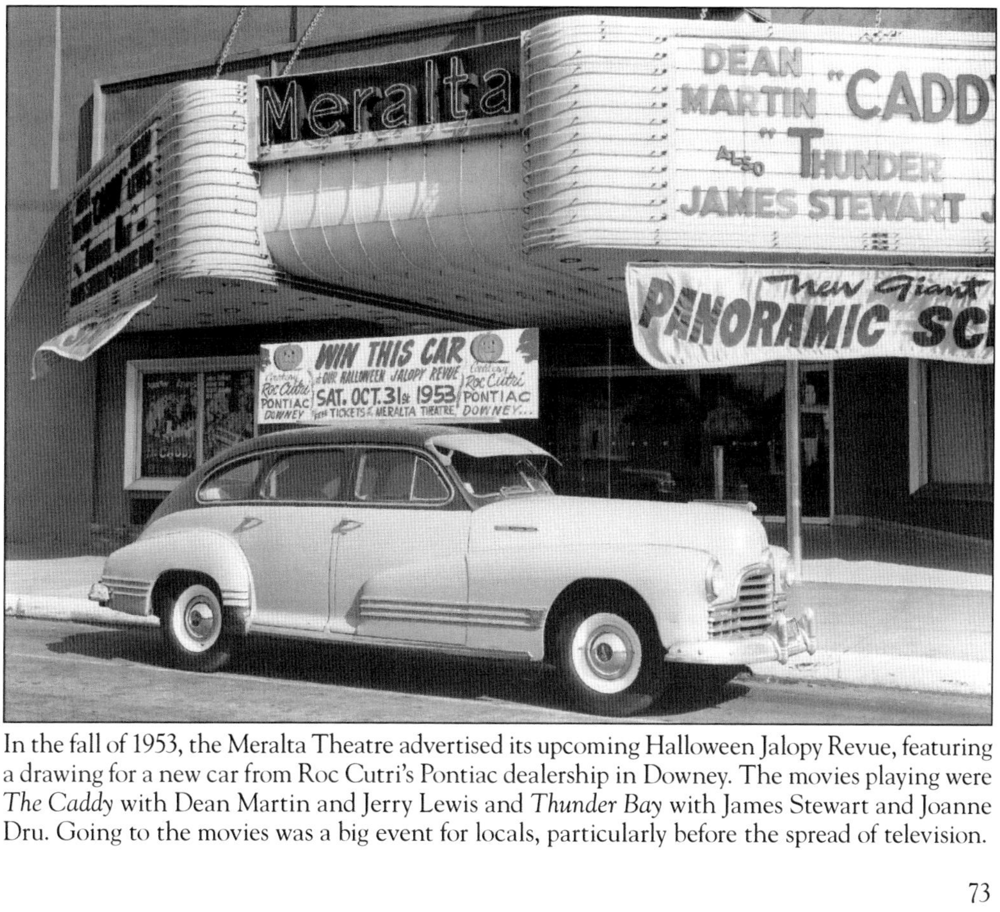

In the fall of 1953, the Meralta Theatre advertised its upcoming Halloween Jalopy Revue, featuring a drawing for a new car from Roc Cutri's Pontiac dealership in Downey. The movies playing were *The Caddy* with Dean Martin and Jerry Lewis and *Thunder Bay* with James Stewart and Joanne Dru. Going to the movies was a big event for locals, particularly before the spread of television.

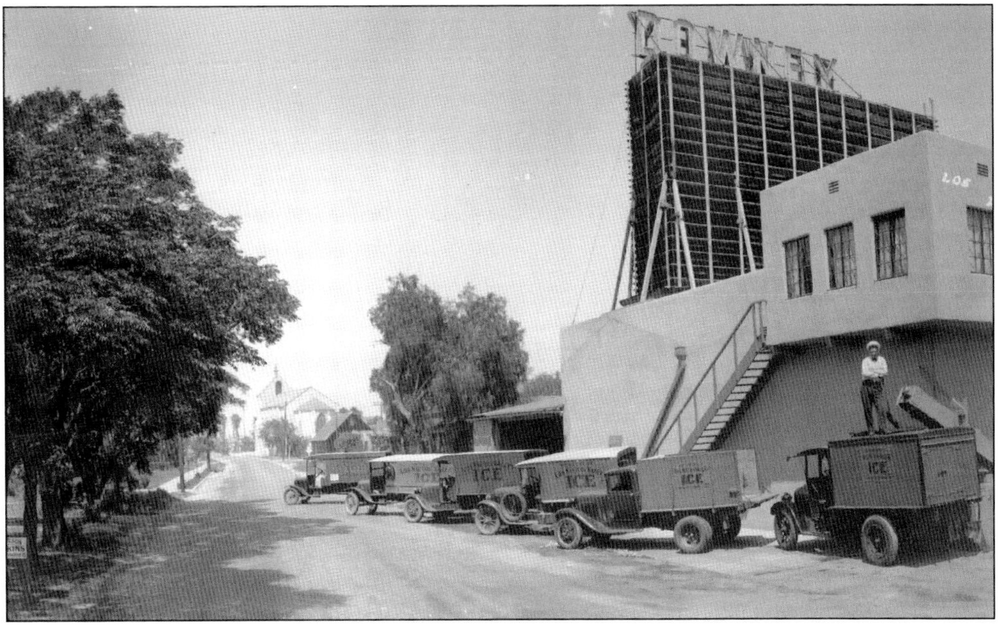

Los Nietos Valley Ice Company on Fourth and New Streets in 1932 used these delivery trucks. Ice delivery was critical for families and businesses to keep food fresh. This picture is half of a "roll" or wide angle picture, and was taken standing on New Street facing north towards Our Lady of Perpetual Help Catholic Church.

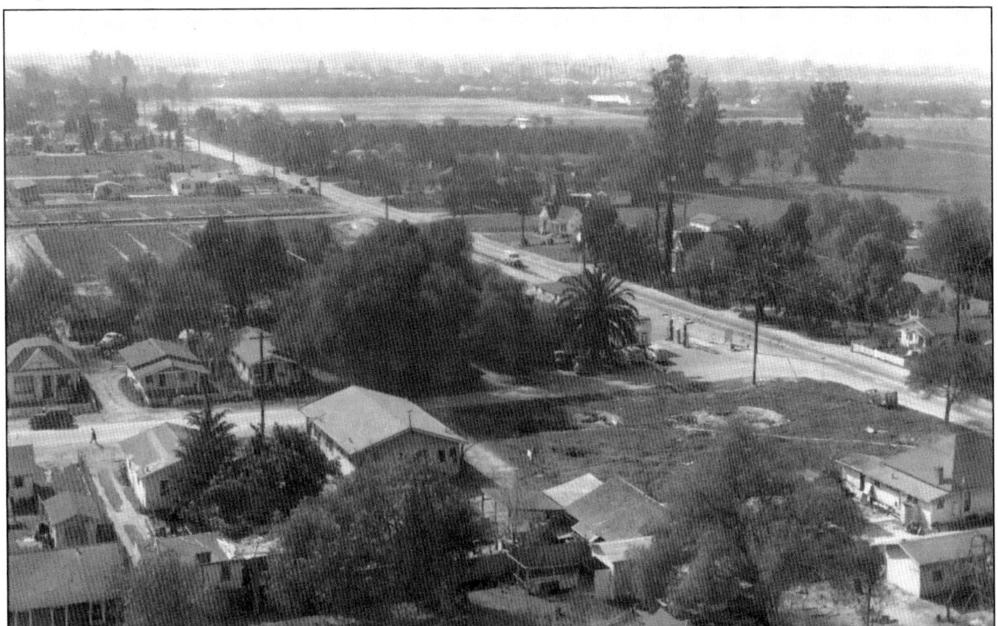

Taken in the 1930s, this picture shows Downey Avenue running past Texas and Cleta Streets (left) north of Stewart and Gray Road and south of the railroad tracks near Firestone Boulevard. In the distance (right) the palm trees lining College Avenue (Paramount Boulevard) are clearly visible running north-south. Up until the residential development of the 1950s, Downey was a very rural city. In 1940 Downey's population was 12,000 people, and by 1960 it was 86,000.

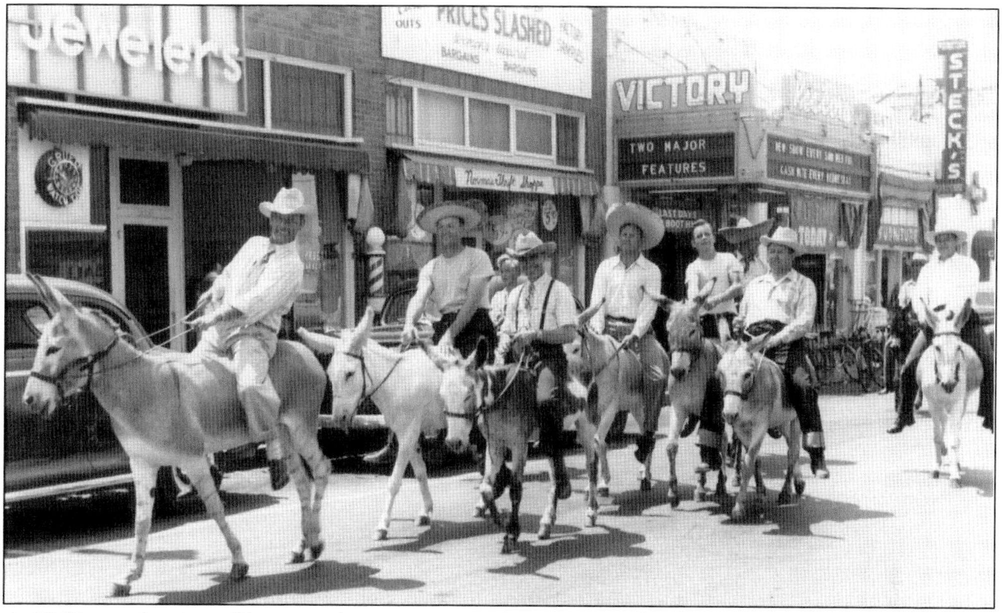

A 1947 parade along Downey Avenue passes the Victory Theatre and Steck's Hardware and Furniture. The Victory Theatre is playing *Last Days of Boot Hill*, a western starring Charles Starrett and Smiley Barnett. The Victory Theatre would later become the Avenue Theatre. Also seen in this photograph are Norma's Thrift Shoppe and Pruette's Barbershop.

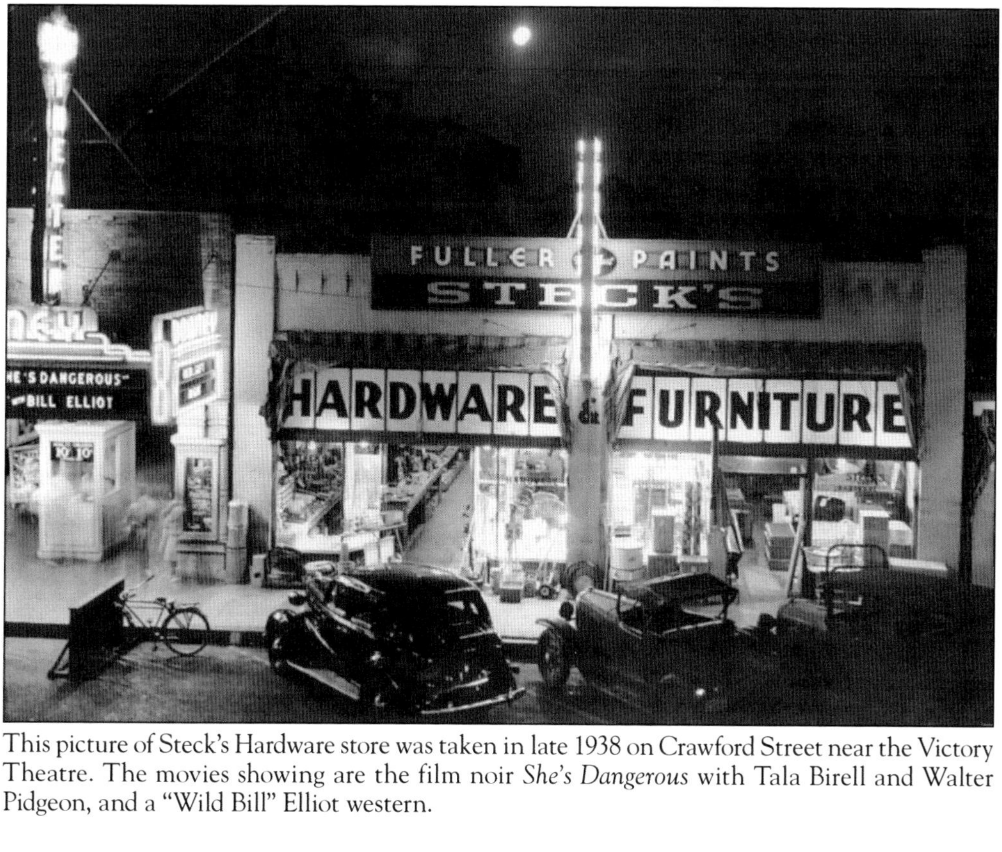

This picture of Steck's Hardware store was taken in late 1938 on Crawford Street near the Victory Theatre. The movies showing are the film noir *She's Dangerous* with Tala Birell and Walter Pidgeon, and a "Wild Bill" Elliot western.

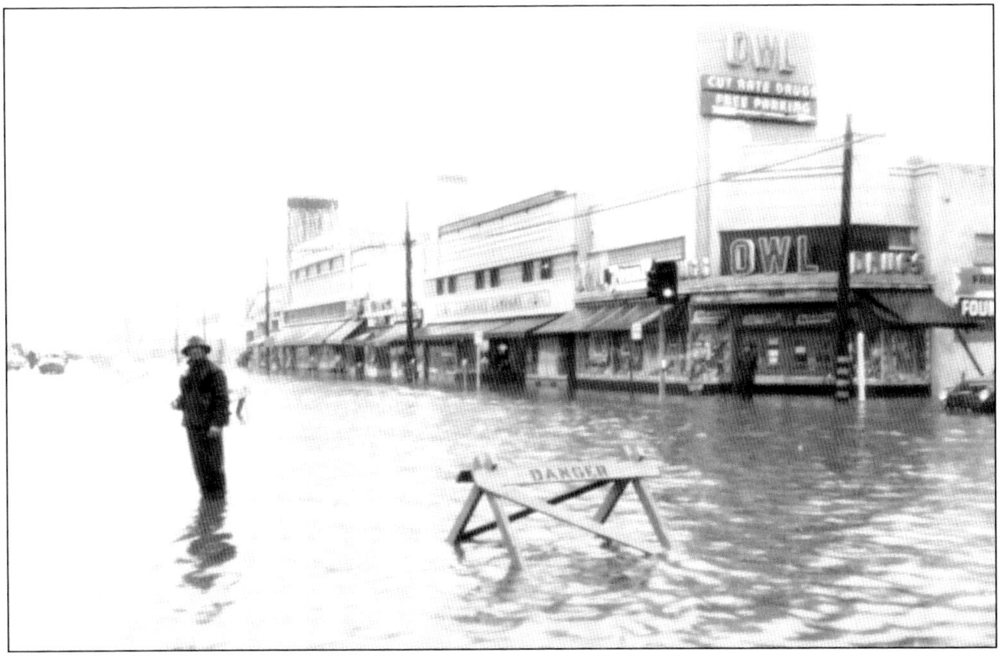

In 1951 and 1952, the Los Angeles area experienced heavy rainfall, resulting in heavy flooding in Downey. This photograph of Firestone Boulevard looking east from Paramount Boulevard shows the flooding in Downey before storm drains. This is the corner of La Reina and Firestone Boulevard in Downey's shopping district. J. J. Newberry's, J. C. Penney, OWL Rexall Drugstore, and other businesses are flooded up to their doorways.

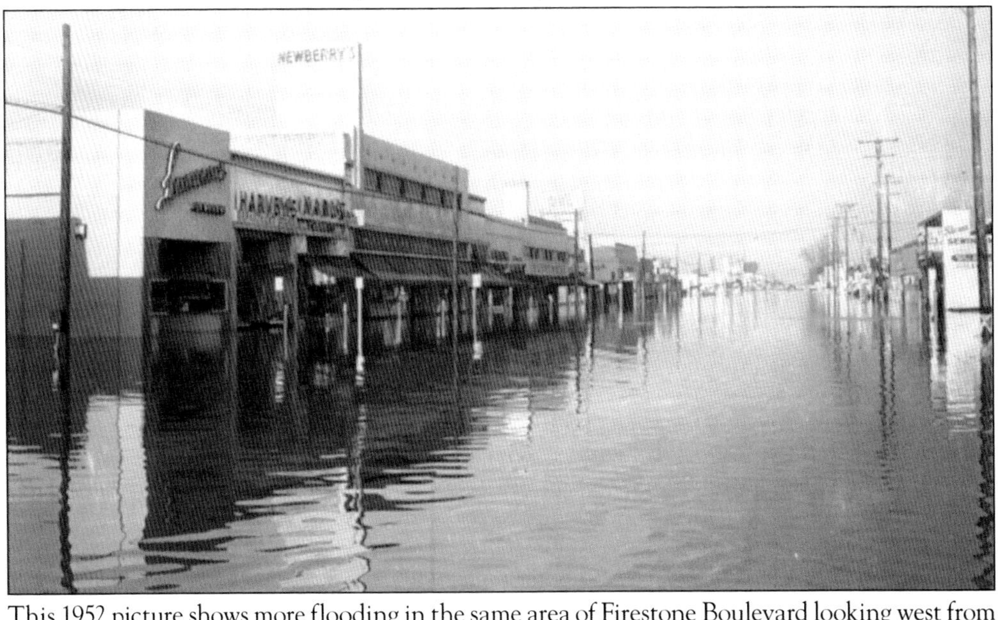

This 1952 picture shows more flooding in the same area of Firestone Boulevard looking west from Downey Avenue. Old Downey residents can remember flood after flood until dams, channels, and storm drains were built. In December 1889, the Old San Gabriel River, the New San Gabriel River, and the Los Angeles River all swelled their banks until their waters joined and they formed a single lake over a huge area between Downey and Los Angeles.

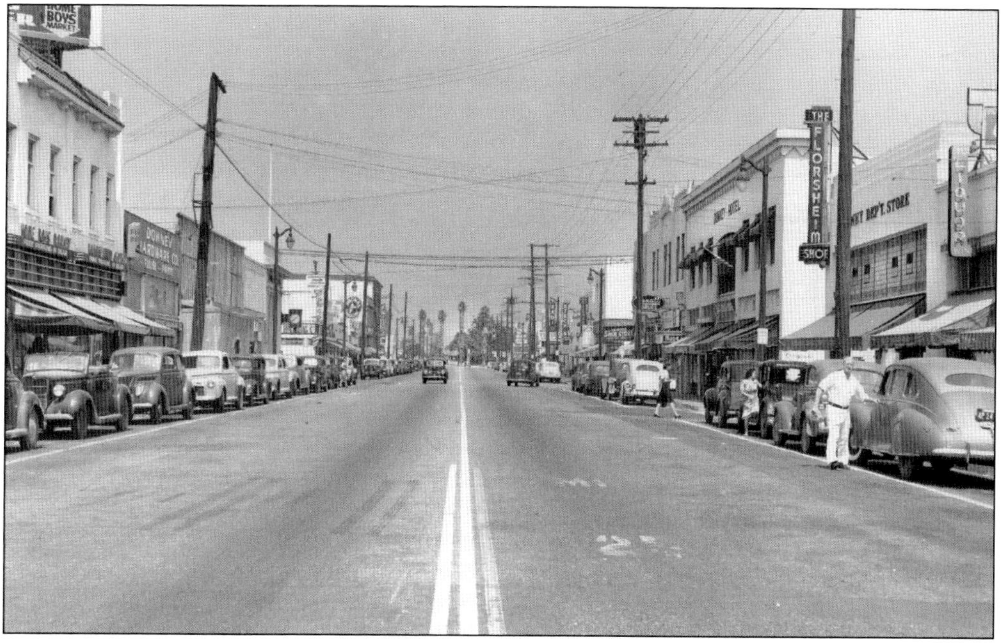

Here is a picture of Downey's main street, Downey Avenue, looking north from Firestone in 1945. On the left is Home Boys market next to Downey Hardware. Across the street is Steck's Hardware, Furniture, and Paint; Krueger's Shoe Store; and Rexall Drugs. Steck's was next to the Victory Theatre, which eventually became the Avenue Theatre. On August 13, 1875, druggist James O. Bailey purchased property with the Odd Fellows Association and erected a two-story building on the spot where the Home Boys market stands in this photograph.

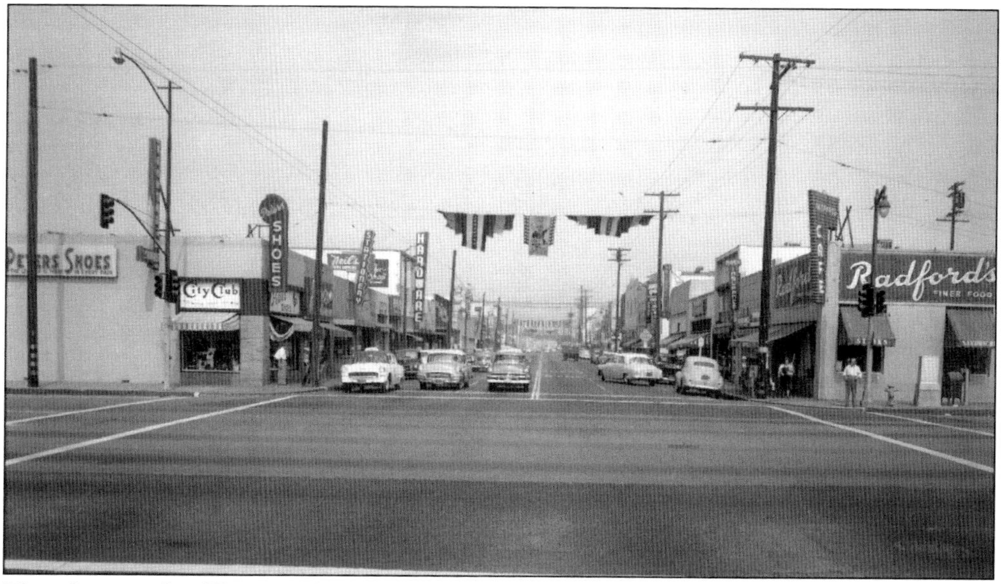

This photograph of Downey Avenue in September 1955 was taken at noon from the middle of Downey Avenue and Firestone Boulevard looking north. Radford's Restaurant is located on the northeast corner across the street from Neil's Stationers, Peter's Shoes, and Downey Hardware. The banners across the street advertise the Los Angeles County Fair. The first LA County Fair was held in Downey north of this intersection in 1884.

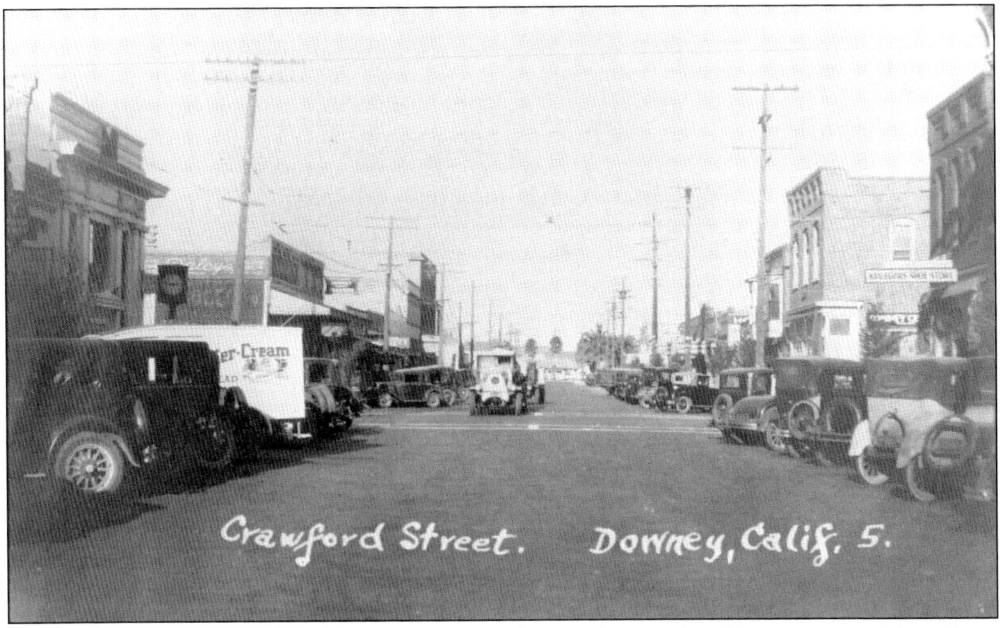

This picture of Crawford Street (Downey Avenue) was taken in the 1920s. Krueger's Shoe Store and the Downey Hotel are seen on the right side of the picture at Second Street. Across the street is Hull's Drug Store and the Los Nietos Valley Bank. H. A. Scott and O. Mahone formed the bank in 1887; in 1889, James T. Blythe bought into the business. The bank was incorporated in June 1891 with a capital of $50,000.

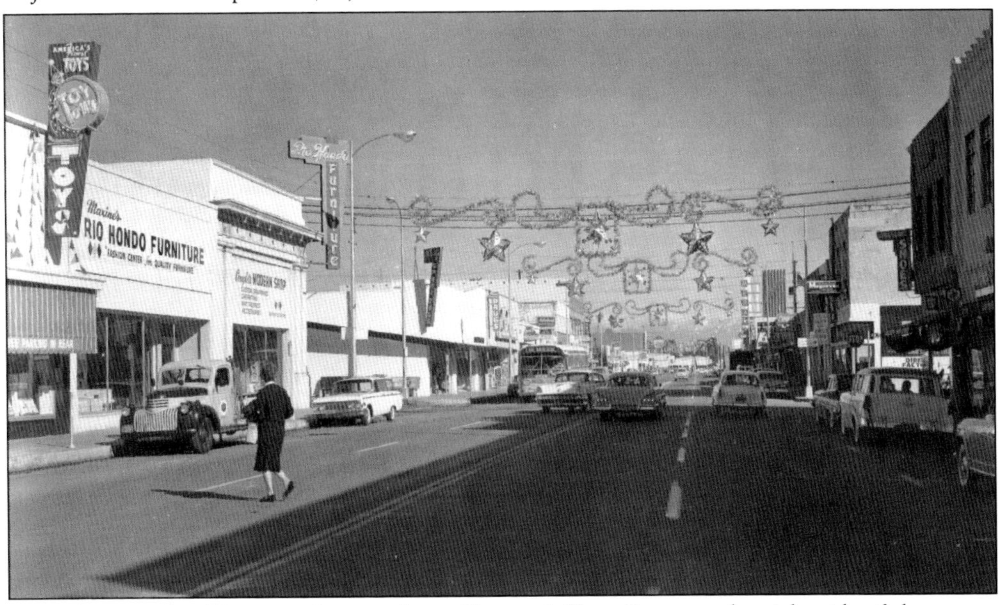

This photograph of Downey Avenue shows Krueger's Shoe Store on the right side of the street. Here in 1961, many stores have changed since the 1930s. Facing north from Firestone Boulevard you can see Sachs Lincoln Mercury in the distance at Fifth Street, near the tower of the Presbyterian Church on Seventh Street. On the west side is the Downey Masonic Lodge at Third Street, and on the east side of the street, the Avenue and Meralta Theaters are also visible. These Christmas decorations were used for many years in downtown Downey.

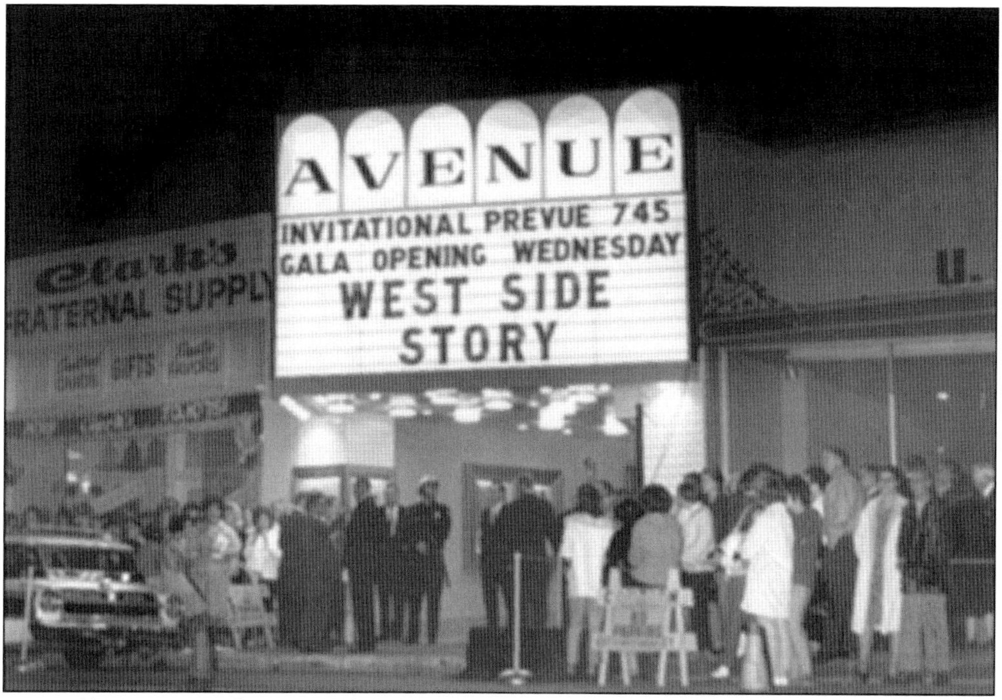

Pictured here in December 1961 is the Avenue Theatre, located on Downey Avenue between Second and Third Streets. The Avenue was built in 1922 and featured a brick facade with a beautiful arch, which at one time marked the entrance to the theater. Originally called the Downey Theater, it later became the Victory Theater, and finally in 1948 the Avenue Theater.

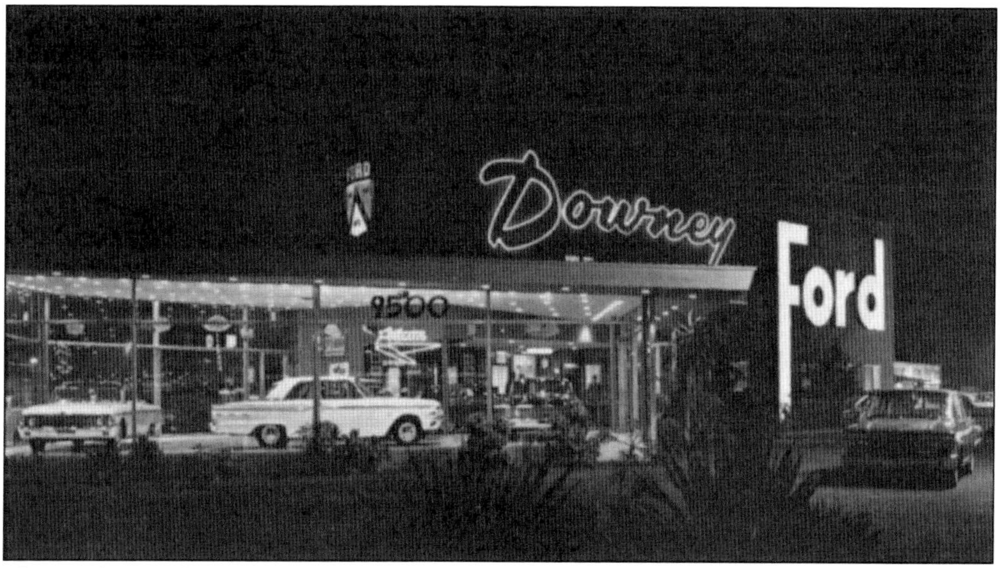

This is a photograph of Downey Ford, formerly Graham Ford, in the early 1960s. In the early 1950s, Ralph Graham began selling Fords at 7859 Firestone Boulevard in Downey. In the early 1960s Graham moved north to Lakewood Boulevard at Gallatin Road. In the 1980s Graham's son, James K. Graham, took over Downey Ford and continued a long tradition of good service and community involvement.

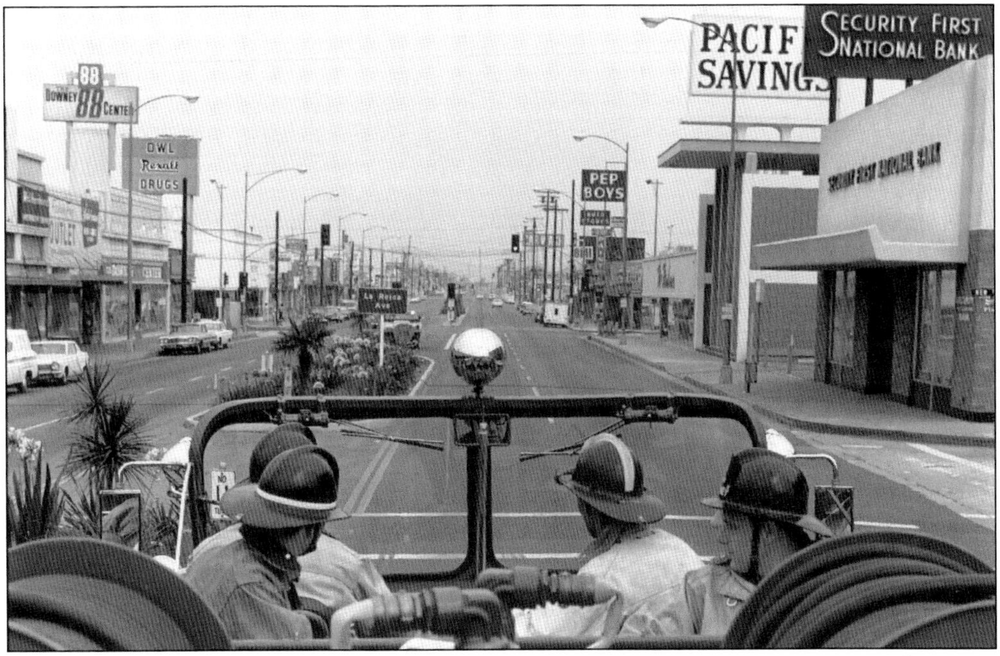

This 1960s photograph was taken from atop a Downey Fire Department engine traveling west down Firestone Boulevard, approaching La Reina Street. On the south side of Firestone is the Downey 88 Center, Owl Rexall Drugs, and Beneficial Finance. On the north side are Security First National Bank, Pep Boys, and the car wash. The traffic signal at Paramount Boulevard is in the distance with Paramount Chevrolet on the left-hand side.

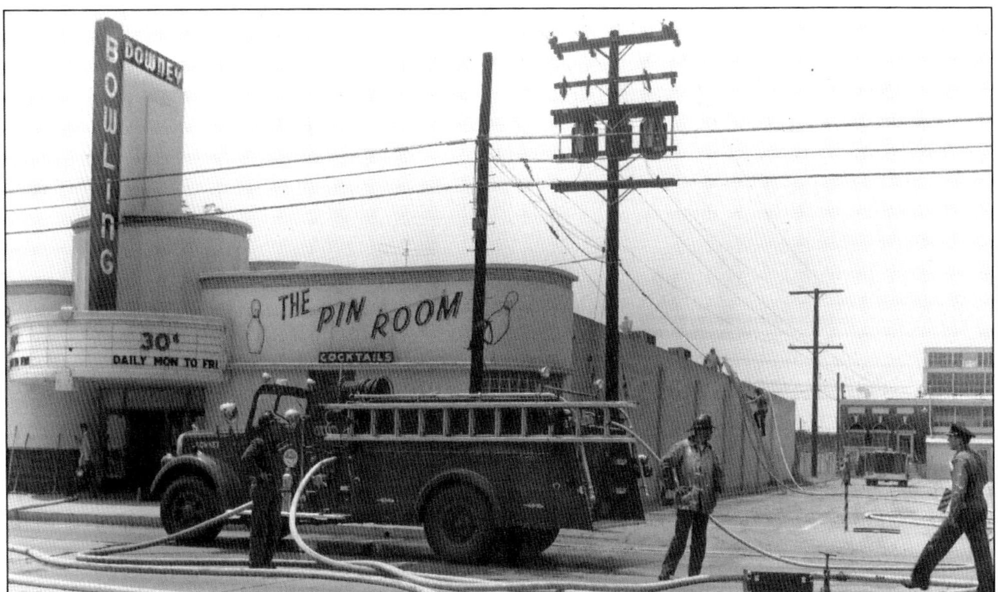

The Downey Fire Department responds to a fire at the Downey Bowling Alley and Pin Room Cocktail Lounge in this 1964 picture on the southeast corner of Brookshire Avenue and Firestone Boulevard. To the right near Dolan Avenue is the Ball and Tweedy Sunkist Packing House, torn down later that year.

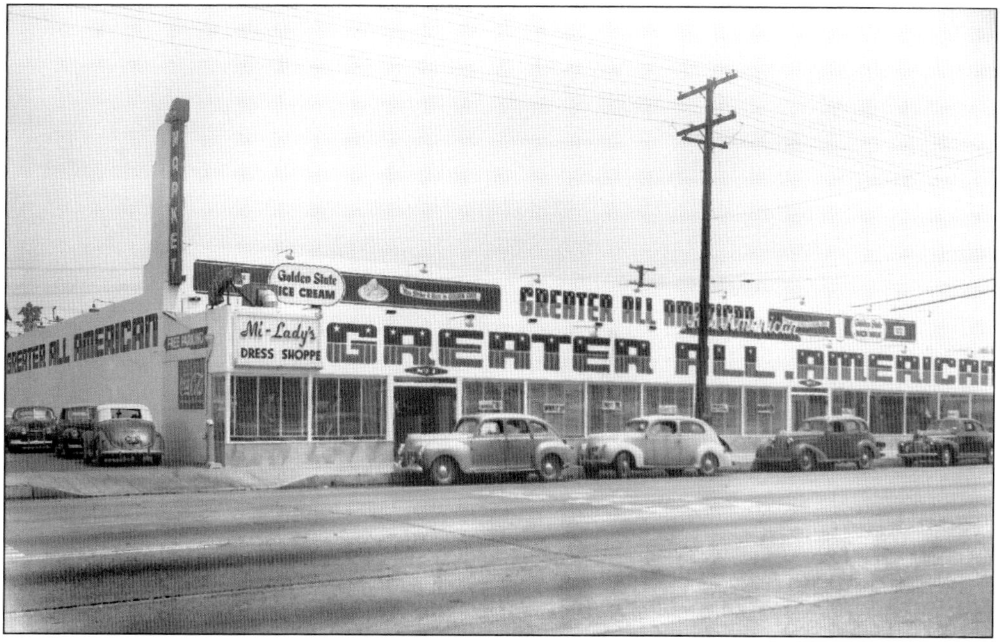

The Greater All-American Market on Firestone Boulevard and Dolan Street later became the All-American Home Center, and moved west on Firestone Boulevard. The building shown here was then occupied by Supply Sergeant. In 1959, on vacation to the area, Irving Gertler walked into the All-American Home Center and asked the manager if the store was for sale. After meeting with the owners of All-American Markets, Gertler purchased the store for a handshake, $5,000, and five years to pay for the inventory.

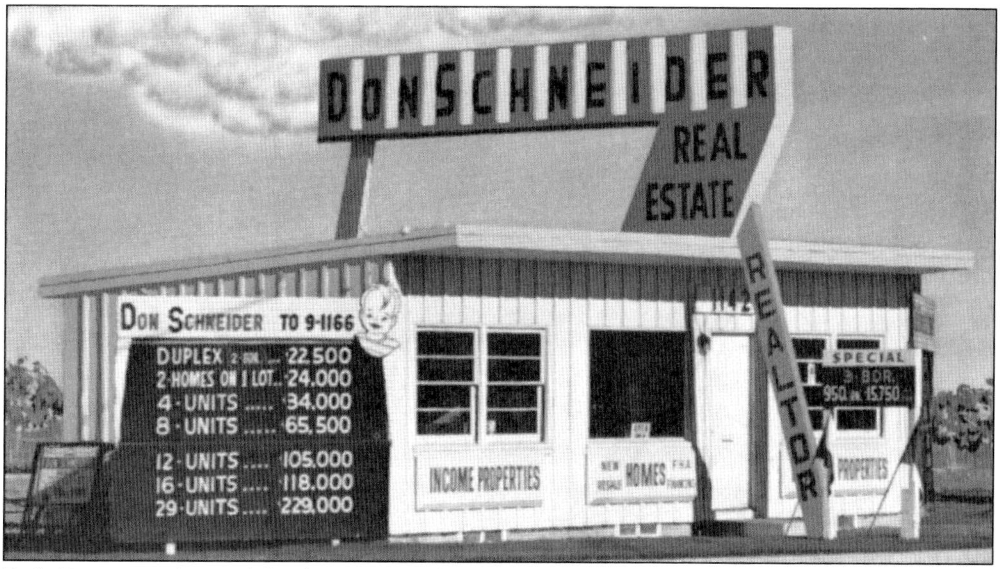

Early Downey realtor and developer Don Schnieder first opened shop here on Paramount Boulevard. In later years, he moved his office to Florence Avenue between Downey and Brookshire Avenues. Schnieder, like many of Downey's real estate agents during the housing boom, lived to see Downey become the beautiful city it is today.

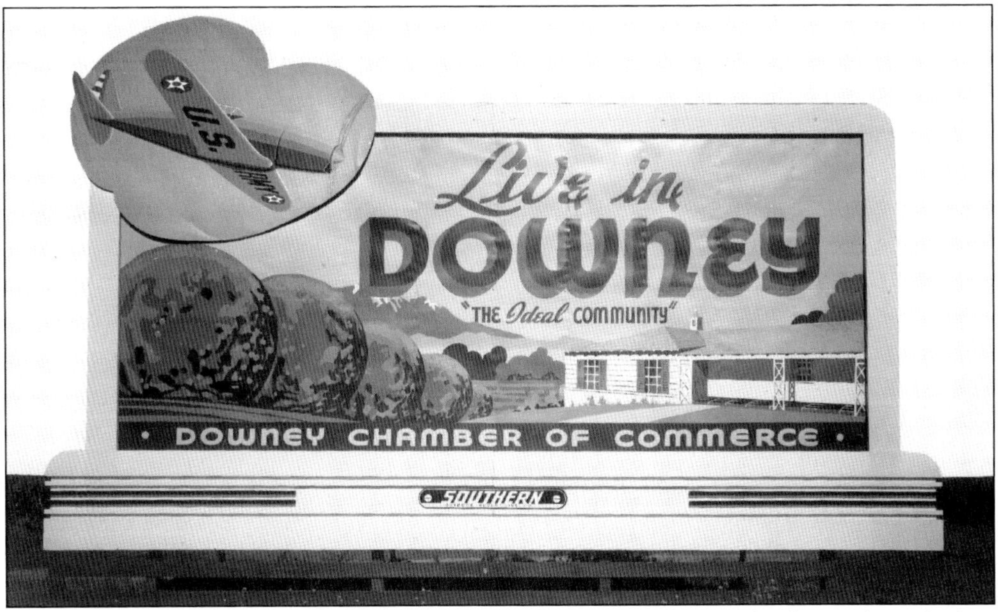

The Downey Chamber of Commerce used this sign to promote the thousands of homes being built in the 1950s. The chamber's stated purpose was to foster "the continuation of an expanding economic climate and to explain and promote the American business system to local residents."

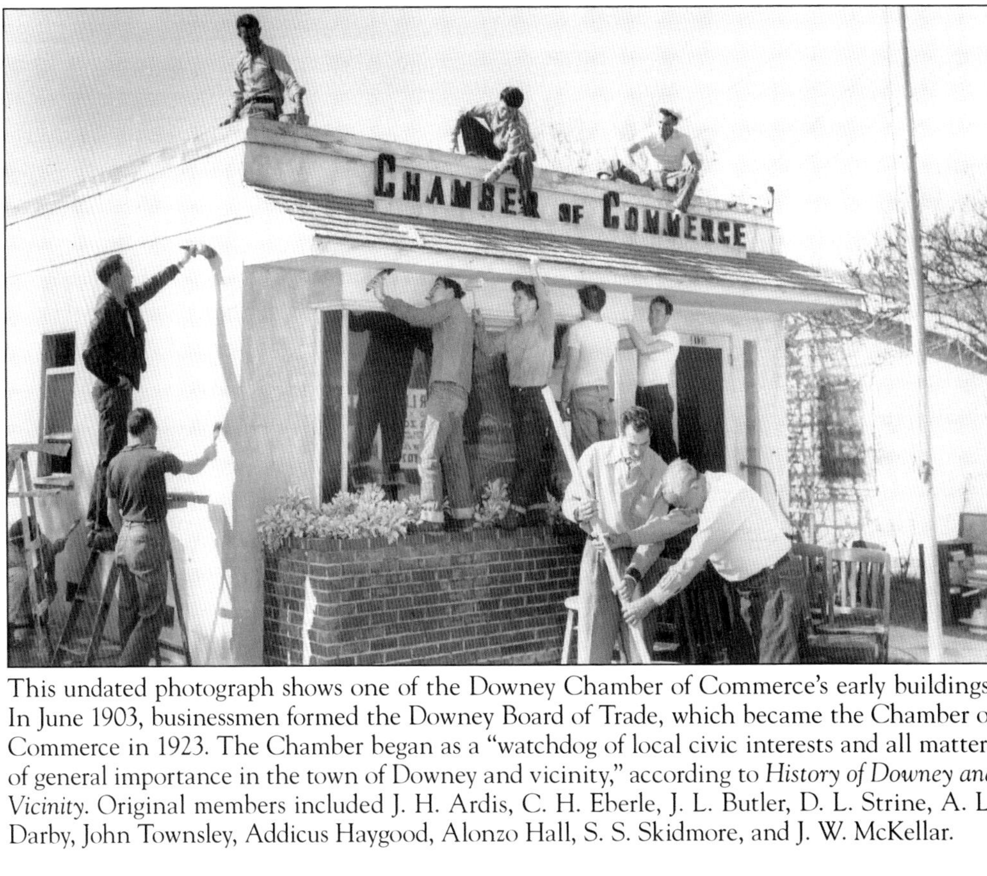

This undated photograph shows one of the Downey Chamber of Commerce's early buildings. In June 1903, businessmen formed the Downey Board of Trade, which became the Chamber of Commerce in 1923. The Chamber began as a "watchdog of local civic interests and all matters of general importance in the town of Downey and vicinity," according to *History of Downey and Vicinity*. Original members included J. H. Ardis, C. H. Eberle, J. L. Butler, D. L. Strine, A. L. Darby, John Townsley, Addicus Haygood, Alonzo Hall, S. S. Skidmore, and J. W. McKellar.

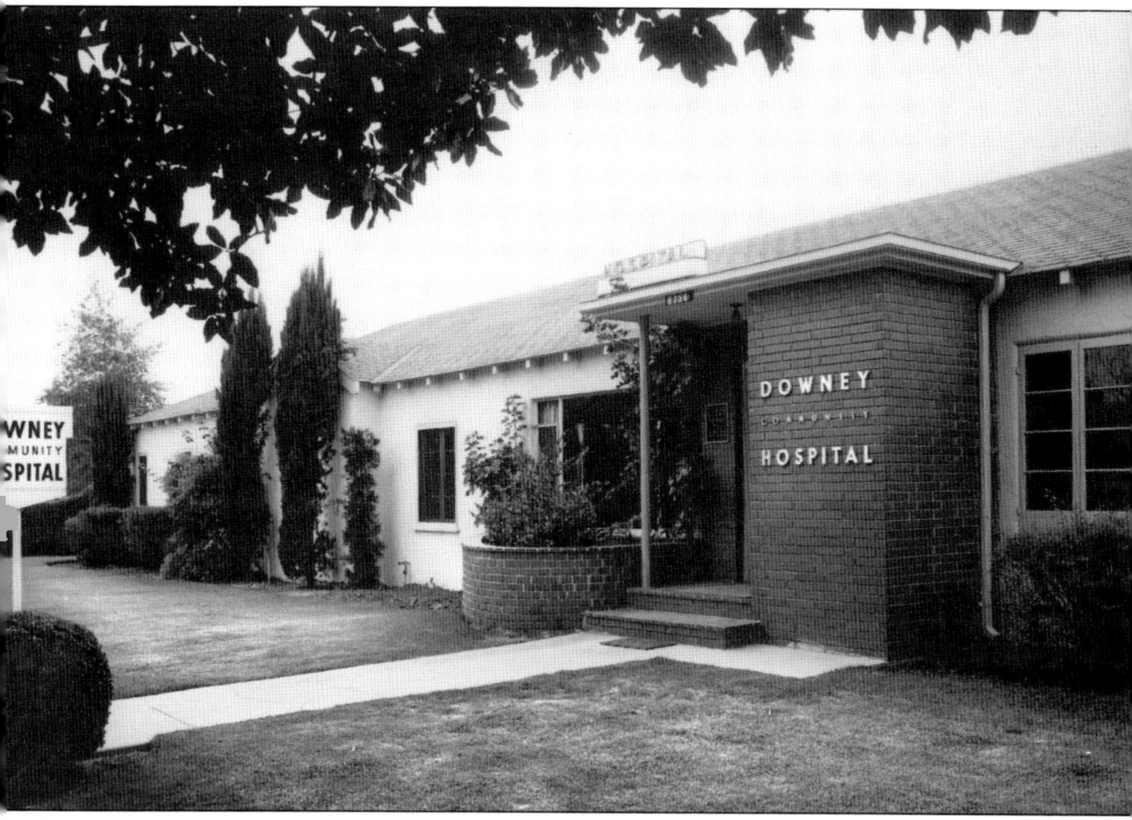

Downey Community Hospital, seen here in September 1955, was located between Church Street (Brookshire) and Downey Avenue. Its origins were in 1920, when Dr. E. H. Welcome and a group of businessmen established a health-care enterprise. By 1924, the hospital moved from Crawford Street to a cottage-style facility on Fifth Street. In 1933, Welcome reorganized and took the helm of the new Downey Community Hospital. The Morris family acquired a controlling interest in 1956, and by the end of 1969, a new hospital was complete on Brookshire Avenue.

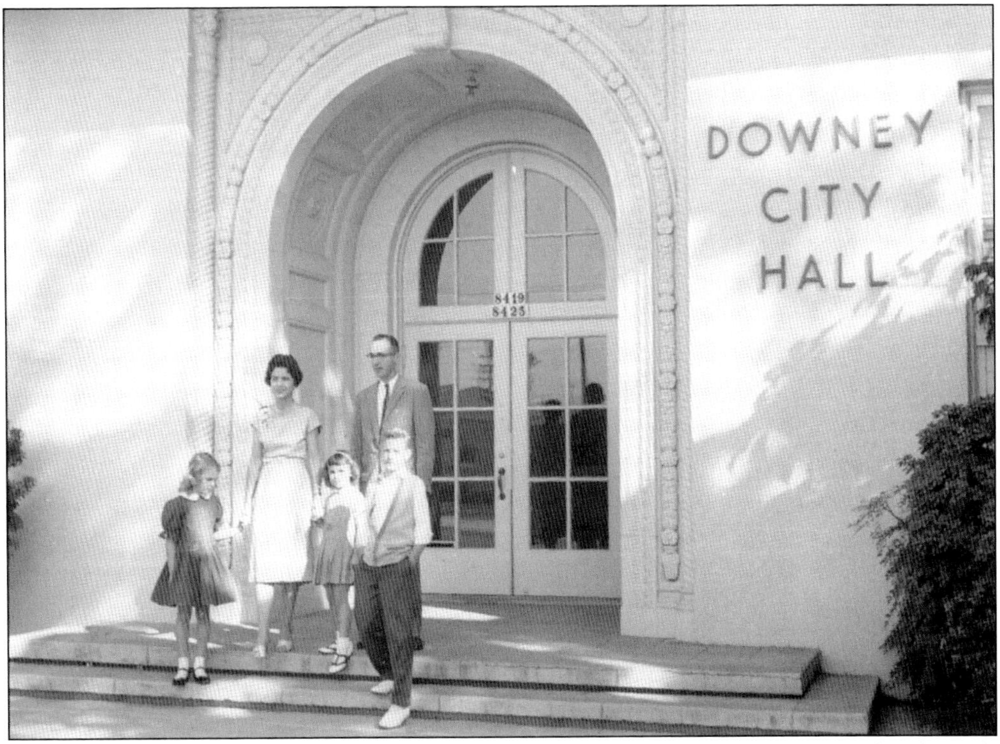

This 1960s image shows a Downey family who just walked through the Downey Arch. The arch was the old entrance to Downey Grammar School, built in 1916 by Willard Brent Company and designed by noted school architect John C. Austin. A school for 40 years until Downey's 1957 incorporation, the building became Downey's new city hall, police station, and library.

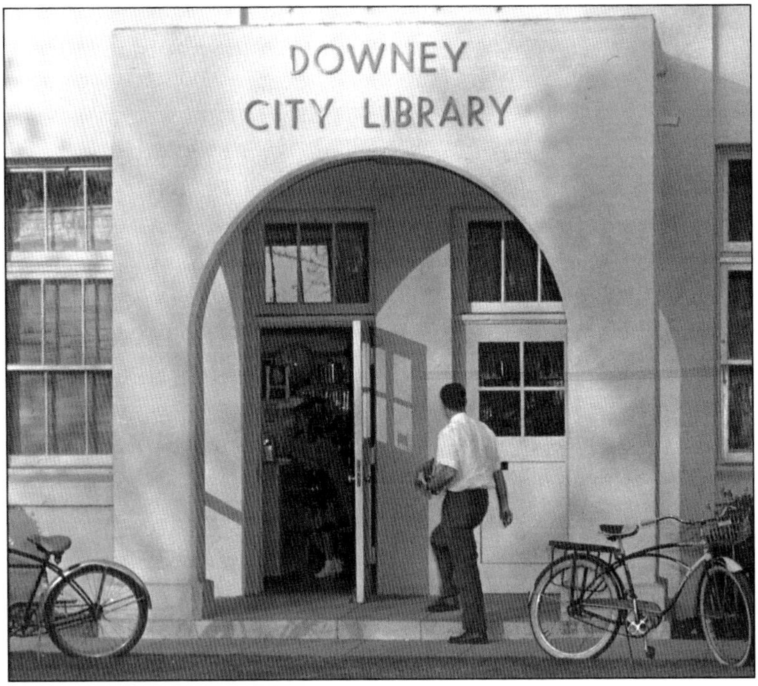

The Downey City Library dates back to 1901 when the Saturday Afternoon Club and Downey teacher Josie McKellar spearheaded the library's establishment and growth. When the city purchased the former Downey Elementary School for its new city hall, the library opened in the old cafeteria. A new building with over 16,000 square feet opened to the public on December 17, 1959.

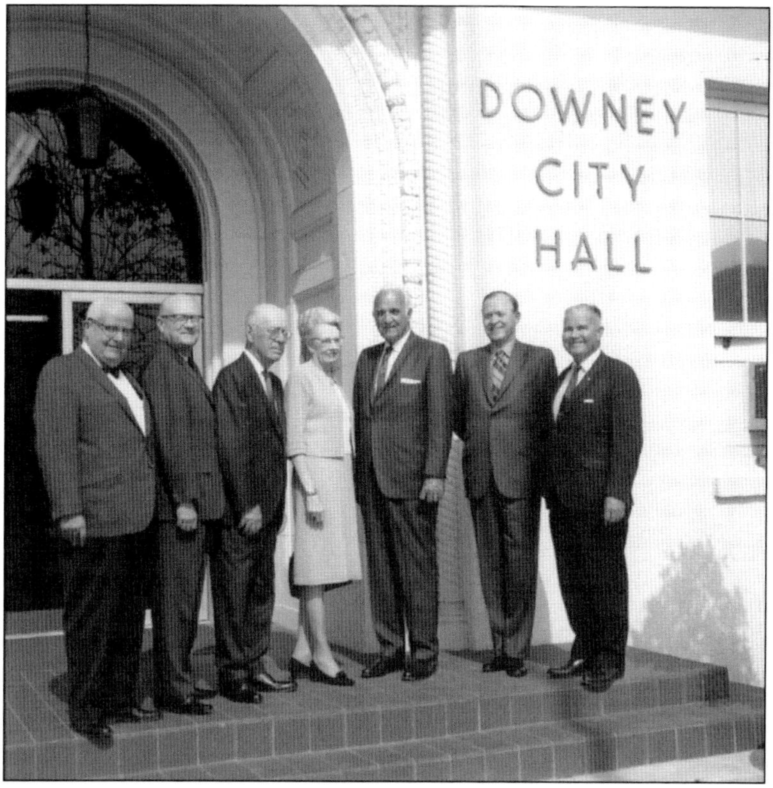

This picture taken in front of Downey City Hall shows Downey's civic leaders of 1970. From left to right, they are Hollis Peavey, Oren King, James Stamps, Della Doyle, Edwin Giddings, Carroll Dunnum, and Scott Temple. Oren King was Downey's first city manager and Della Doyle was the first city treasurer. Peavey, Stamps, Giddings, Dunnum, and Scott Temple all served as mayor of Downey and as councilmen for many years.

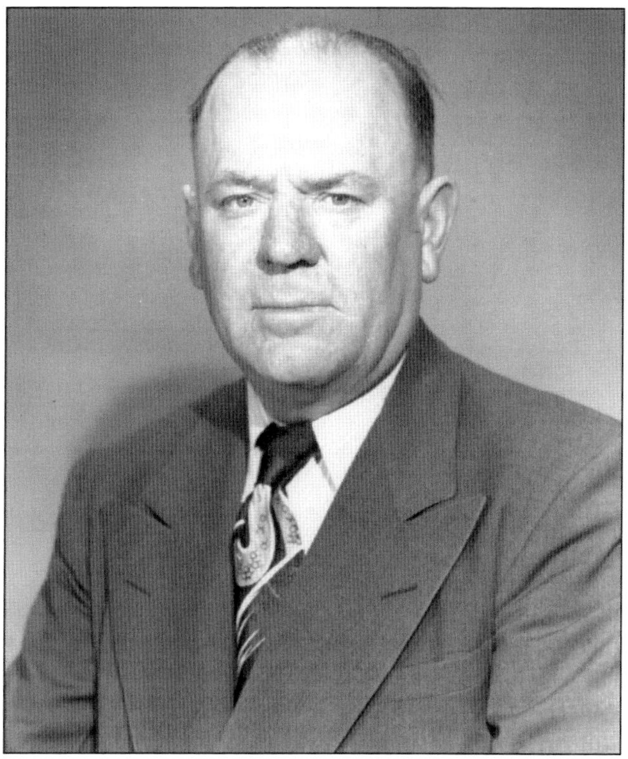

James L. Stamps was born in Lewisville, Arkansas, on July 16, 1891. In 1892, his father L. K. Stamps brought the family to Downey. James attended Gallatin School and then Whittier High School and Woodbury Business School. The Stamps family raised sweet potatoes, sugar beets, alfalfa, cauliflower, barley, and eventually oranges. In 1919, the Stamps family owned hundreds of acres, including land that would become Rio Hondo Golf Course.

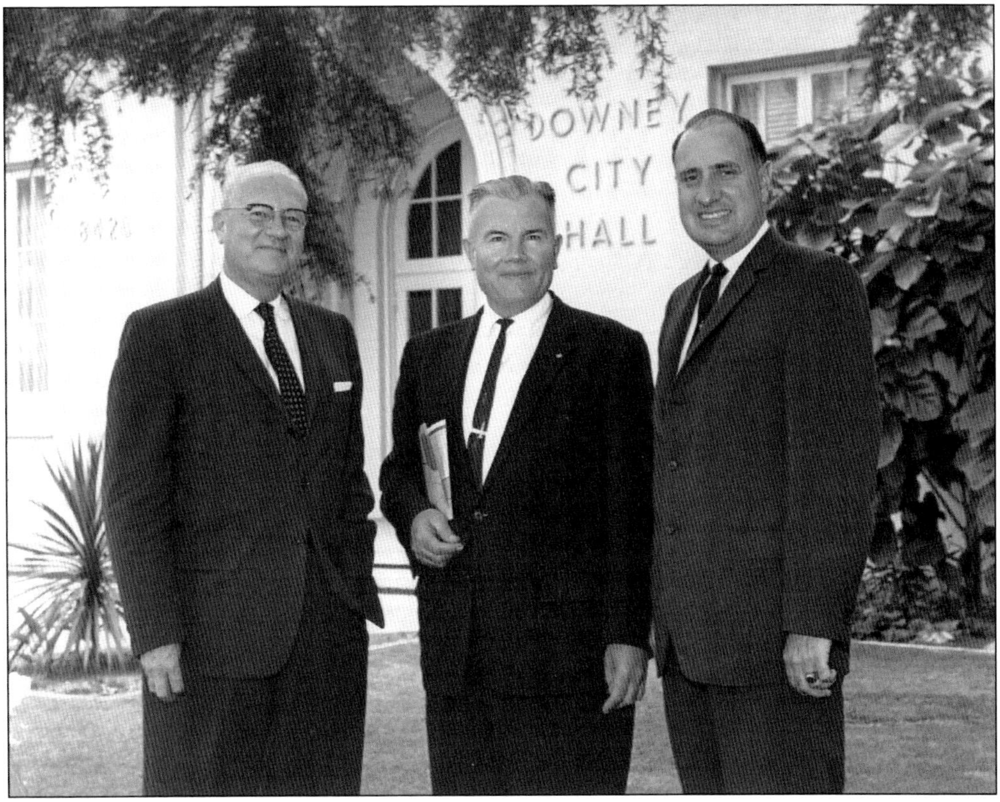

Pictured here are Downey's first permanent city manager, Oren King; four-term mayor Scott Temple; and three-term mayor Thomas Morton. These three men, along with James Stamps and others, would lead Downey through incorporation in 1957.

Three

Schools and Churches

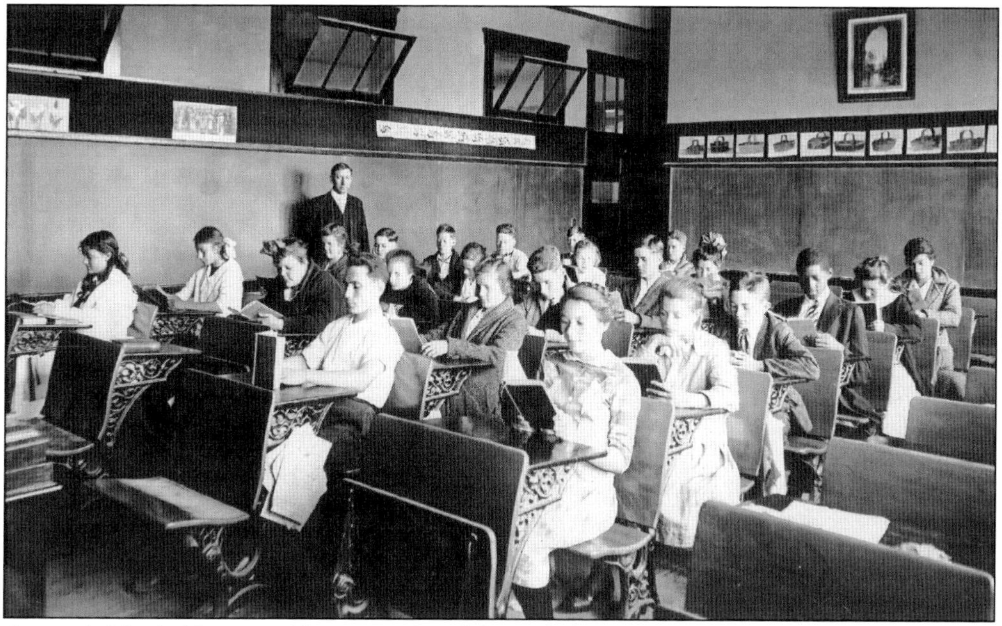

Austin A. Newbold, pictured here in 1917 with his eighth grade class, became principal of Downey Grammar School in 1916. In what would become Downey, the first school was located near the northwest corner of Florence Avenue and Tweedy Lane. That school was part of the Los Angeles Silver School District until Gallatin Settlement and College Settlement merged and became Downey in 1873. Soon the city had Gallatin, Alameda, Old River, and Downey School Districts.

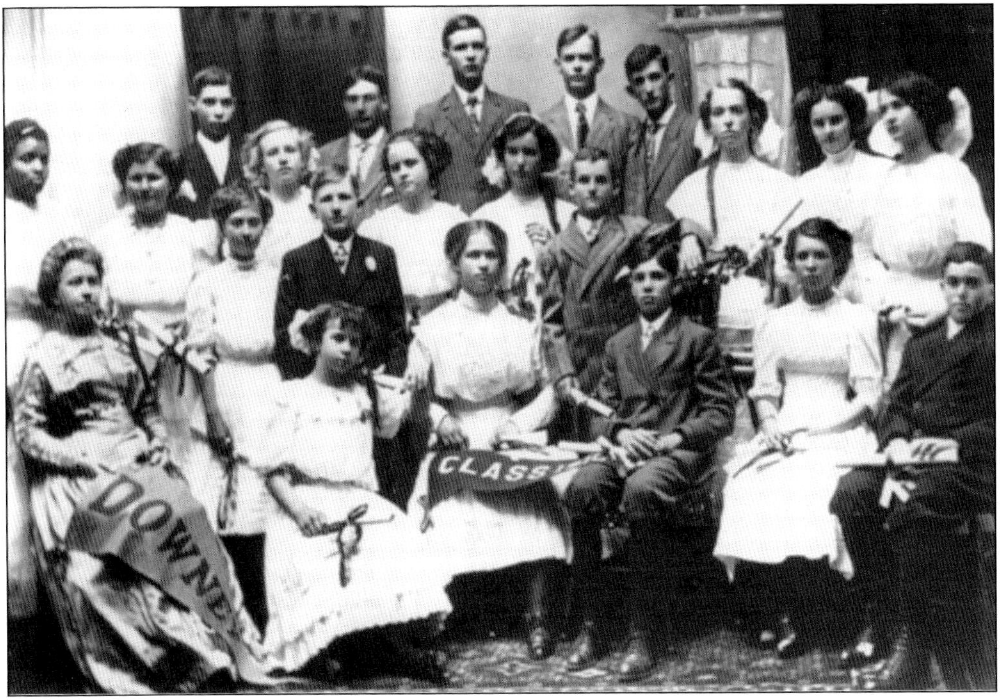

Downey Grammar School's 1910 graduating class is pictured here, from left to right: (first row) teacher Jo (?) McKellar McGee, Lilian Townsend, class president Pearl Witherspoon, May Jewel, Anna Eberle, and Max Rothschild; (second row) Lilly Pearl Brown, Mabel Swanson, Grace Pangborn, Mary Horton, William Cameron Townsend, Vera Henshaw, Edith Price, Howard Rives, Gladys Standlee, Amy Couch, Nellie Branscomb; (third row) Eldon Jewel, Earnest Beaver, Willie McClane, Don Williamson, and Clyde Weirback. William Townsend would become a famous advocate of linguistic research among ethnic minorities and founder of the world's largest Christian missionary organization, Wycliffe Bible translators, which to date has translated the Bible into 2,000 different languages, many of them previously unwritten.

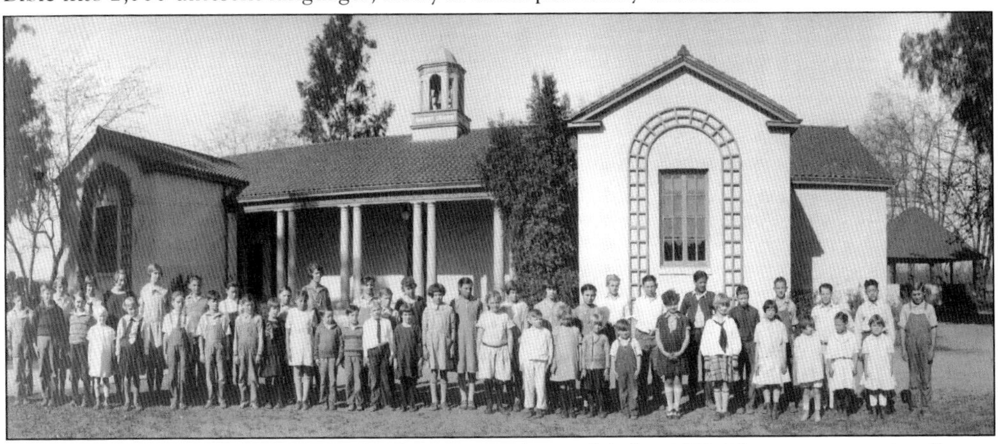

The first Gallatin School House was built in 1871 and remodeled in 1893. The two-room schoolhouse came with a 600-pound school bell. In 1915, the two-room school was demolished, and its bell, books, and desks moved to a new, three-roomed schoolhouse. After the Long Beach Earthquake of 1933, yet another new building was required, and this structure still stands today. The bell seen here is still preserved at the modern-day Gallatin School.

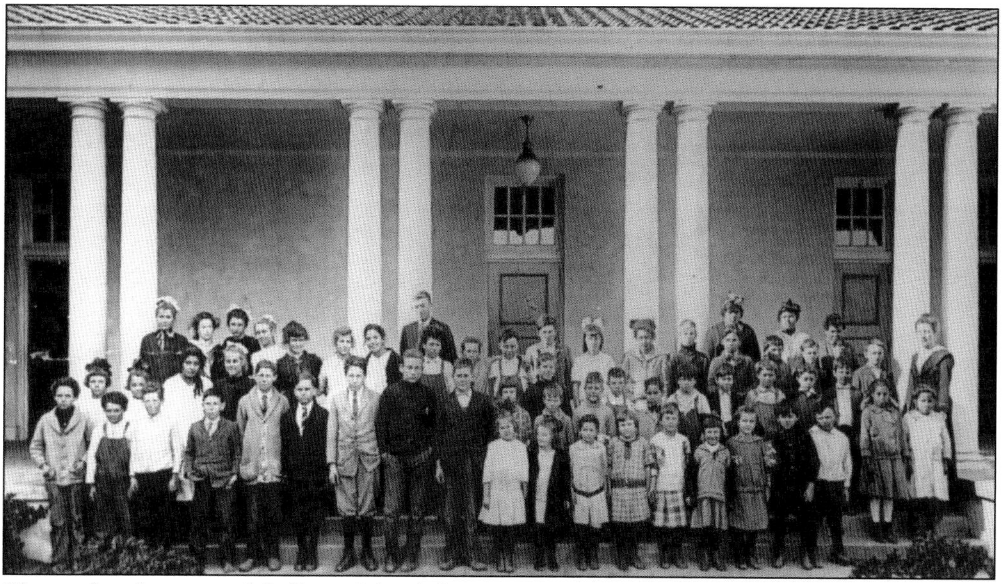

This undated picture of Gallatin School shows Spencer Valentine Williams (born February 14, 1893) in the middle of the photograph behind the children. A longtime resident of Downey who attended Alameda School, Downey High, and Los Angeles Normal School, Spencer was a Downey teacher and also principal of Gallatin, Downey Elementary, and Little Lake Schools.

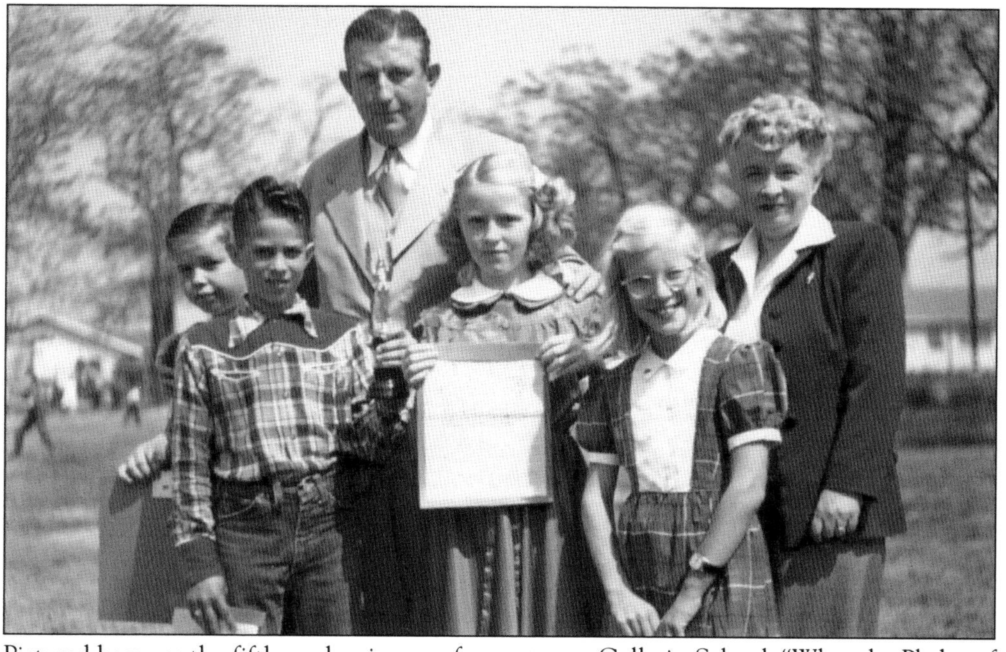

Pictured here are the fifth grade winners of a contest at Gallatin School, "What the Pledge of Allegiance Means to Me," with an unidentified man and principal Maude Price. From left to right are Wayne Cain, Jimmy Galeotti, Glenda Clarck, and Margaret Swain. Marge Swain recalls, "There were four children in the family and we went to Gallatin Elementary, a two-room school completed in 1935 and then staffed by three. Grades one through three were taught by Edith Unsworth, and grades five through six were taught by Maude Price. Both of these incredible women have Downey schools named after them."

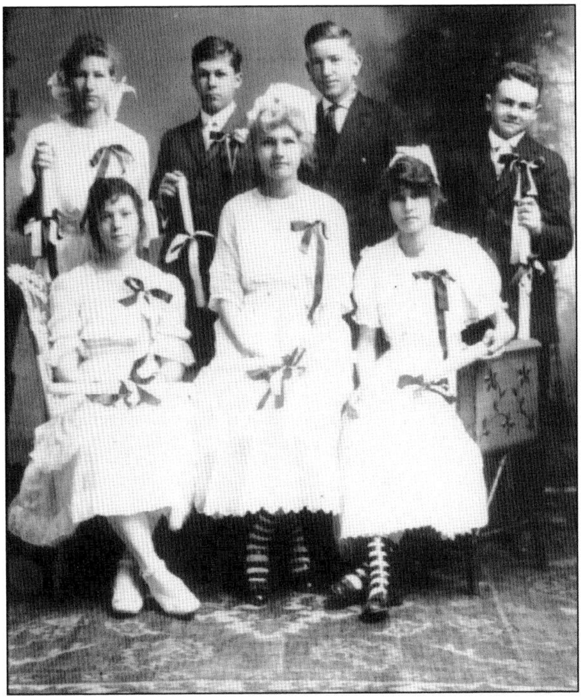

Gallatin Grammar School's graduating class of 1916, seen here, included, from left to right: (first row) Audry Wilks, Maybell Hansen, and Estella Mayes; (second row) Edna Morrow, Amos Redfield, teacher Spencer V. Williams, and Theron Tweedy.

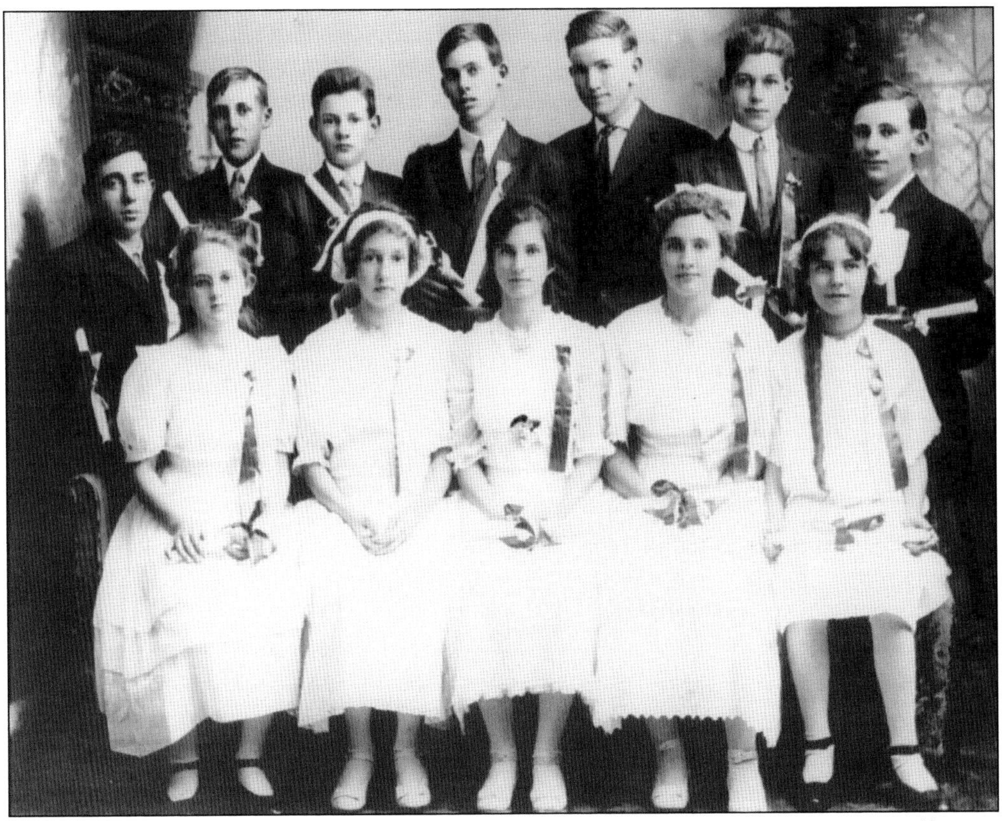

This is Gallatin Grammar School's graduating class of 1919 with teacher Spencer V. Williams.

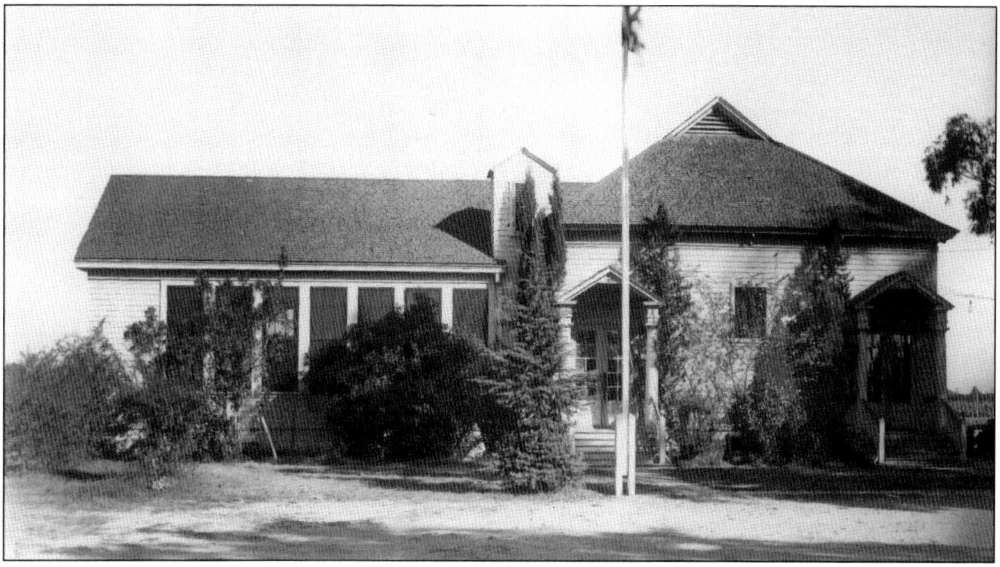

Old River Schoolhouse, on Quill Drive east of Old River Road, served a very rural area where farm children walked or rode horses to school. Hundreds of acres near Old River School were part of the County Poor Farm, which later became Rancho Los Amigos Hospital. As the population grew in the 1950s, Meadow Park and Rives Avenue Schools joined the Old River School District.

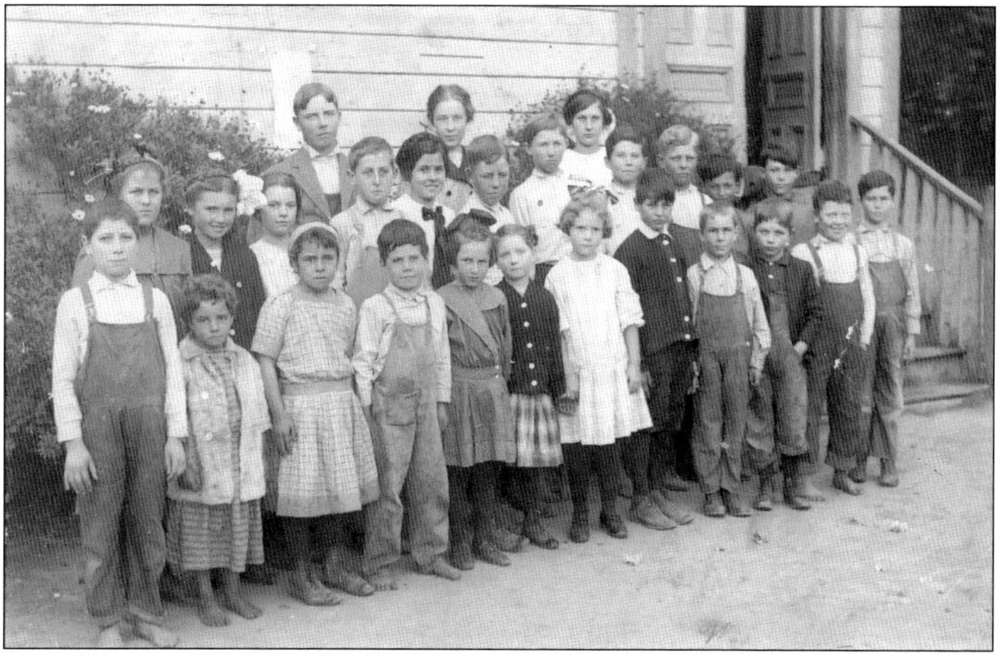

This Old River School photograph is from the 1911–1912 school year. Pictured are Margaret Wilson (the tall girl second to left), Helen McCurdy (left of Wilson), Sam Kelly (tall boy), Leo Leuritz (in front of Sam Kelly), and Ruth Smith (teacher top center). Other classmates, in no particular order, include John Fairbanks, Victoria Leuritz, Raymond Mansfield, Eddie Kelly, Charlie McCurdy, George, Ivy Kelly, and Rozella Kelly. Some of Old River School's teachers were Clara Jamison, Winnie Comstock, Agnes Brown, Mrs. Erickson, Mrs. Cope, Mrs. Payton, Mrs. West, Mrs. Shaeffer, and Mrs. Hogan.

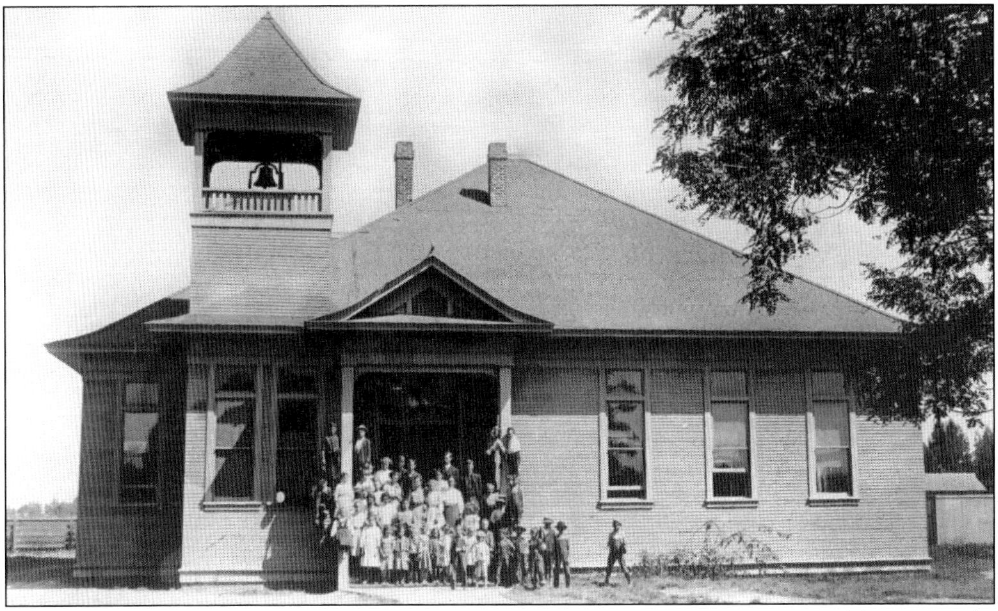

The original Alameda School, located at Imperial Highway and Clark Street, was blown away by an 1871 windstorm. By 1880, a sturdier structure (pictured here in 1907) stood on Alameda Street near Patton Road. That building was destroyed by fire in 1921. In 1922, a fourth was erected.

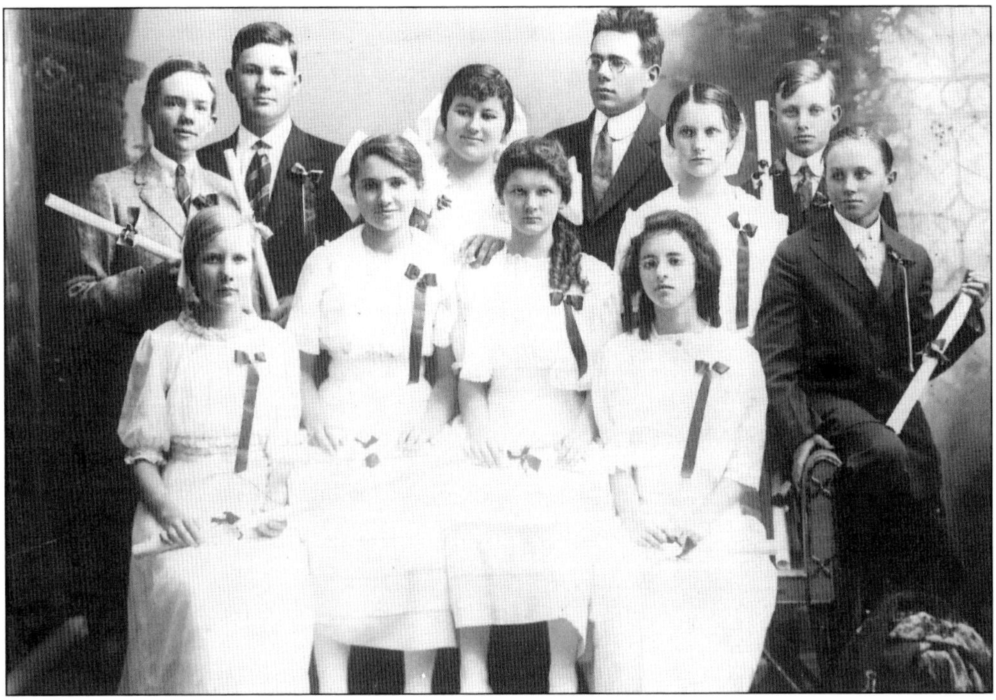

The 1916 Alameda School graduates pictured here are (first row) Ada Ralph, unidentified, Edith Bird, and Rebecca Nelson; (second row) Bruce White, unidentified, Mildred Dilley, teacher Edmond R. Bates, Marjorie Fancher, Willie Stevenson, and another unidentified student. The school's early teachers included Women's Rights and Suffragist leader Mary Foy. The Alameda School District was formed in 1869 by petition of C. Gillett.

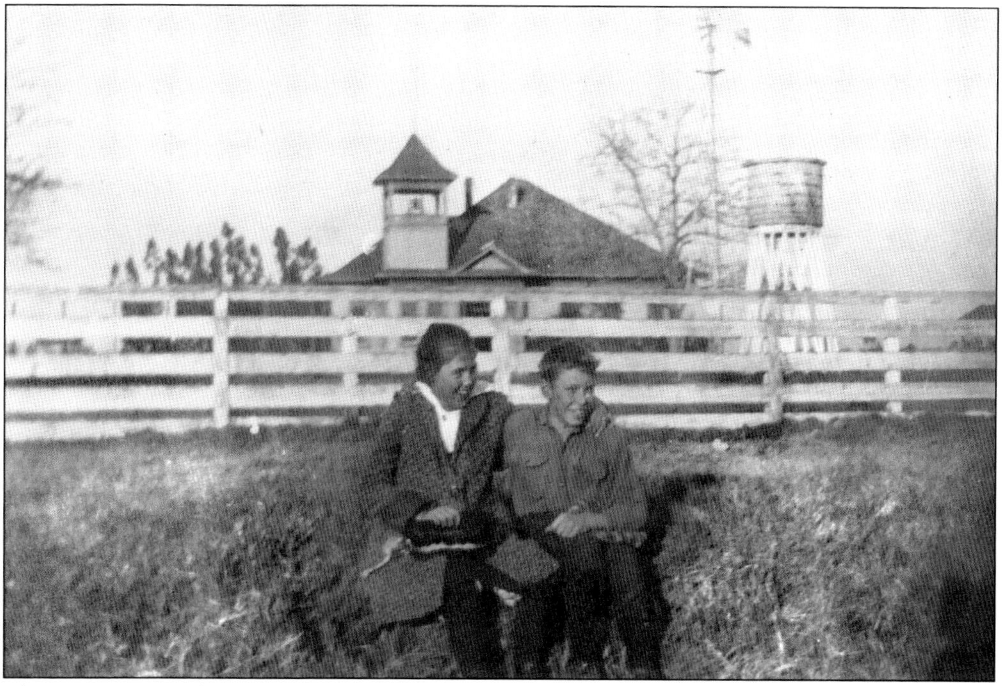

This picture was taken in 1910 and is part of a collection donated to the Downey History Center by Frances Parke Barnes. Barnes grew up in College Settlement on Alameda Street during the early 1900s. She graduated from Alameda School in 1915 and was a lifetime Downey resident. Her father was Sydney L. Parke (1853–1936).

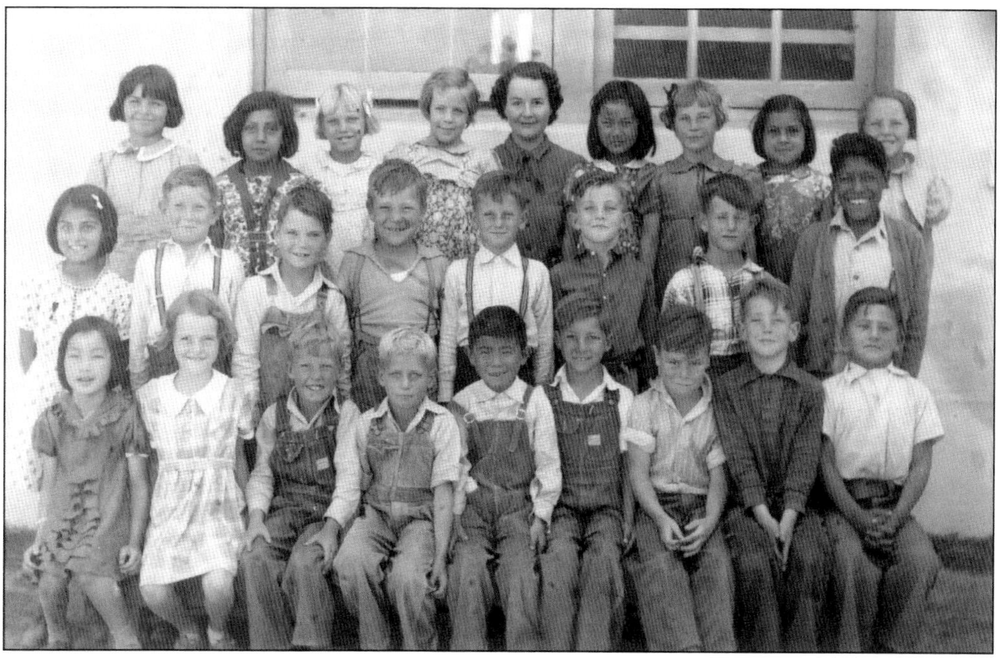

Alameda School began in 1869, and this picture from the early 1900s harkens back to a simpler time. Most of the boys wore bib overalls to school. Many children came to school barefoot.

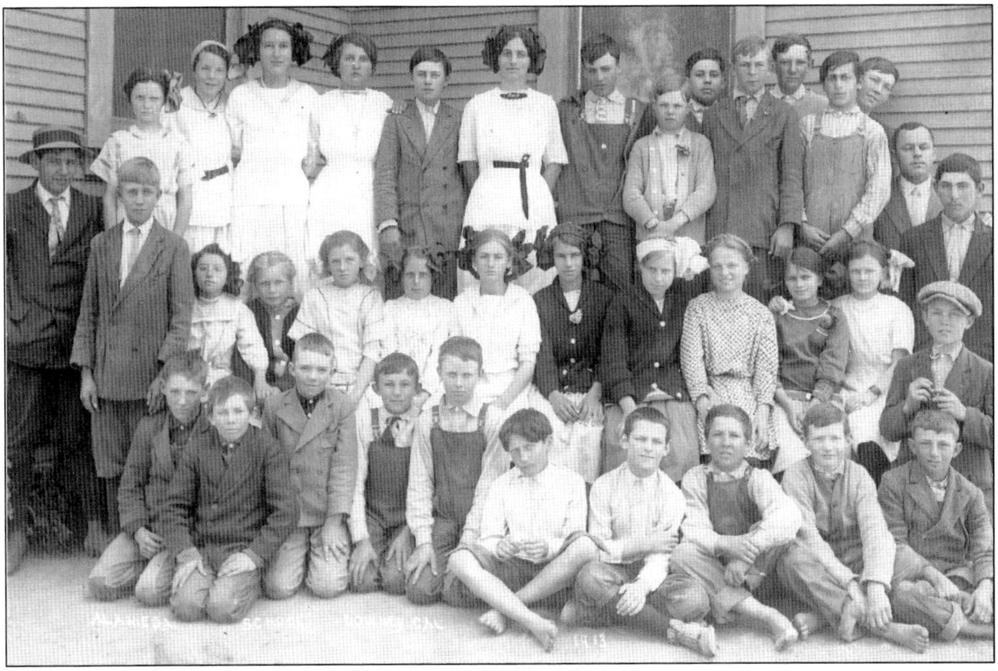

Shown here is the Alameda School upper grade class of 1913. Among those pictured are C. and F. Parke, B. Mooshagian, A. Ralph, E. and J. Boehme, W. Stevensen, E. Ball, R. Nelson, G. and M. Fancher, E. Maw, W. Holcomb, E. Bird, K. Woesner, E. Casey, M. Precido, D. Jones S. Kincaid, E. Jenks, and Mr. Thornton the teacher.

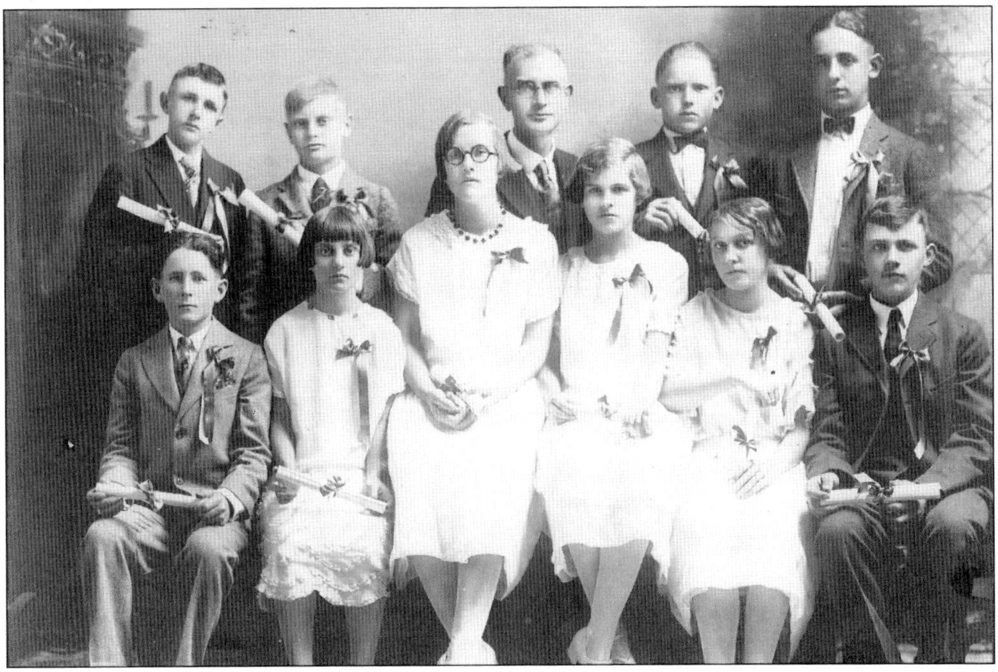

This 1920s picture shows a young Elbert Ward with a group of Alameda School graduates. Ward came to Downey in 1923 as a combination teacher and principal. He retired as the district's superintendent in 1955.

Here is the Downey Grammar School at its opening in September 1884. After purchasing two acres of land between Second and Third Street at Dolan Avenue, town residents built the school. In 1915, a larger, more modern building with better facilities was constructed. More land was purchased from Regina Frankel, and in 1924 a Kindergarten was built with Dorothy Kelly as teacher.

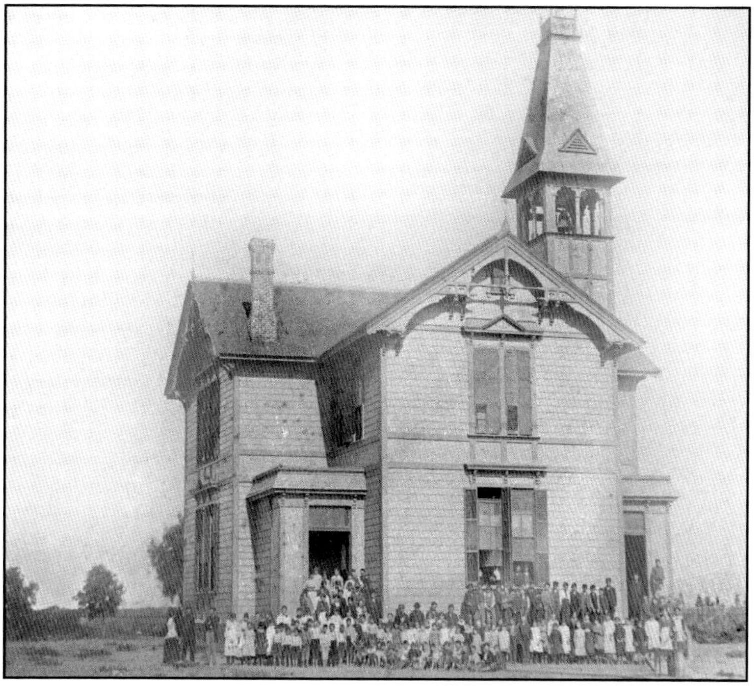

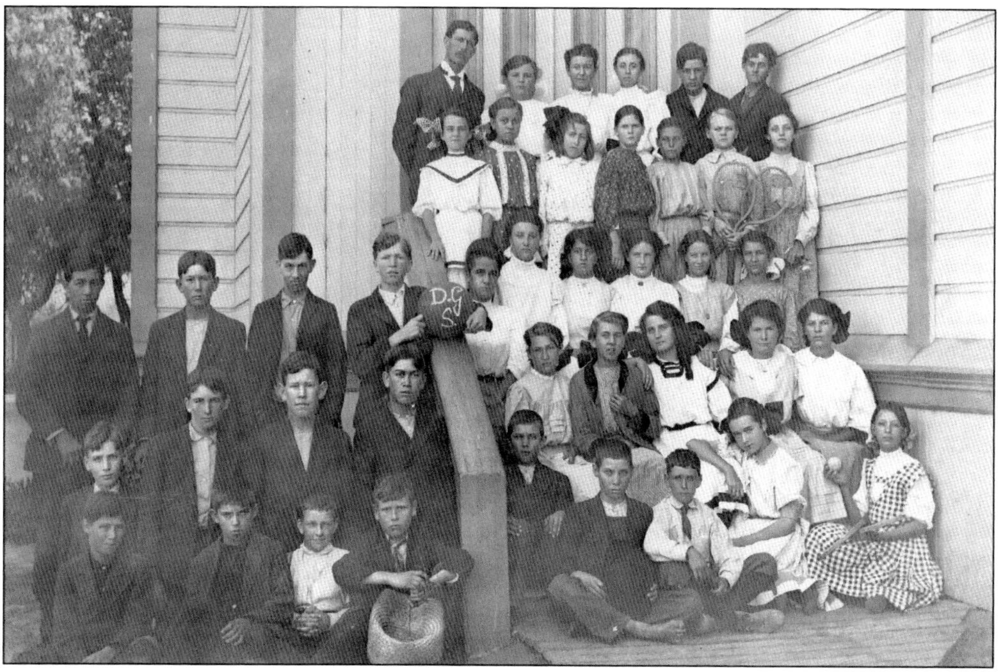

Pictured here is a Downey Grammar School upper grade class in 1907. The Downey School District's fine tradition of educational excellence dates back more than a century to pioneer days. John Downey posted signs at train depots in the south and east advertising land at $10 an acre for purchases of 50 acres or more, with long terms of credit.

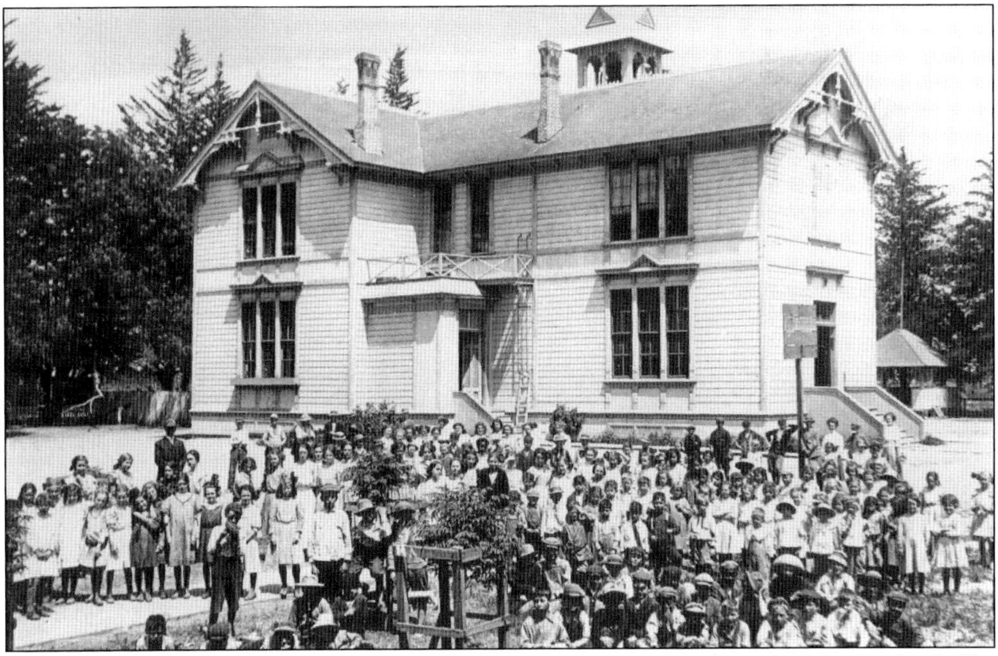

In late 1884, Downey Grammar School moved into a new two-story frame building with a belfry at the corner of Dolan and Third Streets. This side view of the school was taken in 1912.

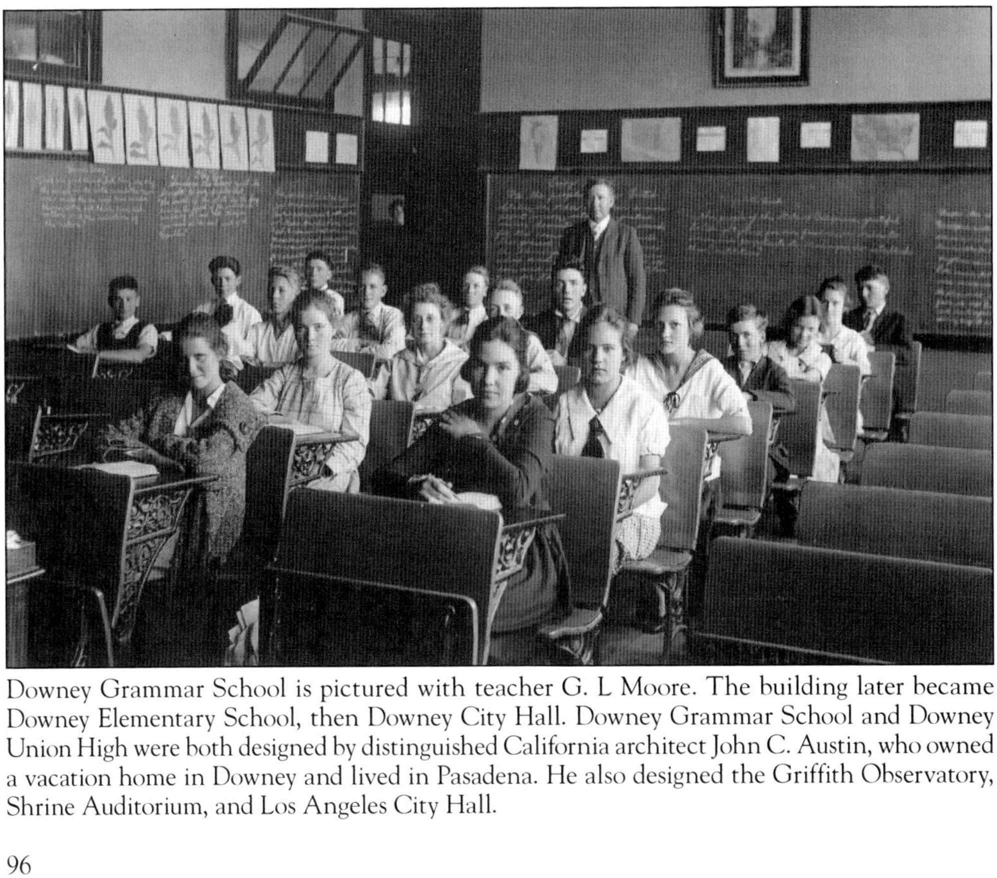

Downey Grammar School is pictured with teacher G. L Moore. The building later became Downey Elementary School, then Downey City Hall. Downey Grammar School and Downey Union High were both designed by distinguished California architect John C. Austin, who owned a vacation home in Downey and lived in Pasadena. He also designed the Griffith Observatory, Shrine Auditorium, and Los Angeles City Hall.

The DOWNEY SCHOOLS

By FRANK F. OTTO

The people of Downey point with pride to the fact that they have been able to vision the future needs of their children and have provided so well that the school organization has not been forced to resort to half day sessions or other expedients to take care of the large number of new pupils.

Our schools believe strongly in masterey of subject matter and in good discipline, but they also believe both of these aims are only a part of the main program, namely, character education, or good citizenship.

The most successful method that has ever been devised for developing character is the "learn by doing" method. Pupils become good citizens by being good citizens. They participate wholeheartedly in good citizenship work only when they are taken into the plan and are helped to understand the aims of the program, the reasons for the program, and the advantages of it.

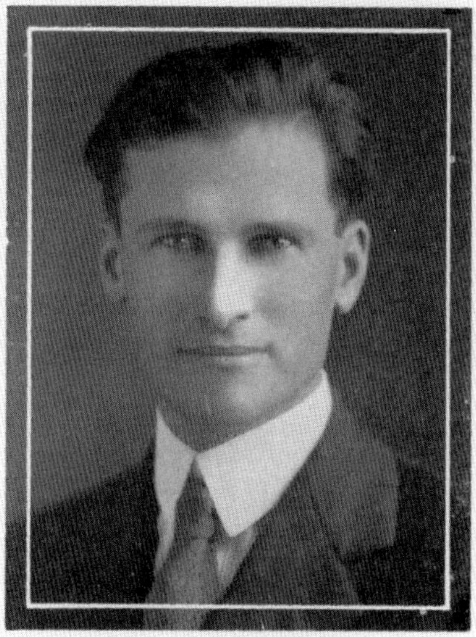

PROF. FRANK F. OTTO
Principal Downey Union High School

In Downey we have four elementary grade schools with equipment and sites valued at $200,000. These schools have a total enrollment of nearly 1000 pupils. Adequate courses are arranged to take care of all grades from kindergarten through to the eighth grade.

Thirty-one teachers, well trained and specialized, have been employed to teach the boys and girls by use of the latest methods and teaching principles. These include special teachers in music, home economics, art and manual training. A well trained nurse assists in helping

(See the Next Page)

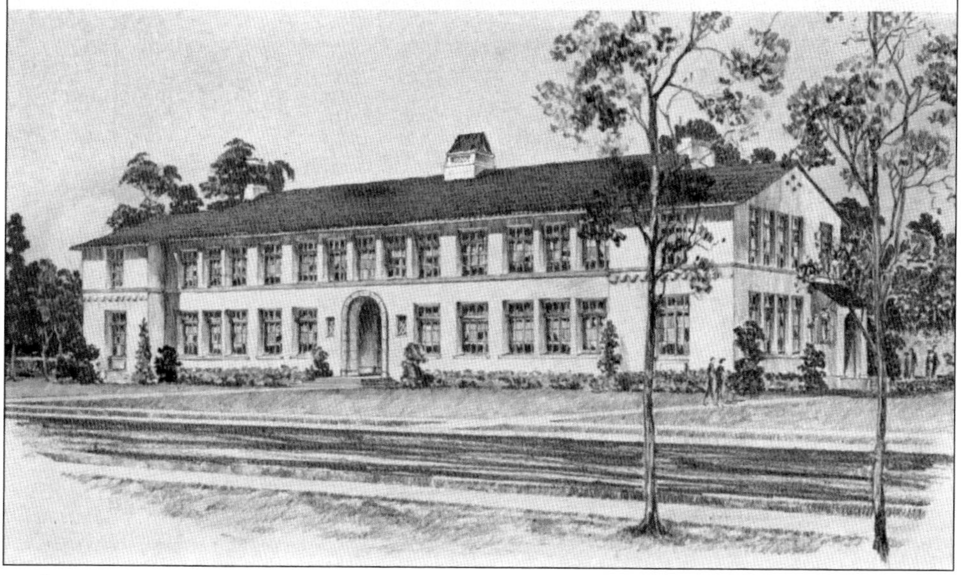

Here longtime Downey High School educator Frank Otto writes about the pride in education found in Downey schools.

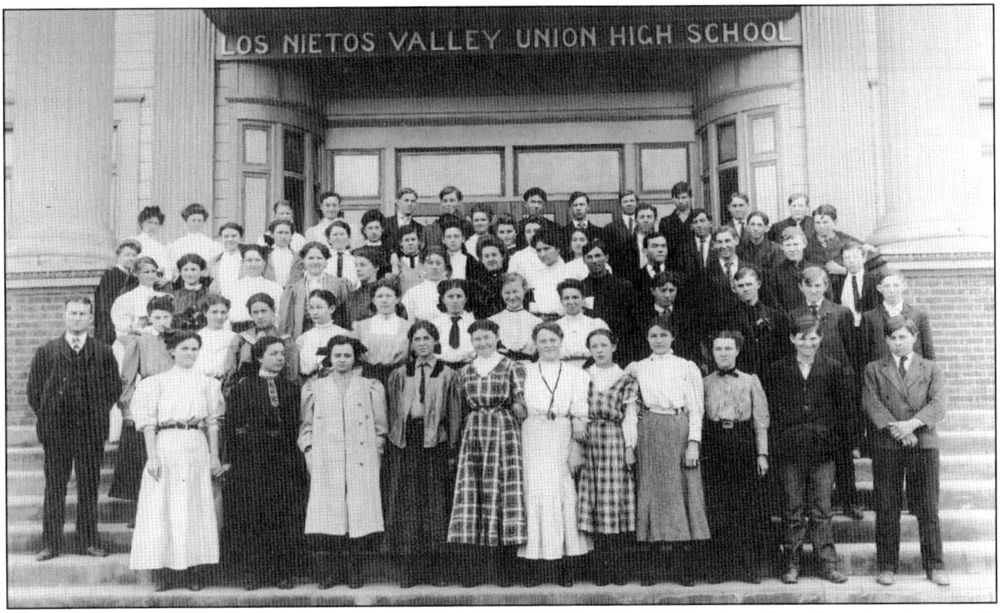

This photograph of Los Nietos Valley Union High School was taken soon after the school opened. The cornerstone was laid on December 9, 1905, and is still preserved in front of the Viking Tower at today's Downey High. A new building was built in 1912. In 1915, the school's name was changed to Downey Union High School.

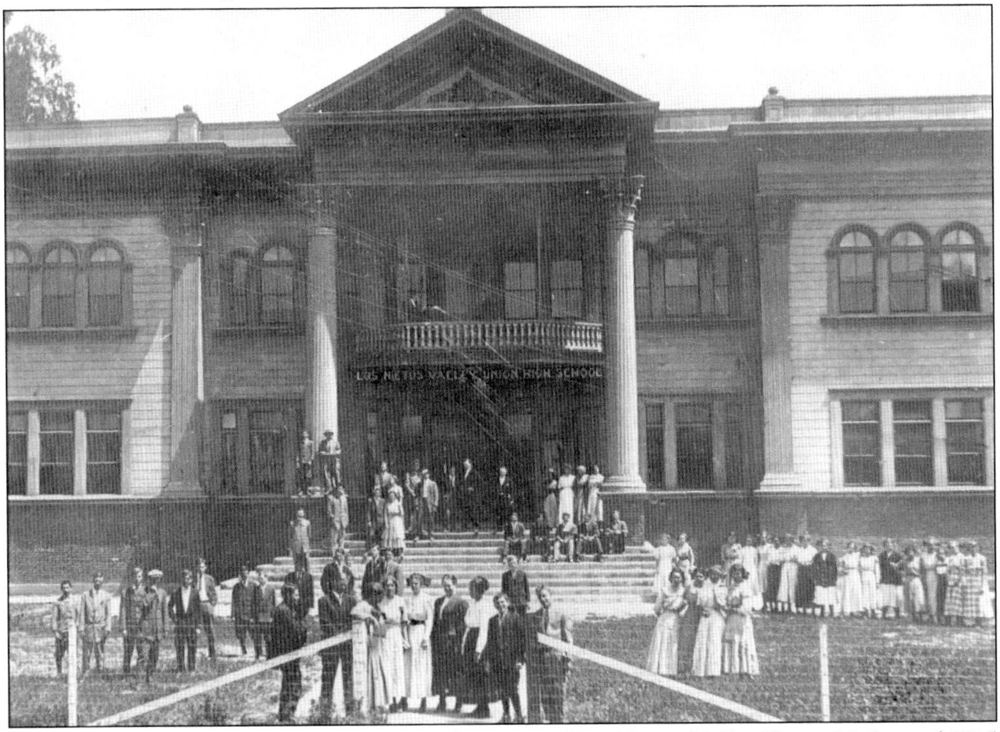

In 1901, a school district was formed under the name of Los Nietos Valley Union High until 1915 when it took the name Downey Union High School District. The schools of the old Los Angeles County Silver School District had finally become the Downey School District.

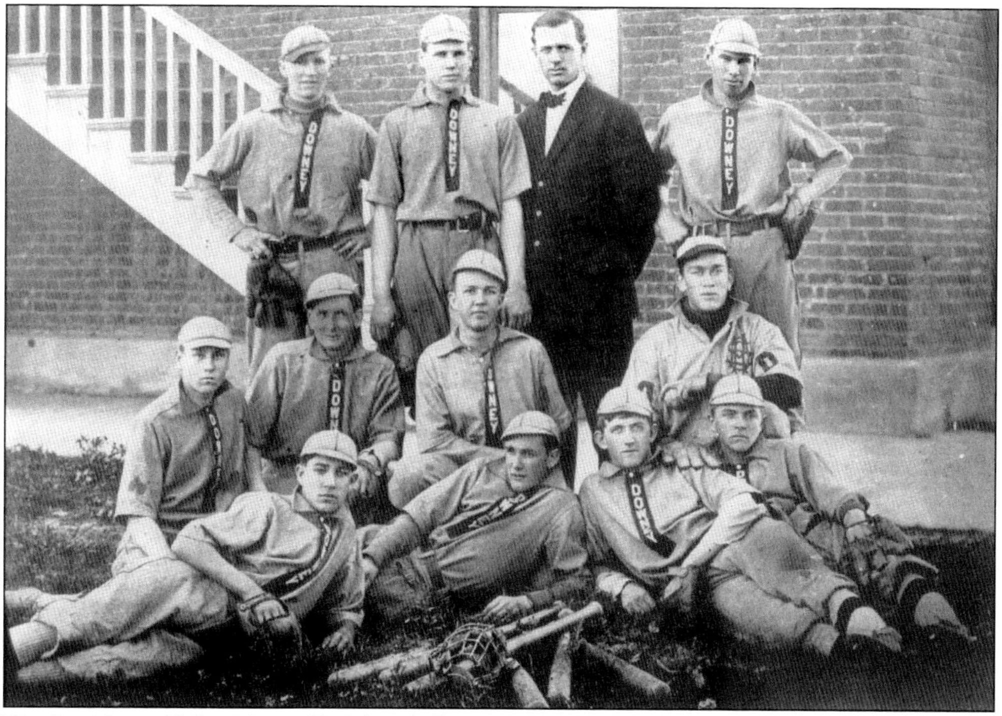

The Los Nietos Valley Union High baseball team is pictured here around 1911. From 1911 to 1913, Downey's championship athletes included W. Brookshire, W. Ball, D. Walk, W. Walk, Day Jewell, McCullough, S. Williams, Dan McKellar, ? Wierback, Bill Porter Johnny Johnson, Sid Foster, H. McIntosh, H. Kirkpatrick, and Dicky Crawford. Their coaches were Duffy Seay and Mr. Taech.

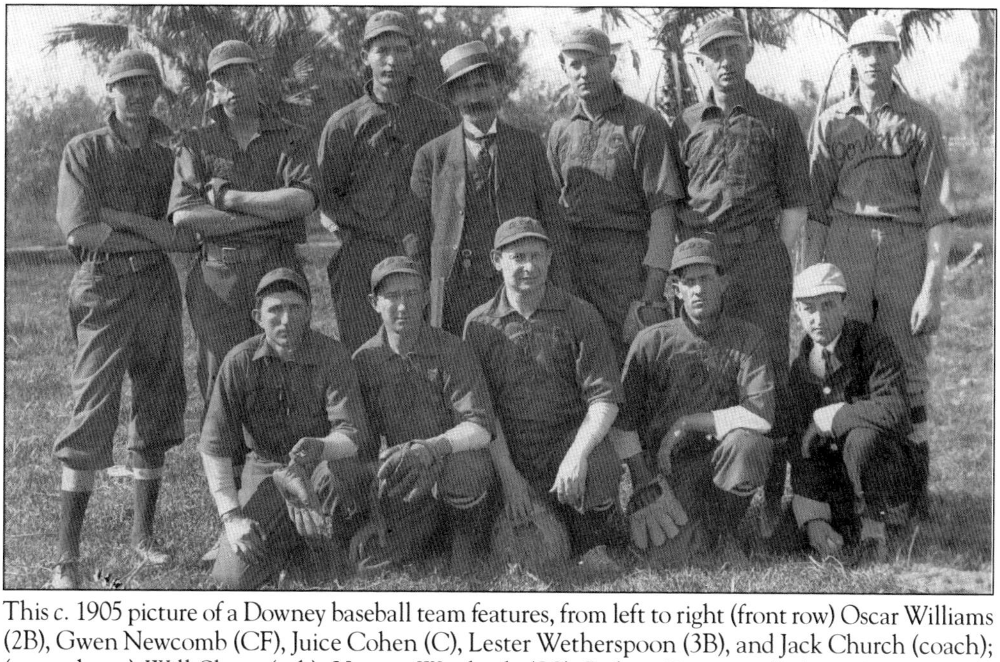

This c. 1905 picture of a Downey baseball team features, from left to right (front row) Oscar Williams (2B), Gwen Newcomb (CF), Juice Cohen (C), Lester Wetherspoon (3B), and Jack Church (coach); (second row) Will Slater (sub), Harvey Weirbach (SS), Robert Freeman (LF), Pinky Goodrich (manager), Rufus Crandal (pitcher), Bill Wierbach (1B), and Owen Wierbach (RF).

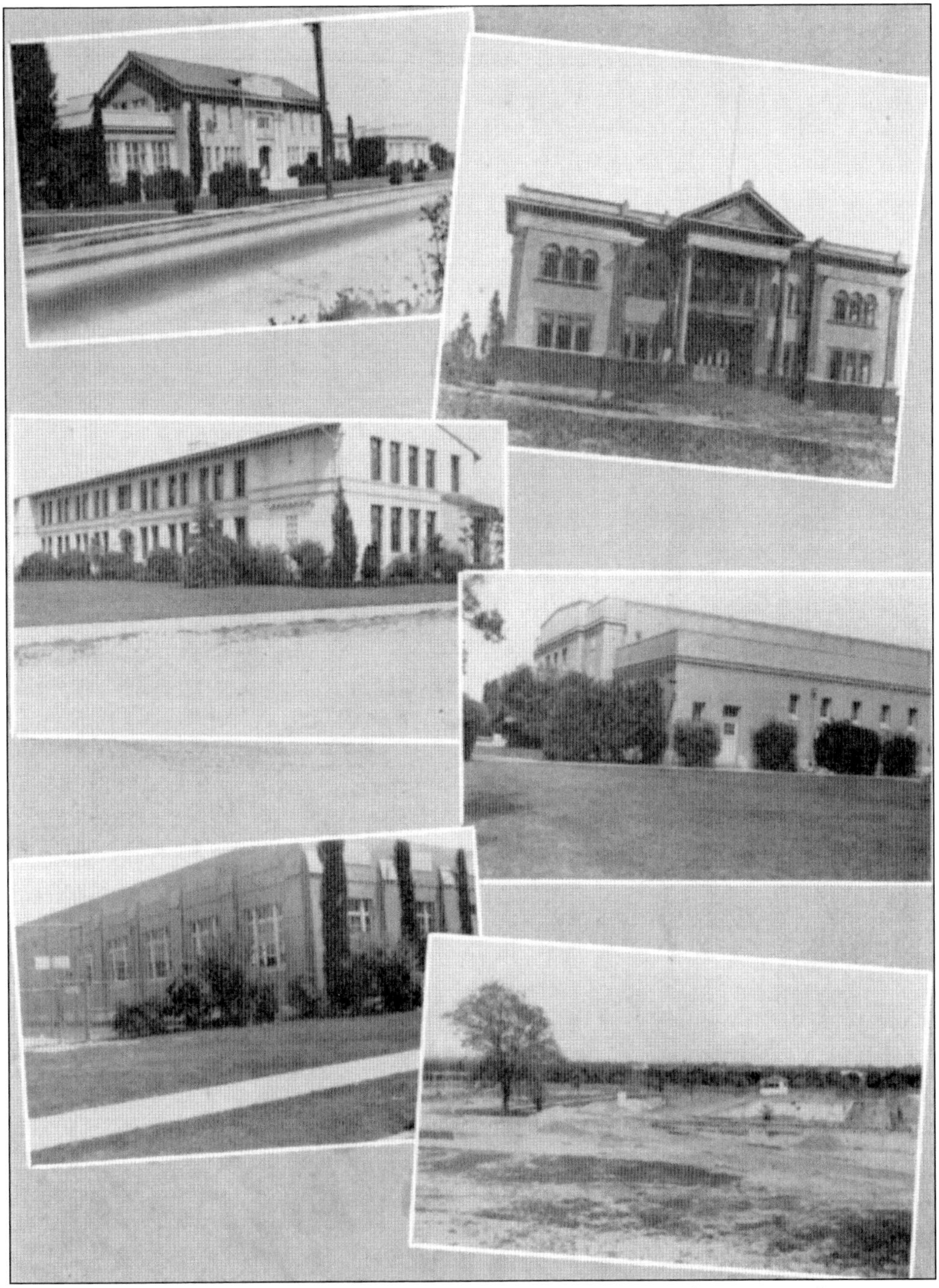

When Downey Union High School was first organized in 1902, its students met in the grammar school's auditorium. The first building went up in 1903 at the end of Second Street. By 1921, a new structure was built to accommodate the growing student body. In 1926, a gymnasium and Manual Arts building were erected on the site of the original high school. In 1928, a junior high school was built (middle left). Downey High had 66 students in 1907; in 1936, it enrolled 562. In 2009, enrollment exceeded 3,700.

On Friday, December 14, 1956, the Downey High School Vikings and the Anaheim High School Colonists met for the Southern California CIF Championship game at the Los Angeles Coliseum. Two extraordinary high school football teams were led by two heroic running backs, Randy Meadows of Downey and Mickey Flynn of Anaheim. Both teams had gone undefeated against their 12 respective opponents during the regular season. Meadows and Flynn were named Co-Players of the Year in the CIF.

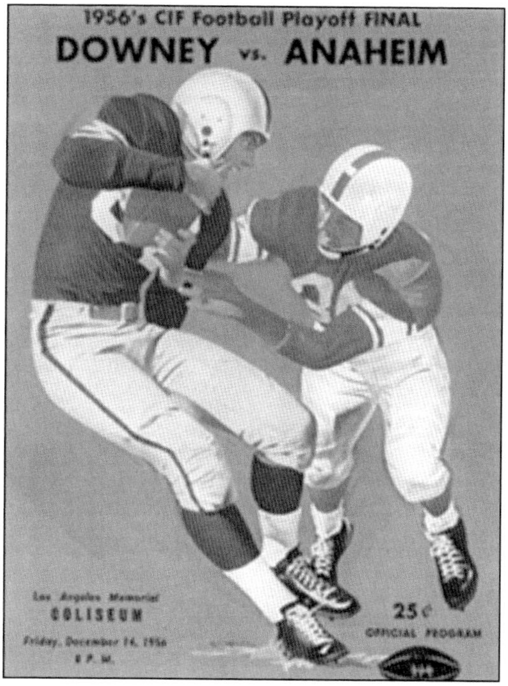

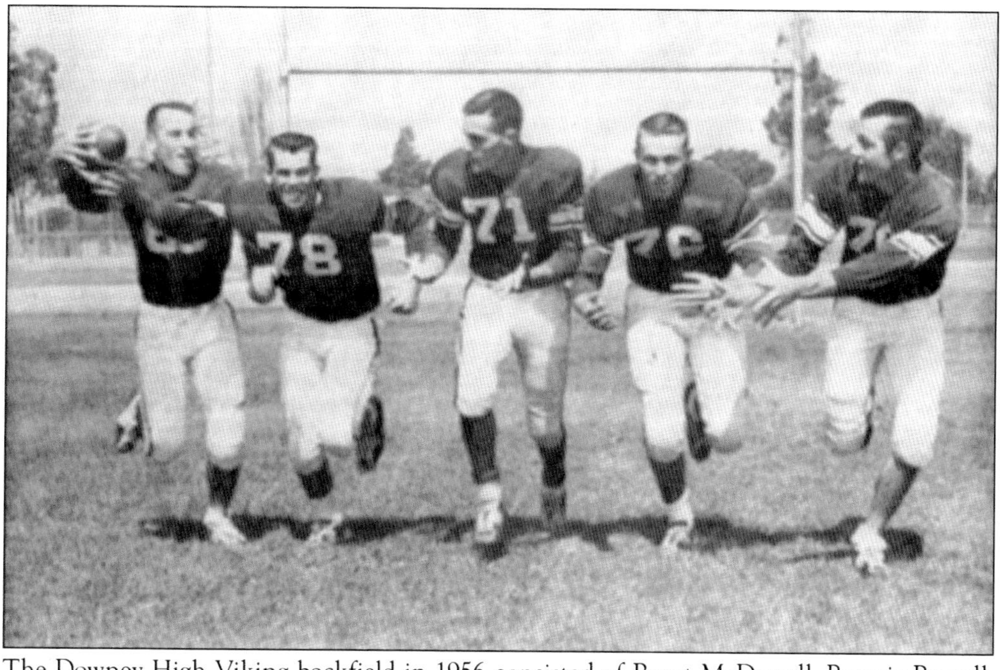

The Downey High Viking backfield in 1956 consisted of Brent McDowell, Ronnie Russell, Randy Meadows, Joe Sallinger, and Jack Trumbo. Longtime Downey coach Dick Hill led the Viking team to the CIF playoffs that year, decided by the championship game in the Los Angeles Memorial Coliseum on December 13. On that foggy Friday night, Downey and Anaheim fought to a 13–13 tie to become co-champions of Southern California. The 41,383 in attendance was the largest crowd ever in California high school history. The two stars of the game were Meadows and Anaheim's Mickey Flynn.

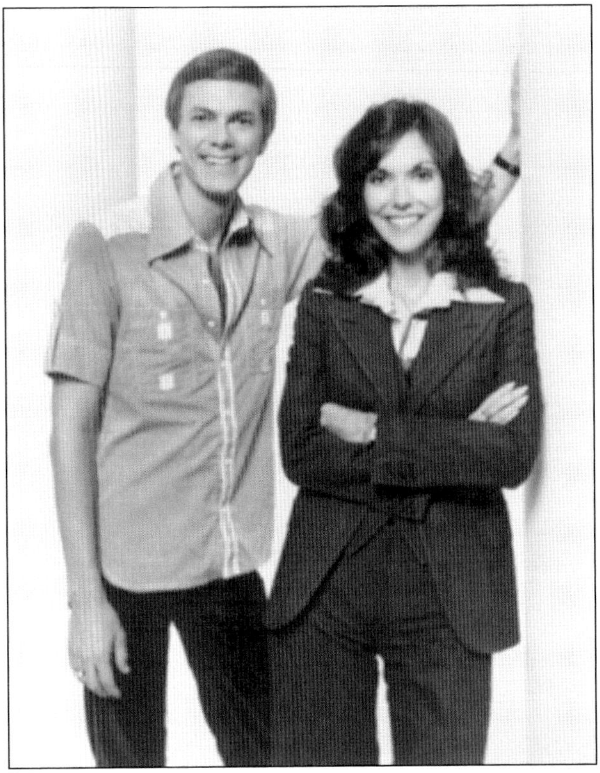

Harold and Agnes Carpenter moved to Downey from Connecticut in 1963 with 16-year-old son Richard and 13-year-old daughter Karen Anne. Richard attended Downey High while studying piano at the University of Southern California. Karen started at Downey High in fall 1964 and played drums and glockenspiel in the marching band. When Karen was still in high school, she and Richard formed the Carpenters Trio with Wes Jacobs. In 1969, they signed a lucrative record deal with A&M Record's Herb Alpert. The rest is history. With Richard's talented arrangements and piano coupled with Karen's softly haunting vocals, the Carpenters became one of America's favorites and Downey's proudest.

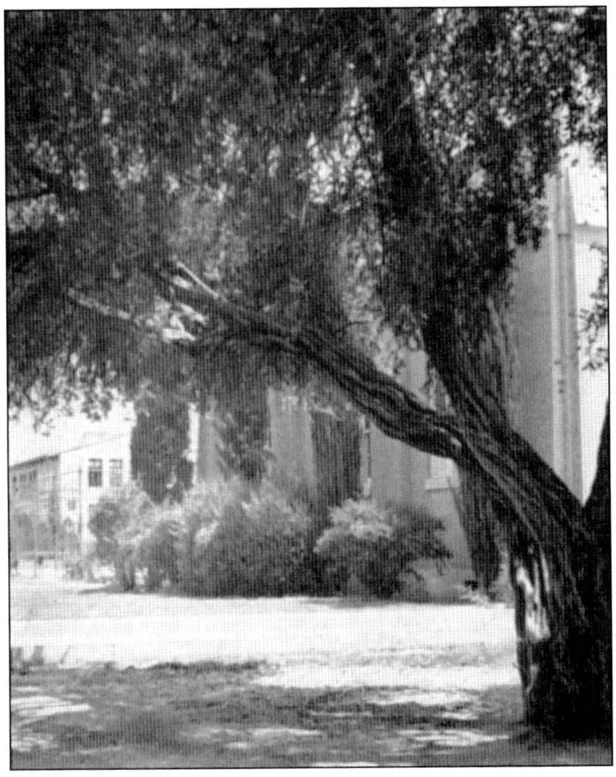

Whether it was known as Los Nietos Valley Union High, Downey Union High, or Downey High School, Downey's always been fortunate to have some of the best schools, teachers, and community support in the Southern California area. Many of today's prominent men and women got their start in Downey's public schools.

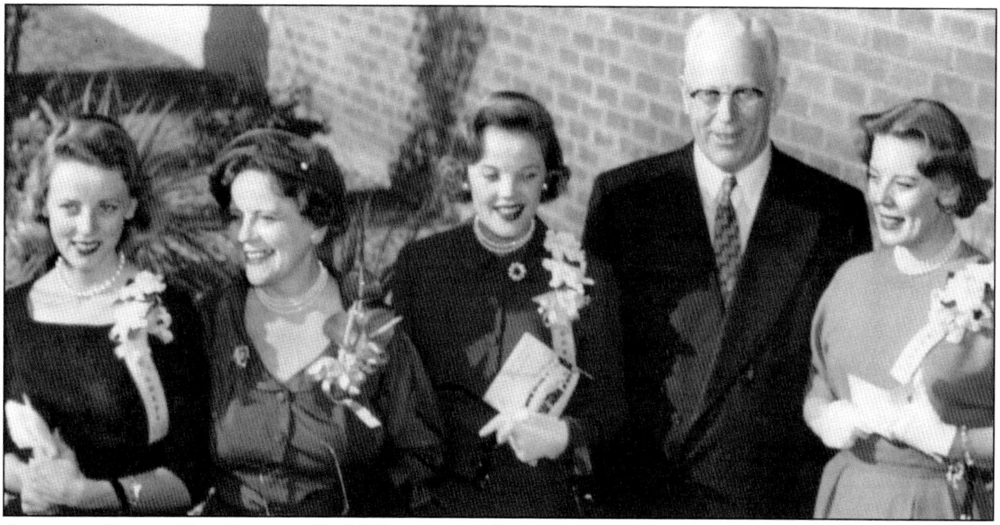

Supreme Court Chief Justice Earl Warren and his wife and daughters are shown in 1955 at the dedication of Earl Warren Senior High School in Downey. Warren, former governor of California, noted that the population of Downey in 1956 equaled the population of California when it became a state in 1850, and the population of Los Angeles County when he was born in 1891. The addition of Earl Warren High School reflected Downey's continued growth and support of education.

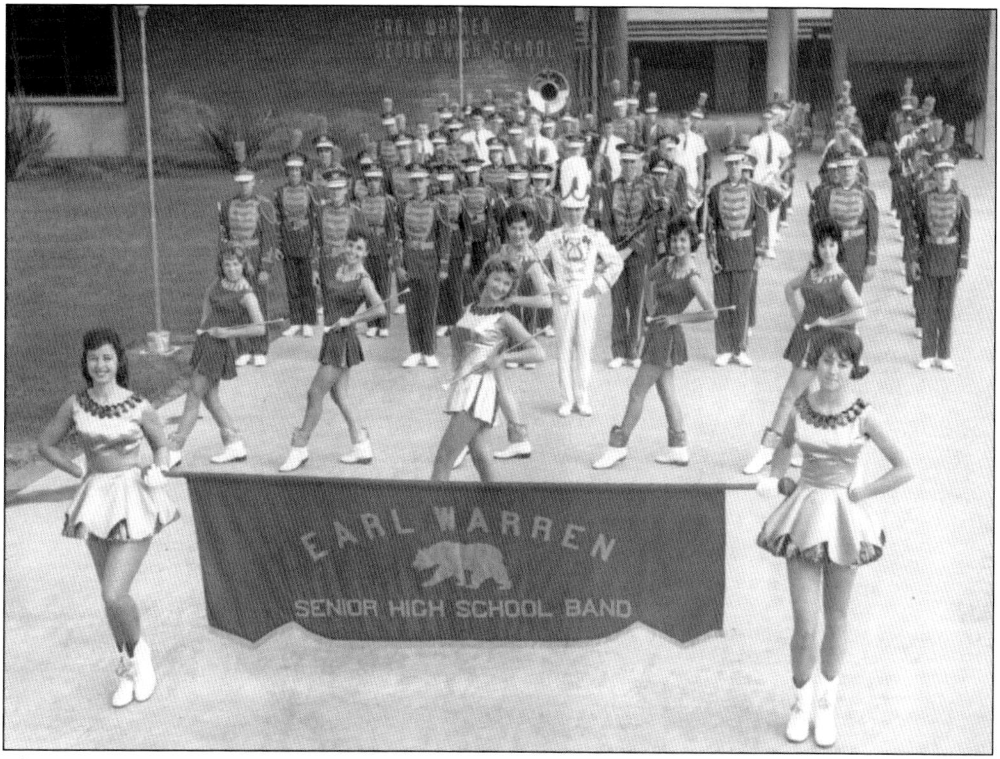

The 1962 EWSHS Band lines up at the school's entrance for a picture. In 1963, the school board simplified the school's name to Warren High School. The school drill team was the Honeybears; Earl Warren's daughter, Nina, was nicknamed "Honeybear." The 1970 WHS graduating class included over 700 students. Warren High School's enrollment today is over 3,500

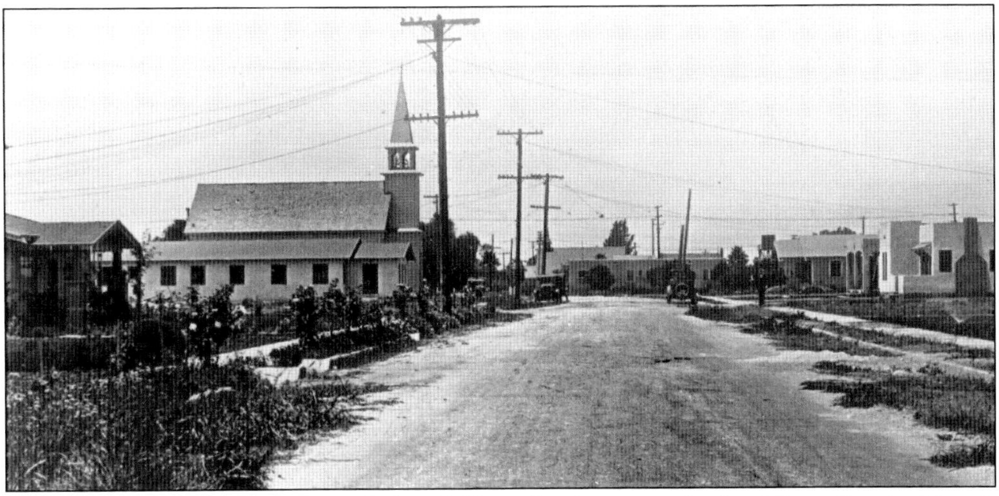

The First Baptist Church was founded in Gallatin Settlement as the Los Nietos Baptist Church on September 19, 1868, under Reverend Isham Fuqua. John Downey and M. D. Crawford donated the property. It was succeeded at Third and Dolan Streets in 1876 by the First Baptist Church of Downey, which served its congregation until 1921, when it was sold to St. Mark's Episcopalian Church and removed to Fifth Street. In 1955, the old 1876 church was moved to Knott's Berry Farm, where it was restored and renamed the "Church of the Reflections." Walter Knott's father, Elgin C. Knott, was a teacher at College Settlement's Los Nietos Collegiate Institute. In 1965, a new First Baptist sanctuary replaced the 1921 church building.

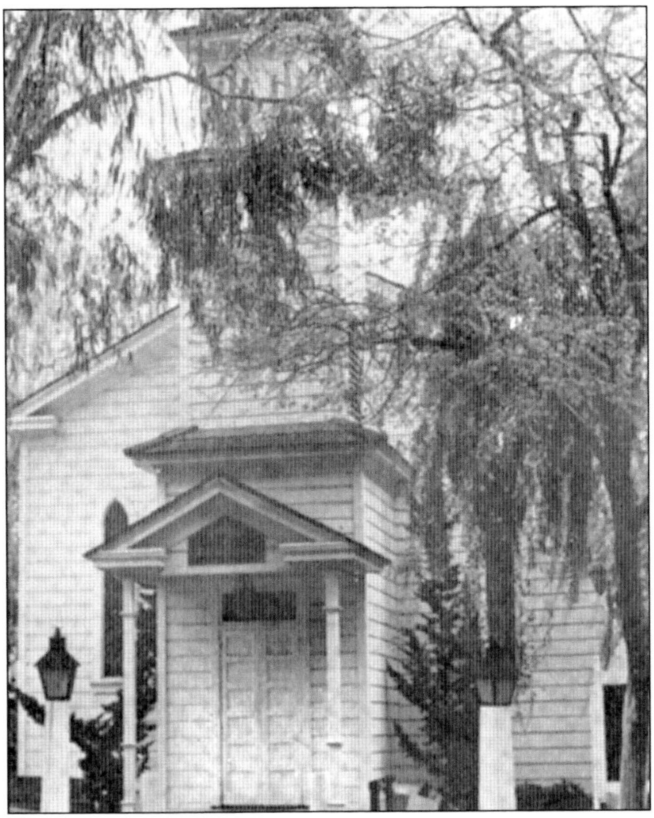

This undated photograph shows the entrance to the old First Baptist Church in Downey, which, for a time, became St. Mark's Epicopalean Church on Fifth Street.

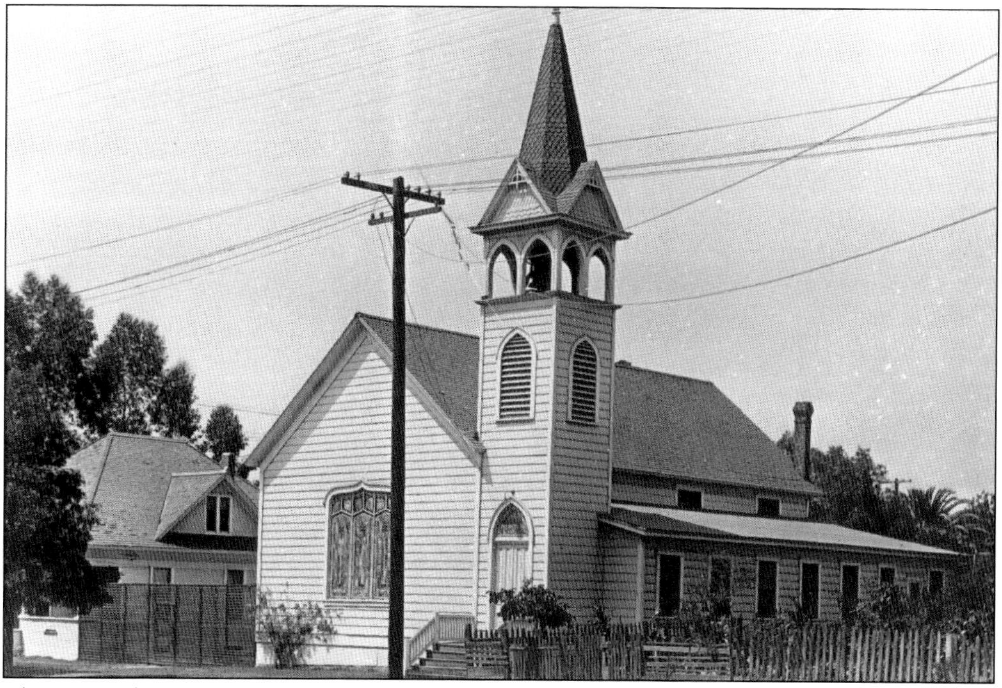

This image depicts the former Cumberland Presbyterian Church building in the late 1920s.

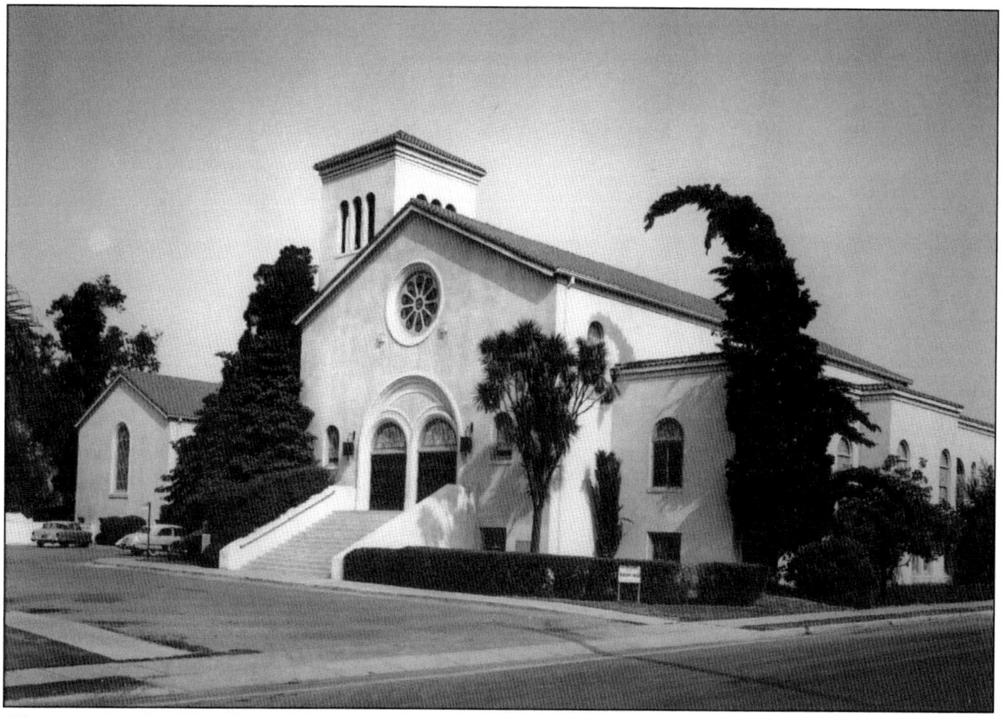

The current First Presbyterian Church building was erected in 1927 at Crawford and Seventh Streets. The first service was held on September 4, 1927. The church is pictured here in 1955. Located on Downey Avenue and Seventh Street, the Presbyterian Church has served the Downey area for well over a century.

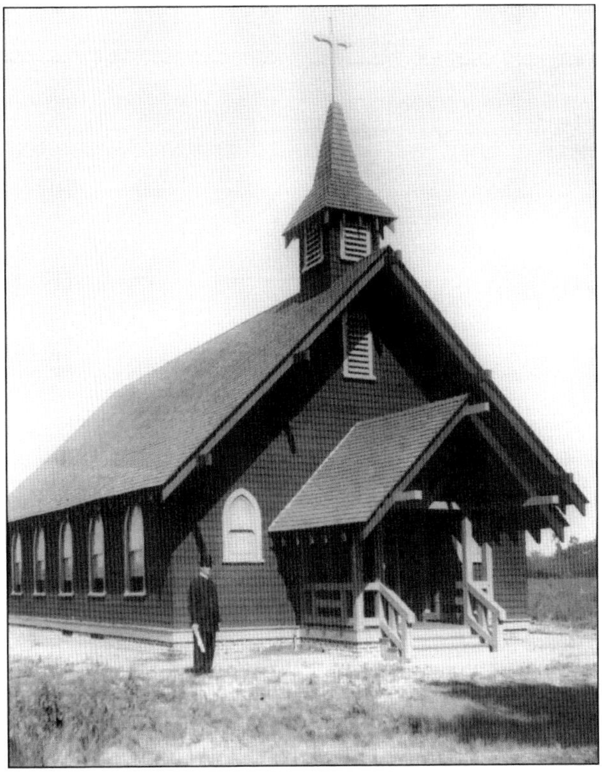

St. Anthony's Catholic Church was built on acreage purchased from the Downey Land and Improvement Association on May 23, 1908. Built on a triangular lot bounded by Crawford, Fifth, and New Streets, the small frame church was blessed in September 1909, and altars were installed in 1911, after which Bishop Thomas Conaty dedicated the church. When Our Lady of Perpetual Help Church was enlarged in 1951, the original wood frame church, which had been used as a parish hall, was demolished.

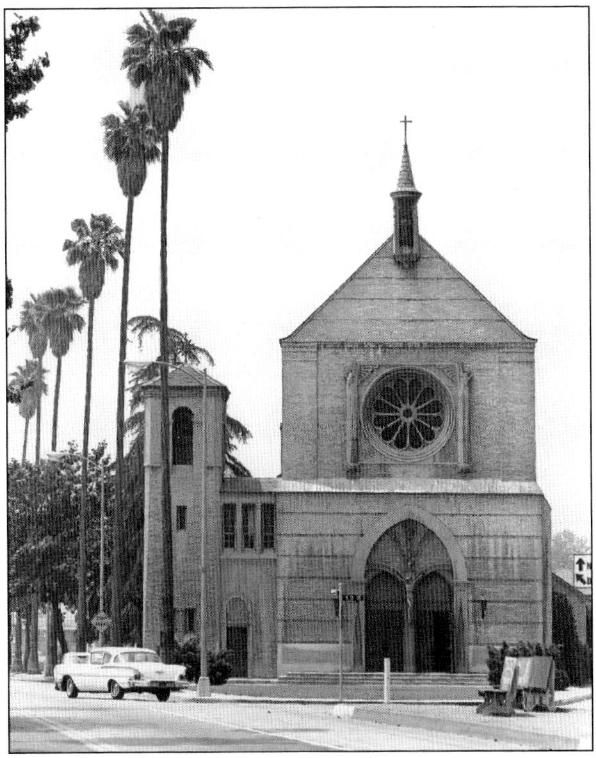

Local industrialist E. M. Smith of EMSCO Aircraft and his wife "Mimmie" were instrumental in the building of Our Lady of Perpetual Help Church. They approached Father O'Brien in 1929, proposing a large church to memorialize their mothers and as a gift to the diocese. Architects Henry Carlton Newton and Robert Dennis Murray designed a historic Italian Romanesque structure, inspired by St. Francis Assisi Church in Italy. On January 25, 1931, Bishop John Cantwell officiated at the dedication. The church was remodeled in 1951, when the sanctuary was moved 47 feet south, and again after the 1987 Whittier Earthquake.

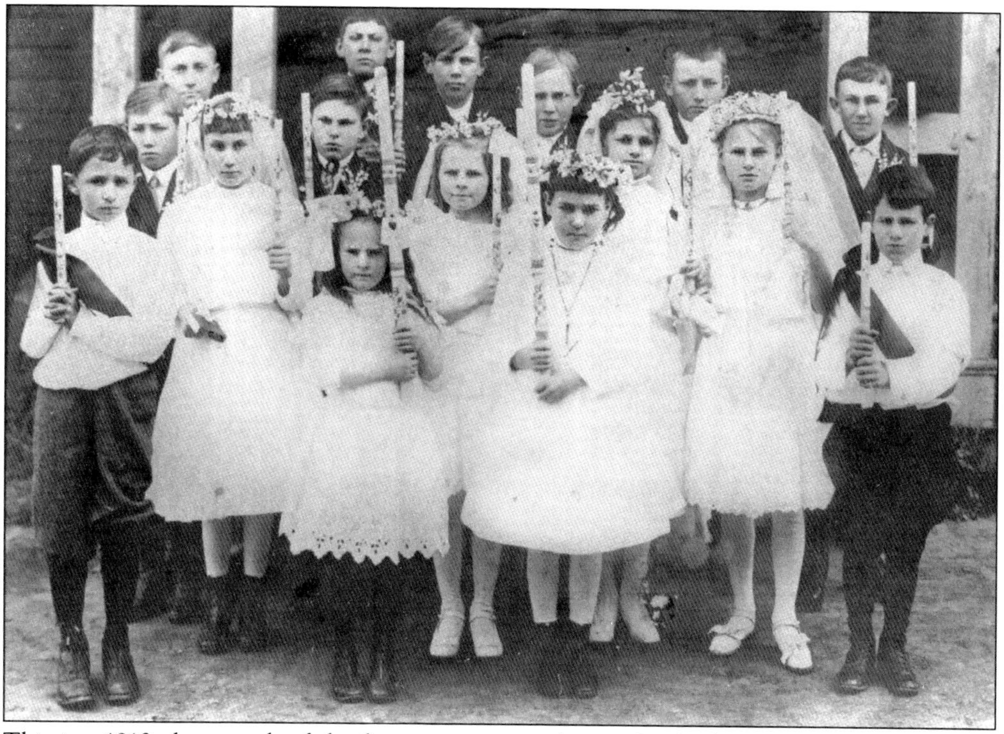

This is a 1913 photograph of the first communion class at St. Anthony's Catholic Church in Downey. Among the new communicants pictured are (front row) Natch Mandella, Florence Mair, and Jessie Maier; (second row) Olive and John Maier; and (third row) Ernest "Pete" Bohme (right). St. Anthony's was a mission church until 1913 when Reverend B. O'Rorke was appointed the first resident pastor. The Catholics of Downey met for regular services at Frankel Hall from 1896 until St. Anthony's church was completed in 1908. St. Anthony's was located on Fifth Street, between Downey Avenue and New Street.

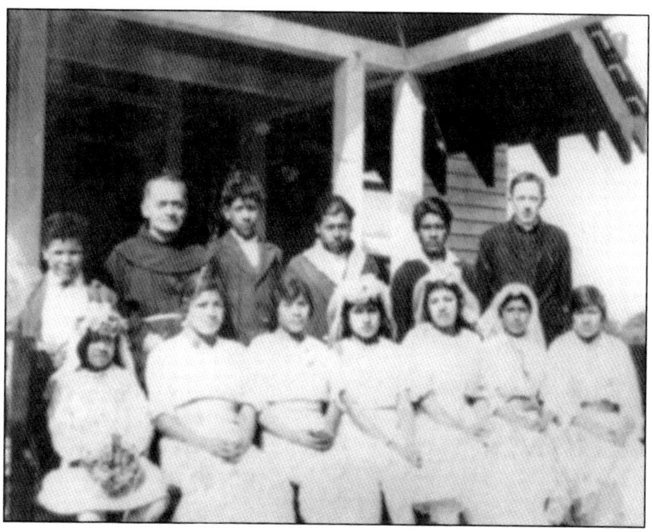

This photograph, taken outside St. Anthony's Catholic Church in Downey soon after the church was completed in 1908, captures Silvestria Samandiego and others at their First Holy Communion. In 1888, following the establishment of St. Joseph's Church at 13th and Los Angeles Streets in Los Angeles, the parish's Franciscan fathers would visit Downey and conduct mass at a local home.

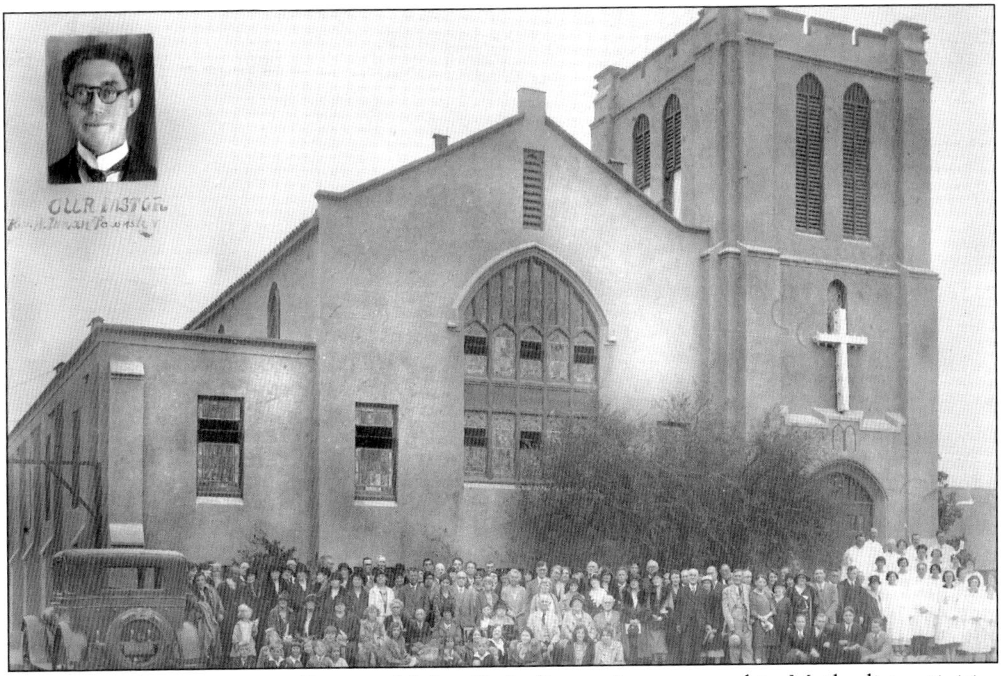

College Settlement pioneer Reverend John C. Ardis was instrumental in Methodist activities and founded the Los Nietos Collegiate Institute in March 1869. In 1873, Downey's Methodists were mainly Southern transplants. In 1877, they built the town's first Methodist Church near the southwest corner of College Avenue and Alameda Street, with a 110-foot steeple mounted with a massive hand pointing heavenward. In the 1890s, elders relocated the church to Dolan and Second Streets. In 1922, church leaders finished a new church at Fifth and Crawford Streets, seen here in the 1930s.

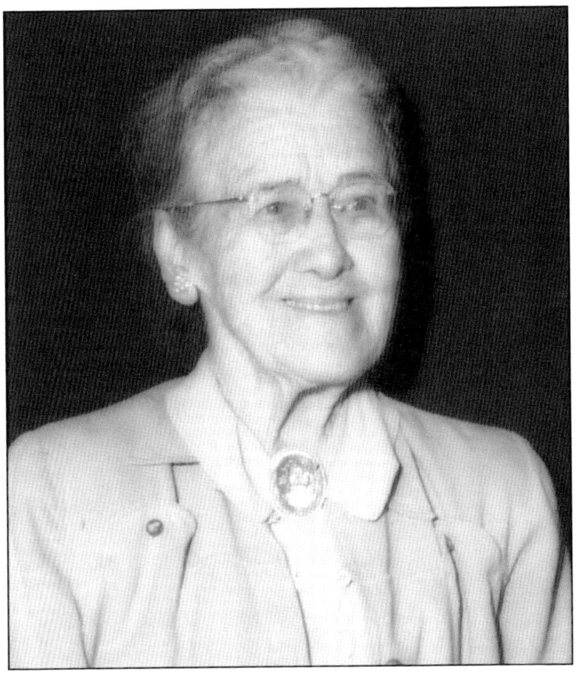

Mamie Haygood Ardis was born January 29, 1868, in Atlanta, Georgia, and was the wife of Julius Harris Ardis, who was the son of Reverend John C. and Francis Ardis, early members of the Methodist Church in Downey. Mamie was the daughter of Atticus G. Haygood Sr., an educator and minister and also president of Emory College and bishop in the Methodist Church South (Downey). Her husband was a member of the Downey Masonic Lodge and was worshipful master in 1898–1899. Mamie Ardis and her extended family were pillars of the Downey community for over 100 years. Mamie was the only woman in her class at Emory University from 1884–1887 and spent her last year at Wesleyan College, earning a B.A. and B.M. in 1888.

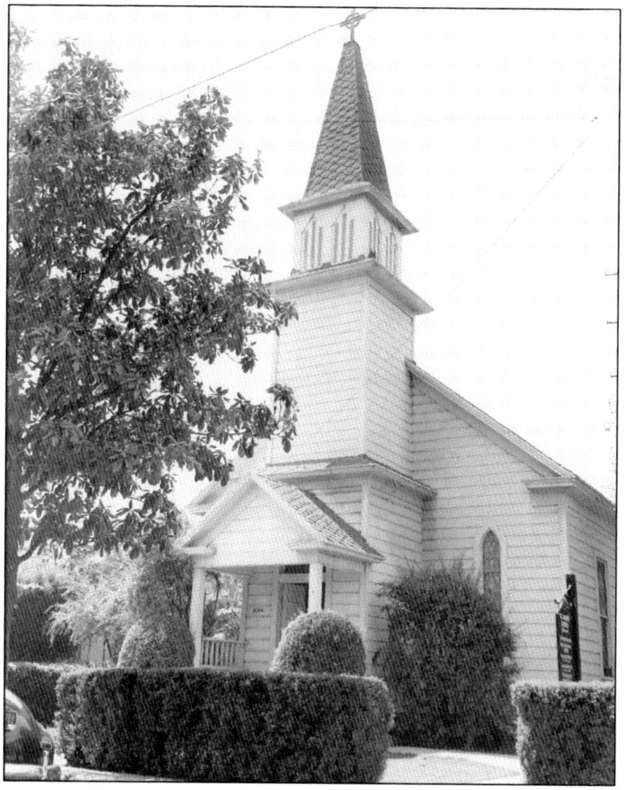

This photograph of St. Marks Church (formerly the First Baptist Church) was taken on May 3, 1954, at 8344 Fifth Street in Downey. Knott's Berry Farm purchased the church in 1955 and moved it beside a pond, renaming it "The Church of the Reflections." There it remained for nearly 50 years as the only active church located within an American amusement park. In 2004, it was moved outside the park's paid admission area and retooled as a scenic wedding chapel. St. Marks Church and School are now located on Downey Avenue.

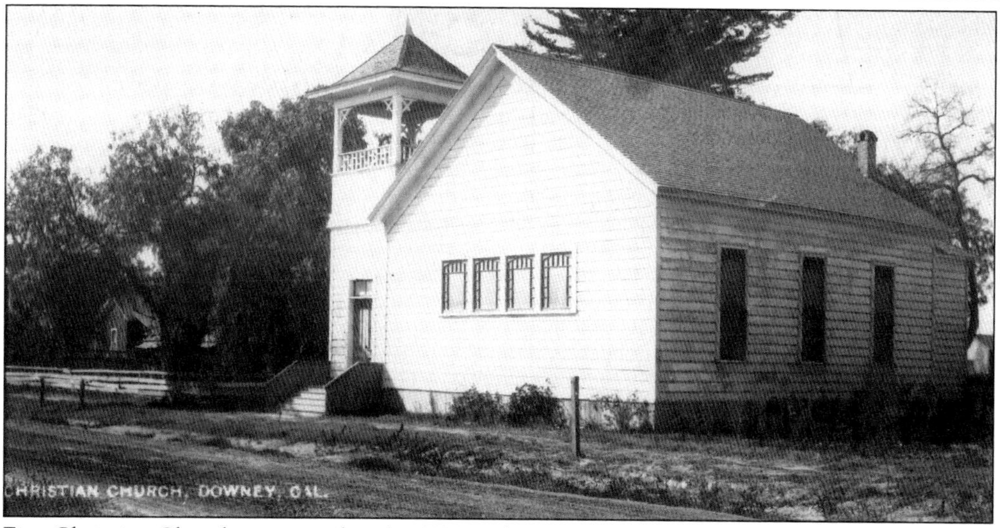

First Christian Church is pictured in the 1920s. The Los Nietos community was invited to College Settlement on January 3, 1869, to hear evangelist B. F. Standefer marking the first service of the Christian Church in Downey. By the 1870s, the church attracted John Downey's attorney, M. D. Crawford, as a member. Crawford helped purchase property for a small redwood frame building at Fourth and New Streets. The church's first two pastors were George R. Hand and James M. Monroe, formerly a professor at Christian College in Santa Rosa. Monroe, with Crawford's help, opened the short-lived Southern Pacific College in 1877. By 1980, an educational building replaced the original 1876 chapel.

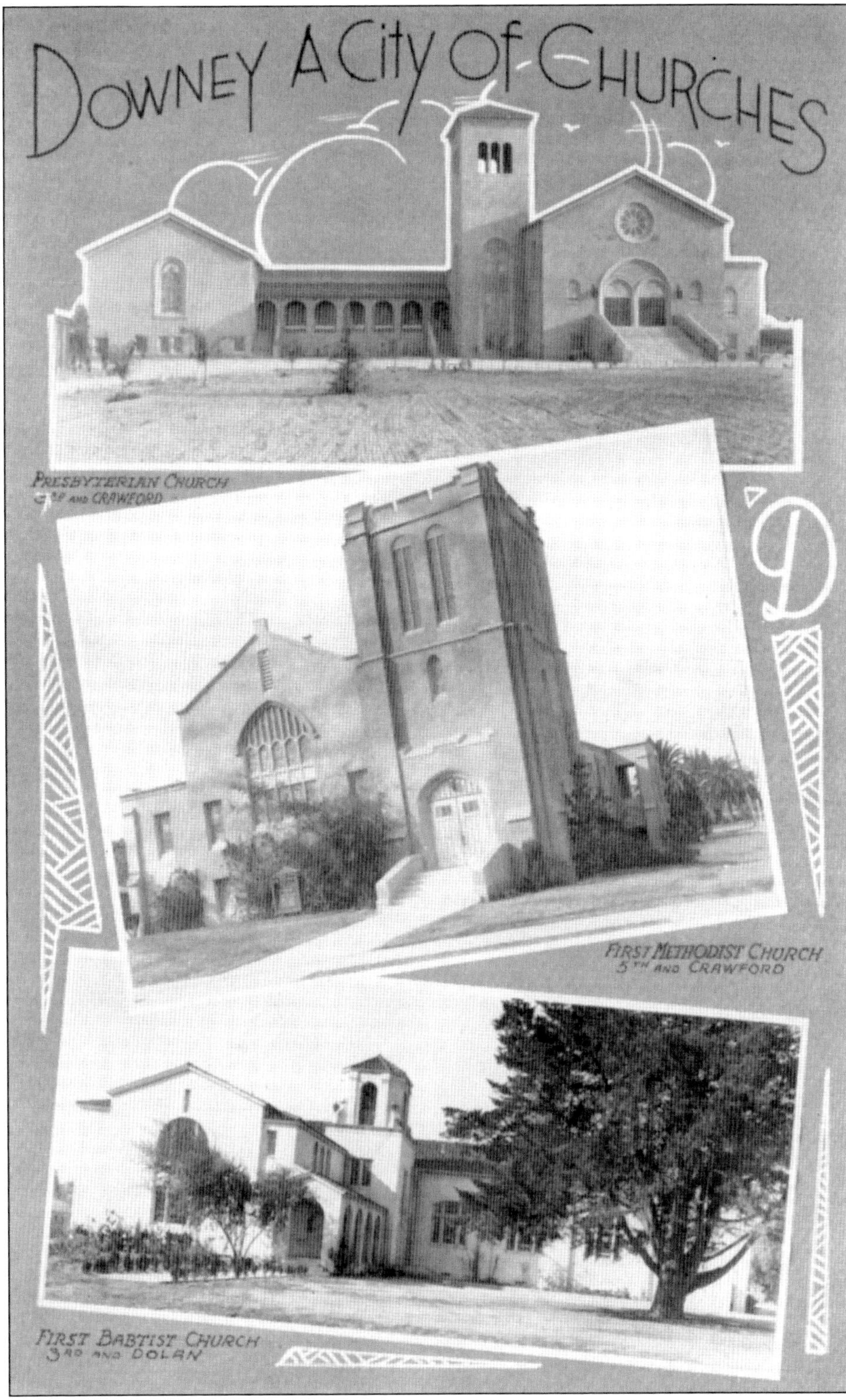

This collage celebrates Downey's early Presbyterian, Methodist, and First Baptist churches.

Four

Aerial Views of Downey, Aviation, and Aerospace

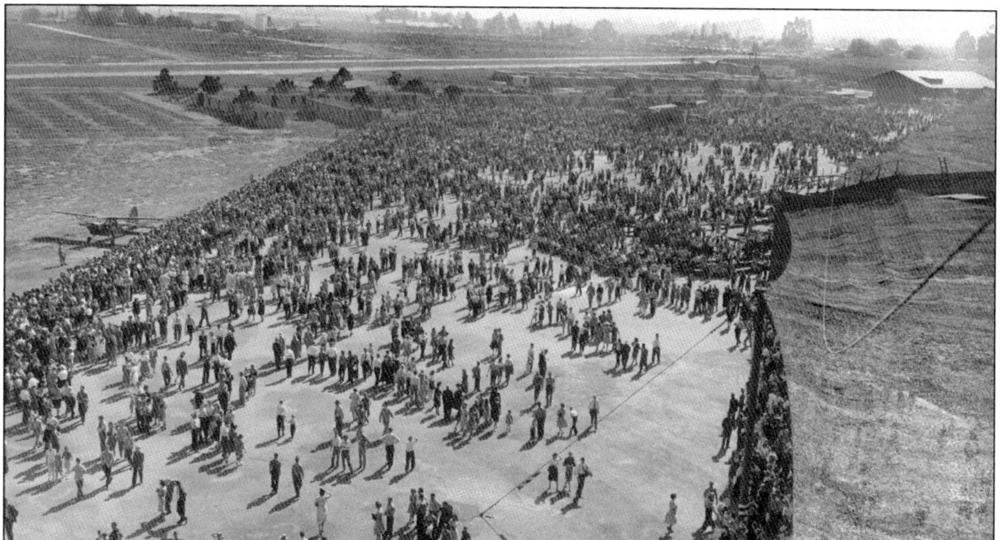

In 1936, aviation pioneer Jerry Vultee bought E. M. Smith's old Downey airstrip and production plant. This aerial view shows Vultee Family Day in 1943. Here, near Washburn Crossing Road, Cerritos Avenue (Lakewood Boulevard), and Alameda Street, was the beginning of a plant that within decades would build the ships sending men to the moon. Vultee built 13,000 airplanes here during World War II. Notice the fake buildings and farm-like look to the property. This site became North American Aviation's Downey Plant and was converted from plane to missile technology in the 1950s. In the 1960s, over 25,000 employees worked here on the Apollo Program.

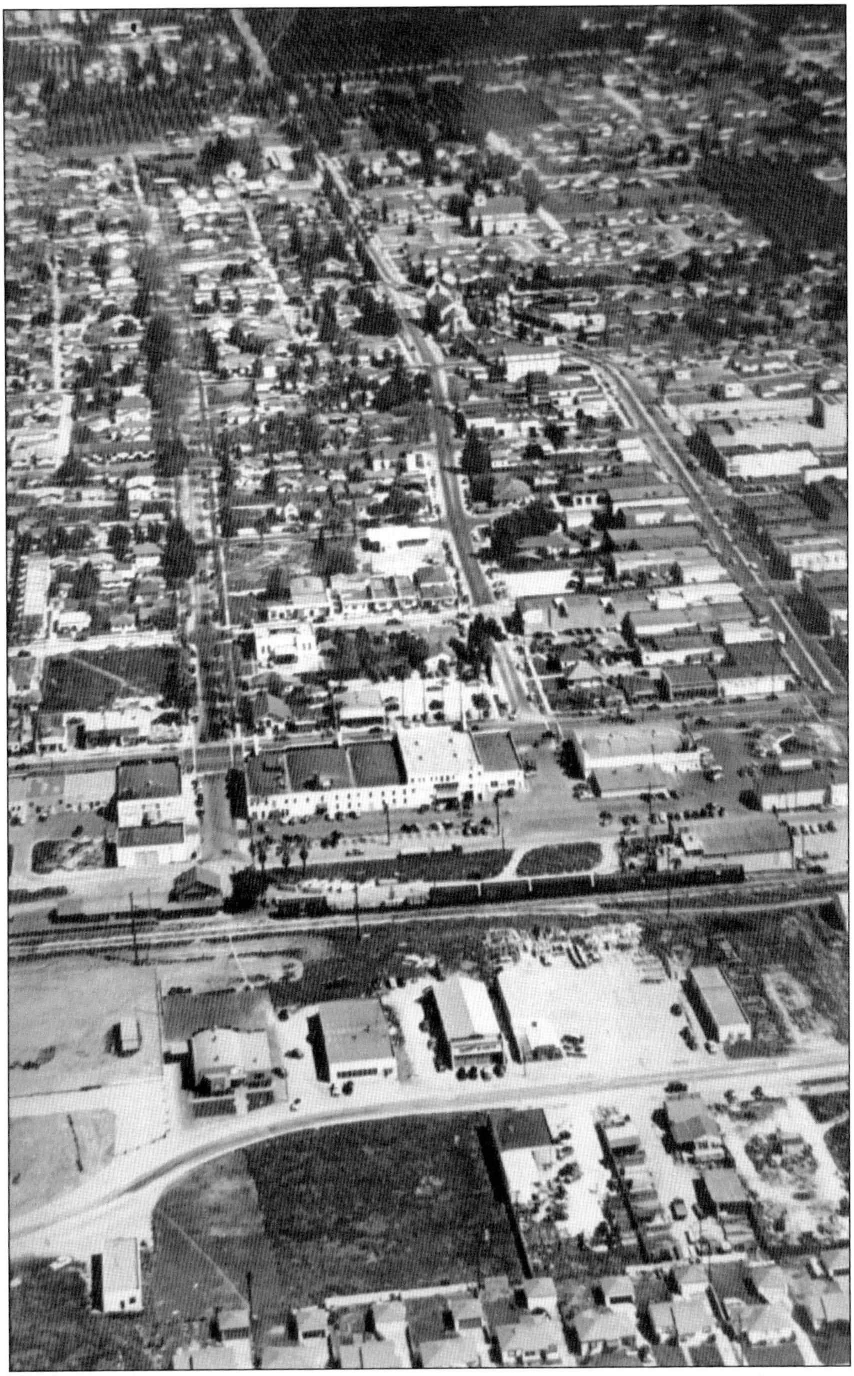

Taken in the 1940s, this aerial view has Downey Avenue in the middle looking north past Cherokee Drive to Florence Avenue. On the left side is La Reina Street running north. Our Lady of Perpetual Help Catholic Church can be seen at the meeting of New Street and Downey Avenue. The large Presbyterian Church on Downey Avenue and Seventh Street can be seen also on the center right. The Methodist Church is also visible just up from the Meralta Theatre (center right) on the west side of Downey Avenue at Fifth Street.

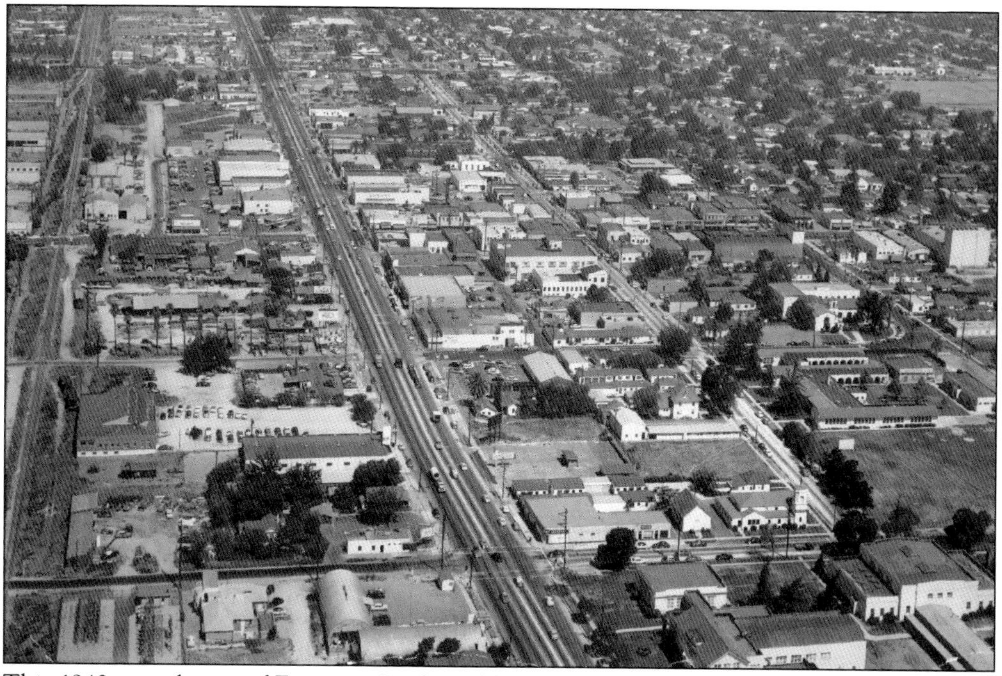

This 1940s aerial view of Firestone Boulevard looks west from Brookshire Avenue. Notice the buildings of Downey Junior High and Downey High School in the lower right. Downey Grammar School, which became City Hall, is located near Second and Third Streets at Dolan. The old high school is facing Firestone Boulevard. To the far left is the Southern Pacific Railroad looking west from just east of Brookshire Avenue.

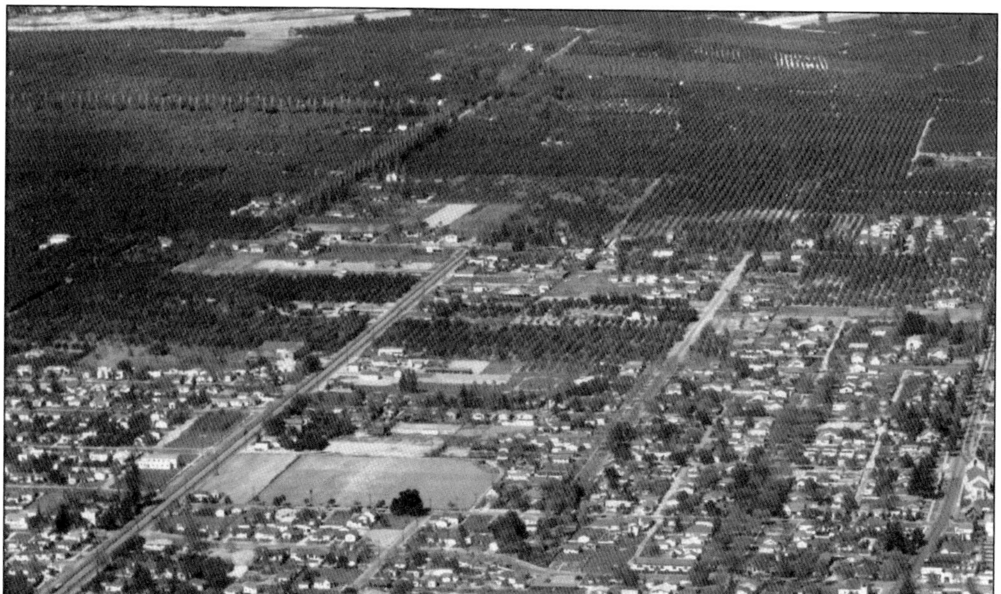

This 1940s photograph shows Tweedy Lane bordered by palm trees and orange orchards. The large Ball Ranch was located on Foster Bridge Road (Suva Street) south to Gainford Street, and from Tweedy Lane to the Rio Hondo. In 1930, it stretched over 107 acres. Paramount Boulevard is on the left meeting Florence Avenue.

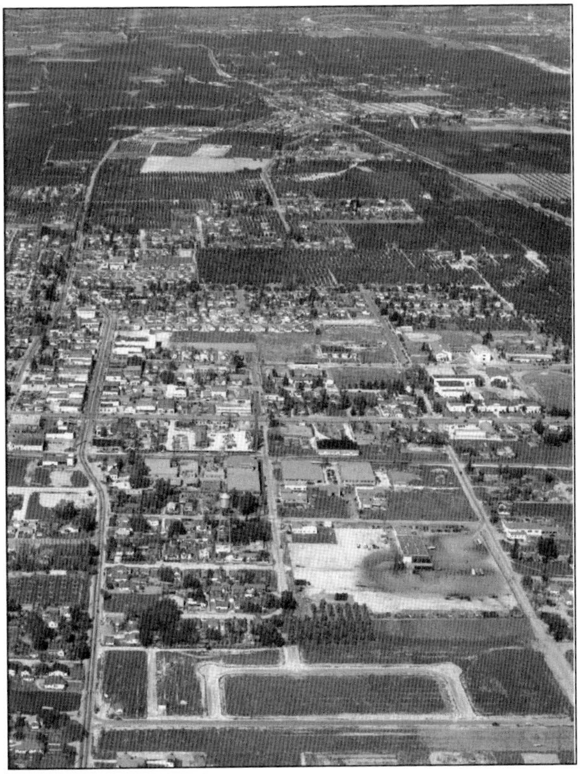

This 1940s photograph shows the eastern half of Downey from Stewart and Gray Road in the south to a fantastic panorama of Rivera and Whittier split by Lakewood-Rosemead Boulevard in the north. Downey Avenue and New Street are on the left side and the Downey High School buildings can be seen at far right center. Just above Downey High to the north is the Ball Home and Ranch built in 1929 at Cherokee Drive west of Lakewood Boulevard. The road in the upper center is Lexington-Gallatin Road, which headed north to Rivera (Pico Rivera) and El Monte. Notice Church Street (Brookshire Avenue) stops at the Ball property north of Fifth Street. On the lower left, surrounded by trees, is the home of Edna Feather, on whose property the YMCA was built.

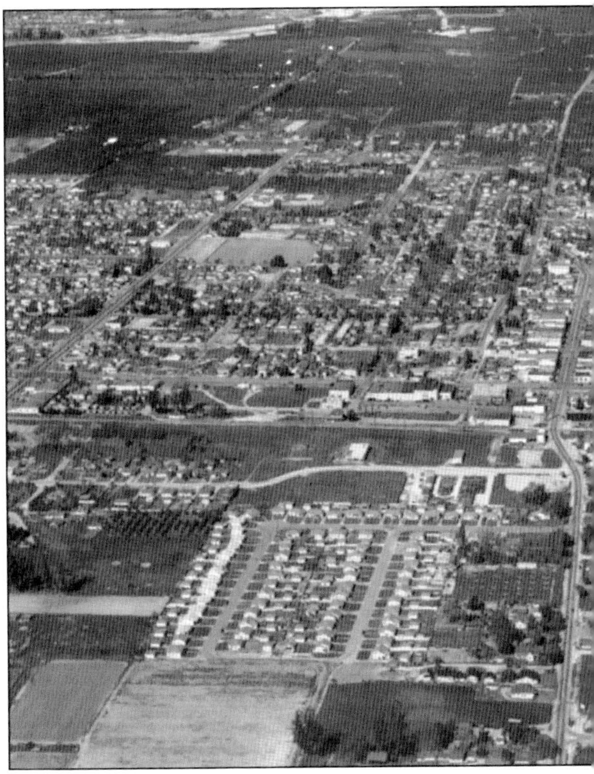

West of downtown Downey on the left in this 1947 aerial view is Paramount Boulevard running north-south, ending at Florence Avenue just southeast of Tweedy Lane, the land where the Gallatin Settlement took root. At the turn of the century, the town between the Rio Hondo and Rio San Gabriel was bounded on the north by orange groves and on the south by dairy farms. Fragrant orange trees and plenty of apple, English walnut, fig, and persimmon trees grew robust in the area's mild climate. Gallatin and Rives Avenues, Tweedy Lane, and many other streets were lined with stately palm trees, magnolia, and pepper trees still common in Downey. The area also had many chicken and rabbit farms. Downey Avenue (Crawford Street) has always been the town's main street. Los Nietos Valley Bank, Strines General Merchandise, Pulley's Drug Store, and Krueger's Shoe Store were common destinations for local residents.

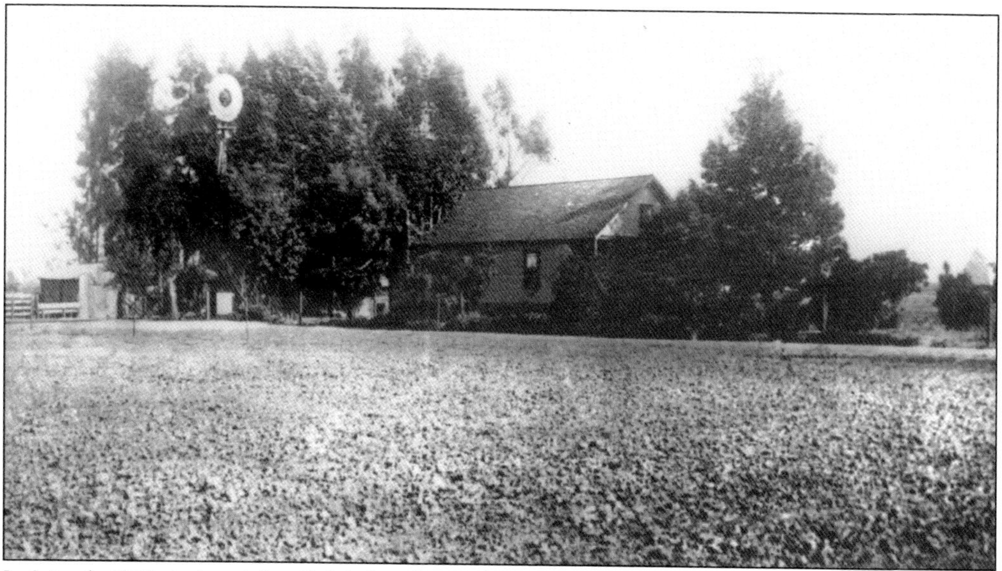

In March 1929, industrialist E. M. Smith purchased James Hughan's 73-acre ranch in southeast Downey, pictured here. It was bounded by Cerritos Avenue (Lakewood Boulevard) on the west, Woodruff Avenue on the east, Zinn Road on the south, and Washburn Crossing on the north. Rancher Hughan farmed castor beans and oranges, and this large piece of property was ideal for an airfield and factory. The first building on the site was 60,000 square feet and the property included 2,400 feet of hardwood runway and associated hangars. Five months after buying the ranch, EMSCO's first plane was flying test flights over Downey.

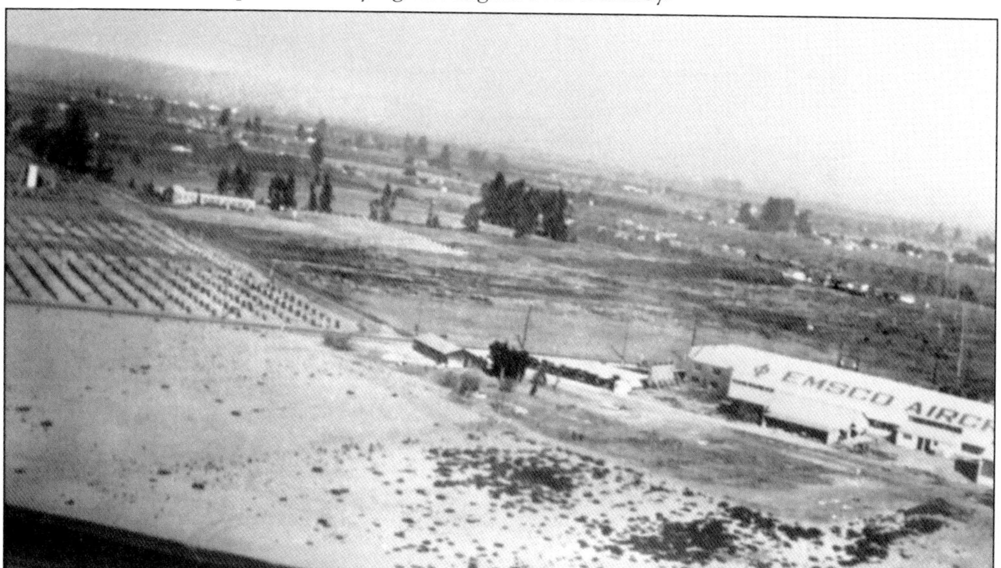

This photograph of EMSCO Aircraft in Downey at Cerritos Road (Lakewood Boulevard) looks west toward Alameda Street. Notice Alameda School in the distance and the hardwood runways in the foreground. Things went well for E. M. Smith until the 1929 stock market crash. After various tenants leased the factory, Bert Kinner moved his Security National Aircraft Company to the vacant Downey plant in 1932. Kinner had pioneered the "folding wing" design and built Amelia Earhart's first aircraft. His most popular aircraft at the time was the Kinner Airster.

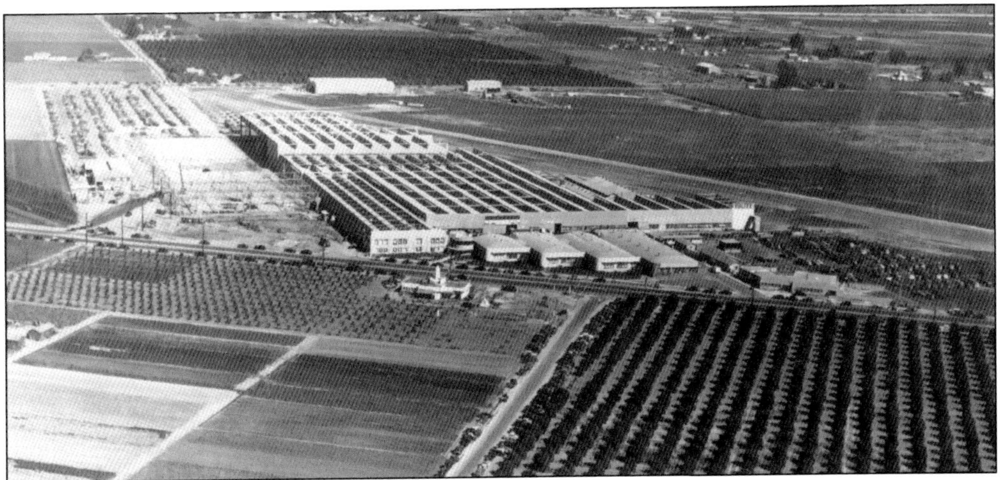

This aerial view of Vultee Field and Vultee Aircraft was taken on September 4, 1940. Named for Gerard F. Vultee, Vultee Aircraft in Downey began in June 1936, moving from Glendale to Downey's former Security Aircraft and EMSCO Aircraft facilities. Jerry Vultee had worked as an engineer at EMSCO Aircraft, Douglas Aircraft, and Lockheed Aircraft before becoming Lockheed's chief engineer in 1928. After the 1929 stock market crash, Vultee left Lockheed in 1930 to partner in 1931 with Errett Lobban Cord, who headed the Cord Corporation. Vultee had plans for a high speed transport plane that Cord would build with a new company, Airplane Development Corporation. Vultee became chief engineer as the company moved into the Downey plant.

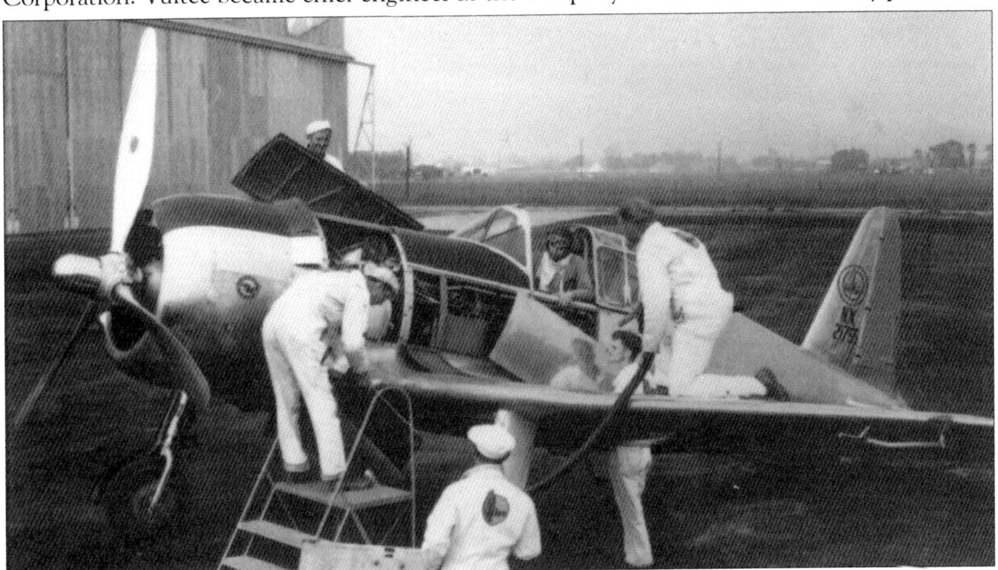

By 1937, the Downey plant was called the Vultee Aircraft Division of the Aviation Manufacturing Corporation. Vultee was selling most of his planes abroad, and making a profit. In 1938, he employed 500 people. This picture shows a maintenance crew posing behind Building One, where Downey Studios is today. After presenting a new aircraft to the U.S. Army, Jerry Vultee and his wife Sylvia were flying back from Washington, D.C., when their plane crashed in Sedona, Arizona, killing them. After Vultee's death the company soon became Consolidated Vultee Aircraft Corporation, or "Convair." Convair went on to produce more than 13,500 aircraft during World War II. By July 1941, Vultee's plant in Downey made 15 percent of all military aircraft in the nation. Even after Vultee's death, Vultee, like North American Aviation, was a family-run company.

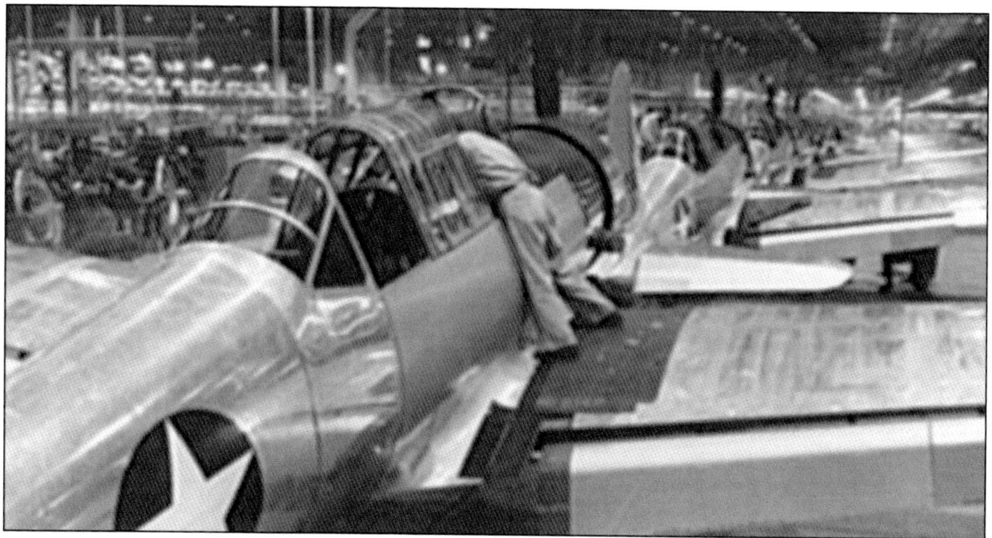

This photograph shows B-13A production in Downey in the early 1940s. Some 11,537 trainer aircraft (Valiants) were produced at the Vultee Field in Downey. The Vultee BT-13 trainer was the lead aircraft in the training of pilots for World War II. During the first six months of 1944, Convair at Vultee Field helped turn out the largest delivery of B-24 Liberator bombers produced in the country. As World War II wound down, production of military aircraft at the Downey plant neared an end. The Vultee Field division of Convair remained at the Downey site to support a contract with the Navy for a short-range missile called the Lark. Another project in the late 1940s was the MX-774, designed to study two types of missiles: a subsonic, jet engine cruise missile and a rocket-powered supersonic ballistic missile. Downey's engineers focused on the ballistic missile concept, using the German V-2 rocket as a starting point.

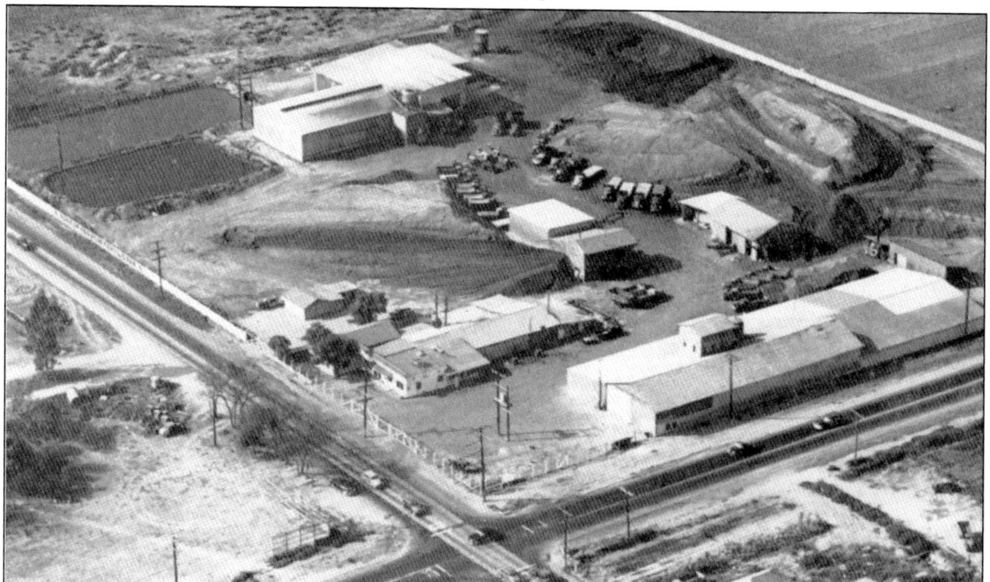

This photograph of Downey Fertilizer Company was taken while flying over the intersection of Bellflower Boulevard and Imperial Highway in 1949. Downey Fertilizer produced Red Star brand and was known for the large mound of fragrant product near Vultee and later North American Aviation. The corner pictured is now a section of Kaiser Permanente Hospital.

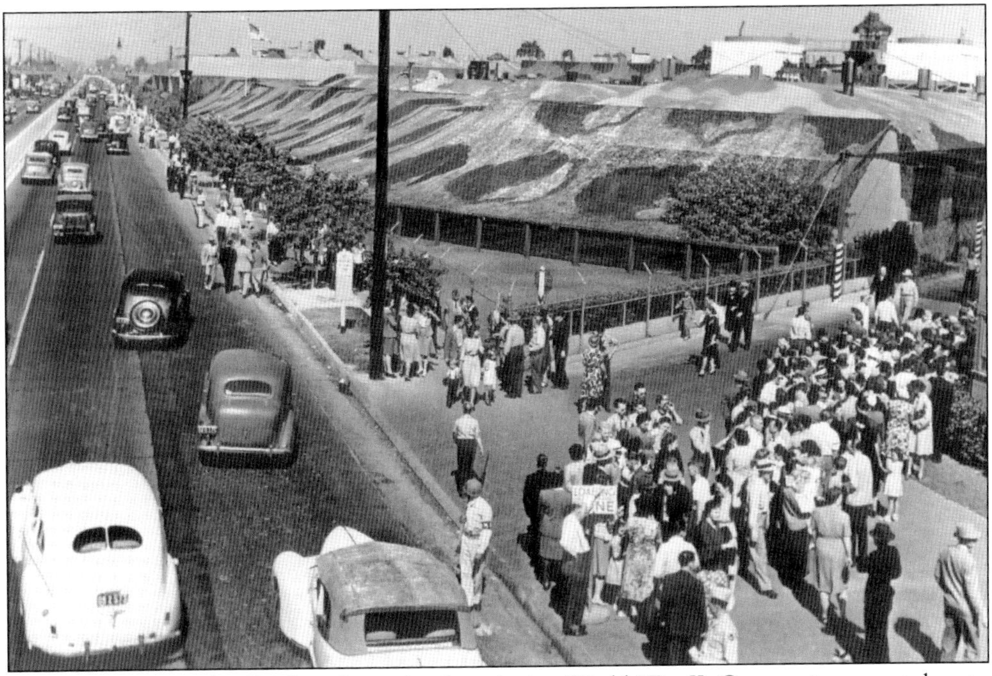

This is a photograph of Vultee Aircraft taken during World War II. Great pains were taken to conceal the aircraft plant with camouflage. From the air this area looked like a large farm with out-buildings, stacks of hay, and trees. This view off Lakewood Boulevard, however, shows that the plant was actually busily producing thousands of airplanes. Women made up a large portion of Vultee's workforce.

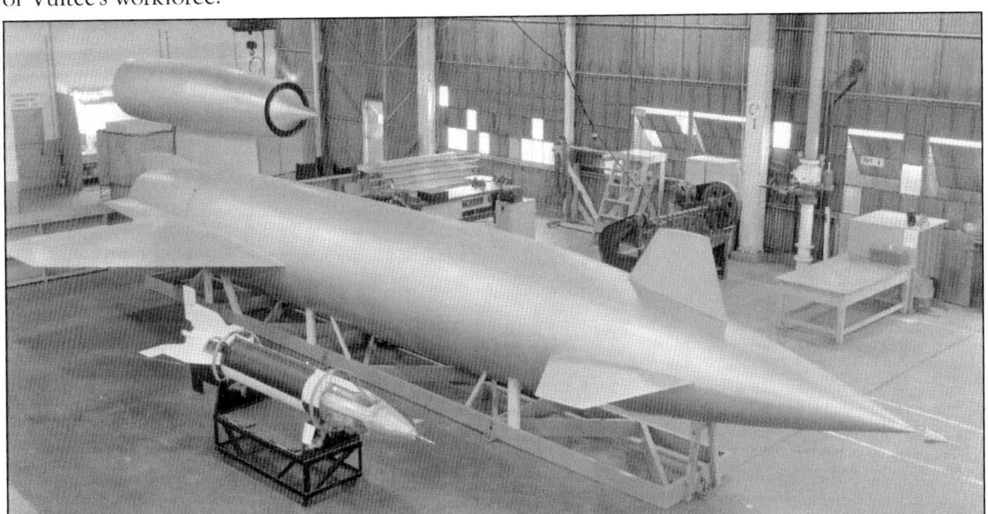

The Downey facility, from the early 1950s to 1964, was officially known as Air Force Plant 16. North American Aviation, under Air Force contract, began to develop a new missile concept called the Navaho. The Air Force eventually canceled the Navaho program in 1957, but in its 10 years of existence, Navaho made many key technological breakthroughs. The company was also experimenting with atomic energy and in 1952 a small, low-power research reactor was tested and placed into operation in Downey and was the first nuclear reactor built and operated in California.

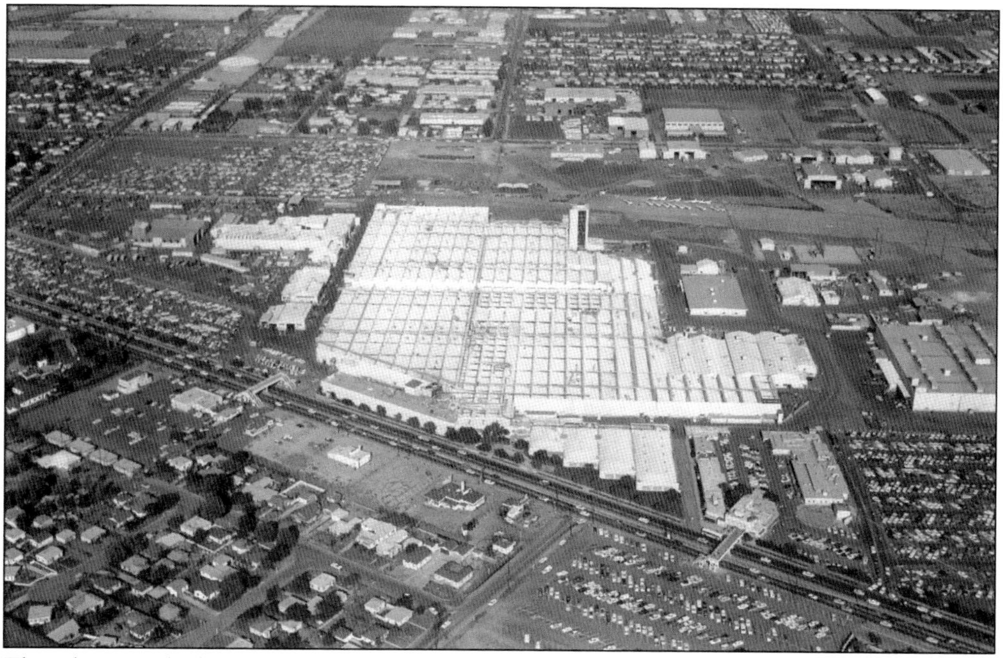

This photograph shows North American Aviation in Downey in 1961. Although the Navaho missile program was eventually canceled, the plant won a major new program— the Air Force's Hound Dog air-to-ground missile (AGM) program. By 1961, North American Aviation was growing by thousands of employees. The plant would expand each year as the company received two large contracts for the Apollo program.

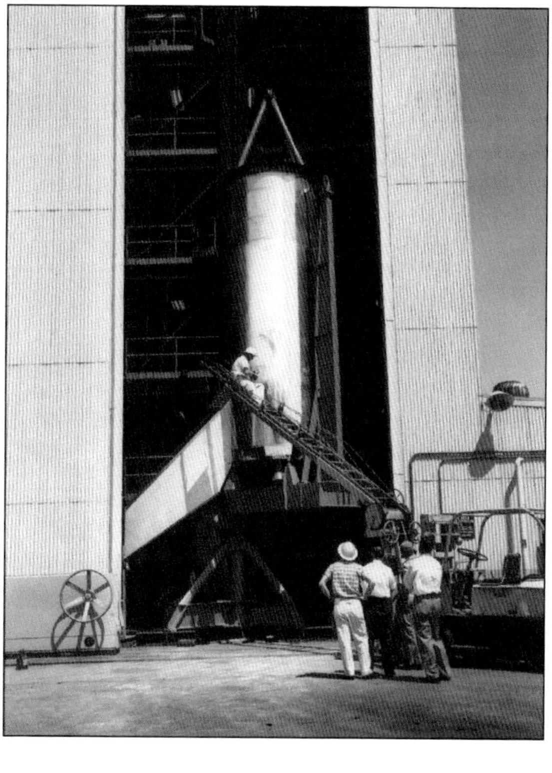

The Hound Dog program was the forerunner of cruise missile technology. Strategic Air Command (SAC) wanted a missile to carry out strategic bombing offensives. North American was also awarded a contract to produce the Little Joe launch vehicle to test the Mercury capsules. A variety of Little Joe configurations were produced for testing, and the vehicle was instrumental to the Mercury program's success. By 1960, Lee Atwood began to redirect the Downey Missile Division away from missile production and toward space exploration. The engineer who led the X-15 rocket plane program, Harrison Storms, became head of North American's Missile Division in 1960.

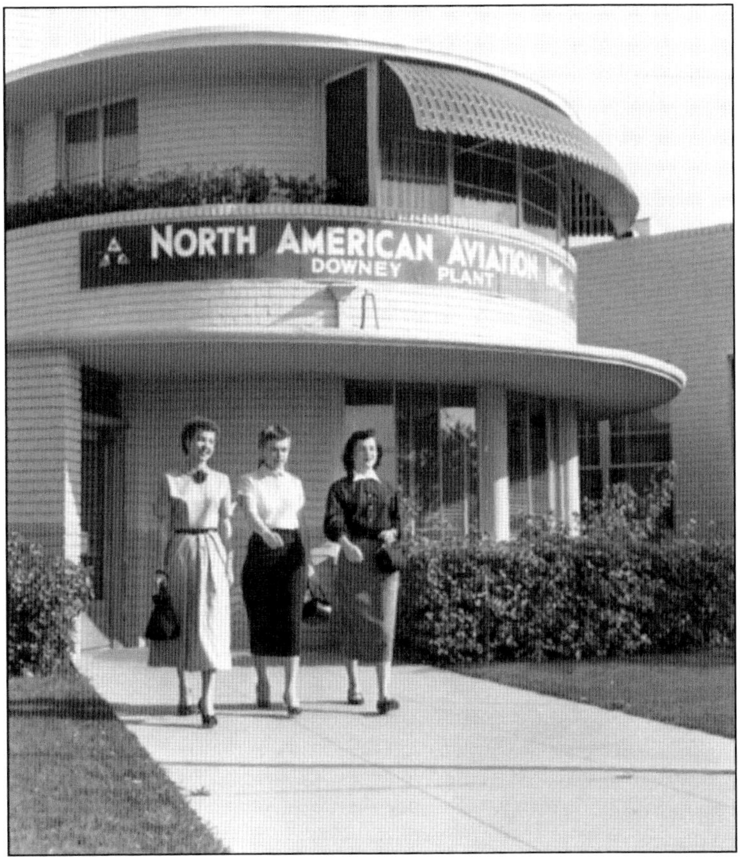

Pictured here in the early 1960s at the entrance to North American Aviation's front offices at the Rotunda on Lakewood Boulevard and Alameda Street is a group of North American secretaries on their way to lunch. North American won both the Apollo spacecraft contract and the Saturn II stage contract for the massive Saturn V rocket that would propel astronauts to the moon some day. Harrison Storms ran the Downey plant for James Howard "Dutch" Kindelberger, president of North American Aviation until his death in 1962.

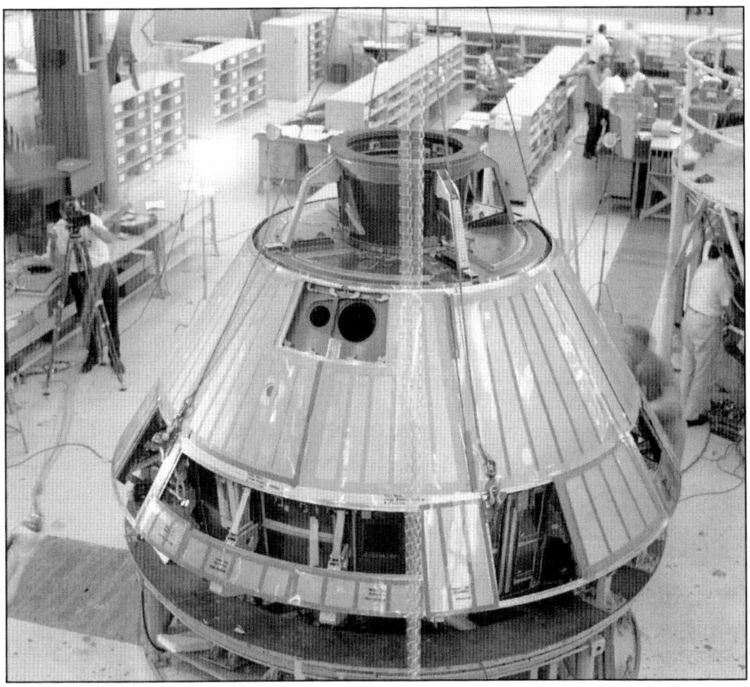

With the Apollo program well under way, Downey's North American Space and Information Division was hiring just about every engineer it could find. By the mid-1960s, the company was employing up to 30,000 people. With the contract secured for the command and service modules, this picture shows engineers involved with the Apollo spacecraft's fabrication.

Both the Apollo command and service modules were built at North American Aviation's plant at Downey, California. This picture is of the Apollo High Impact Test Facility at North American Rockwell in Downey in 1966. The 150-foot tower looked similar to a huge playground swing and provided critical information for crew safety on the lunar lander. Tests were conducted on sand, water, gravel, and boulders. High-speed cameras were mounted in the test pool above and below water.

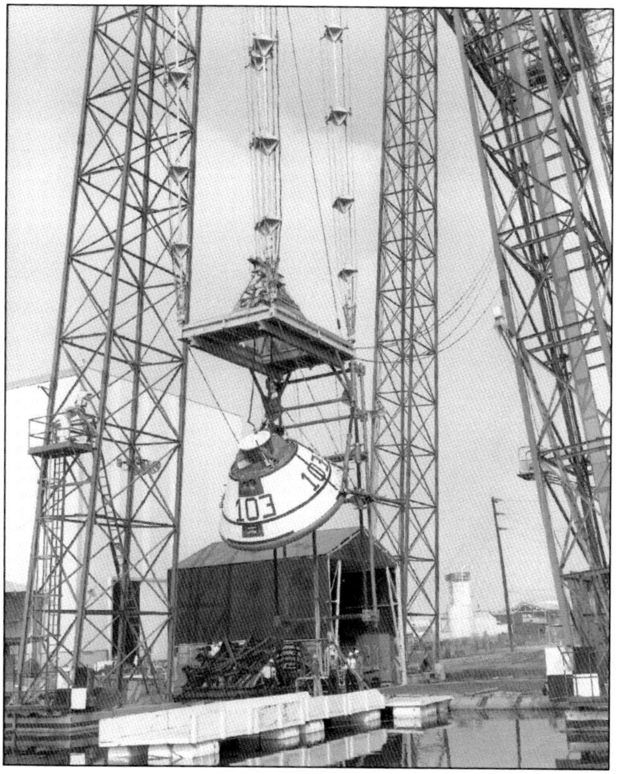

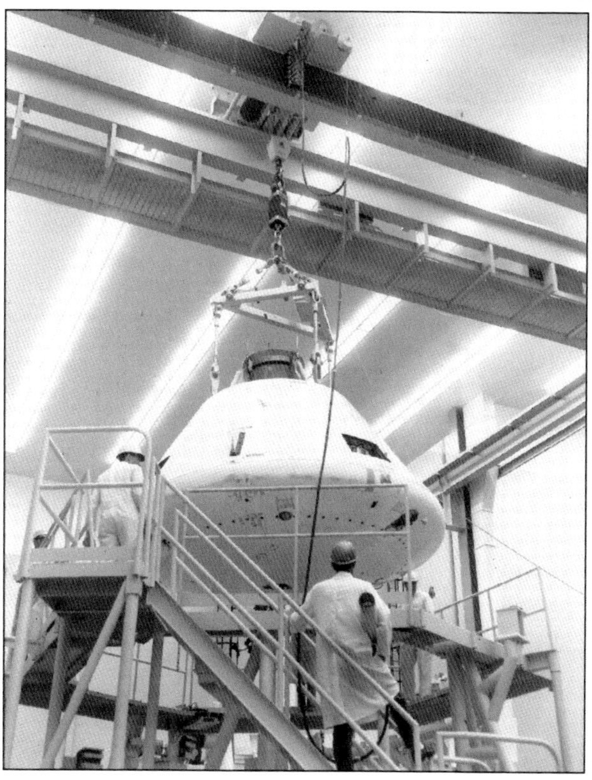

This picture was taken in the high bay Building 290 on October 6, 1965. This Apollo capsule was one of many undergoing testing in the 1960s at North American Aviation in Downey.

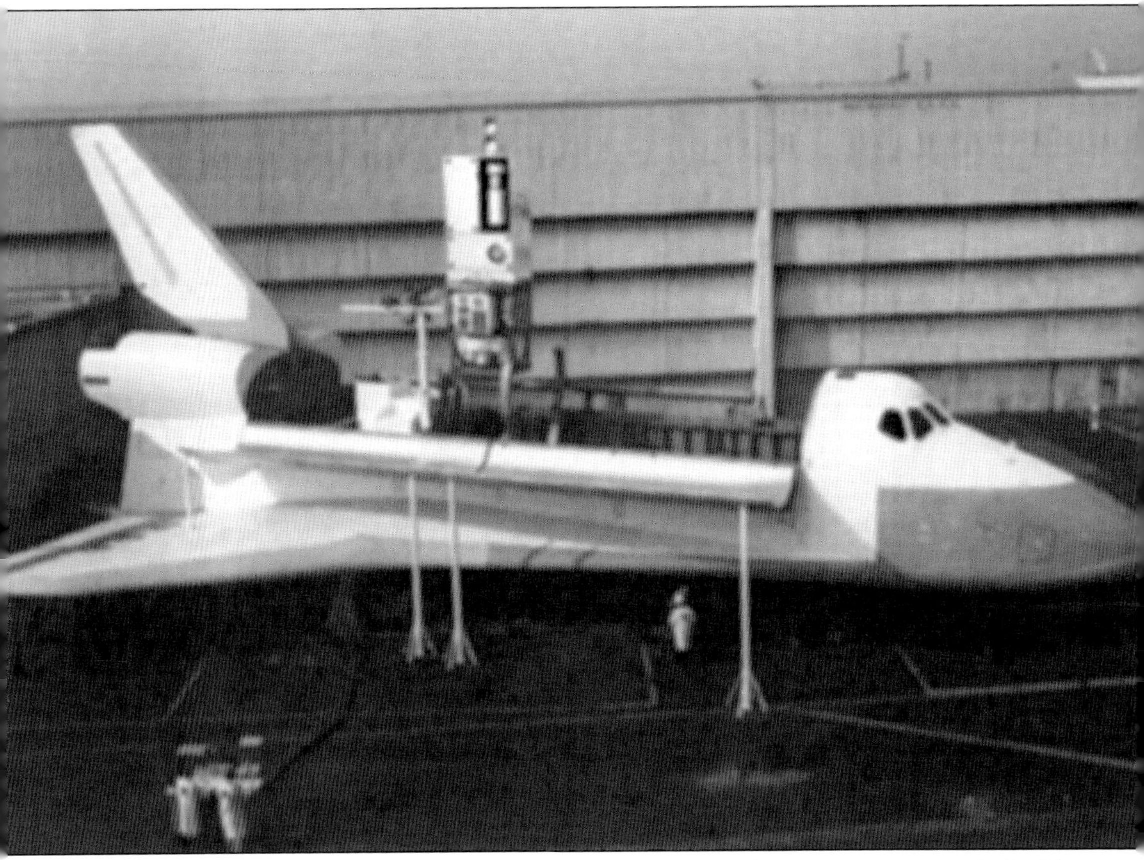

This is a life-size mock-up of the Space Shuttle orbiter in the former DEI room inside Building One at the Boeing plant in Downey. The DEI room was the Design and Integration room, used for employee and public meetings including customer reviews. The City of Downey now owns this shuttle mock-up and hopes to someday showcase it.

Five

Landmarks and Nostalgia

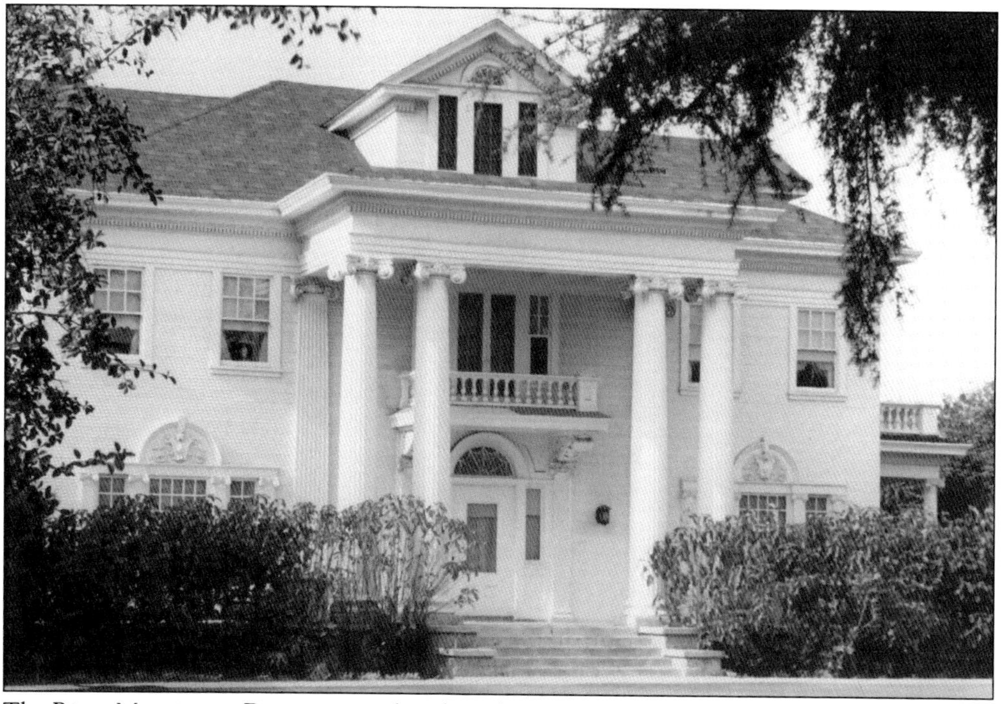

The Rives Mansion in Downey was placed on the Registry of Historic Places in 1978. Work on the home began in 1911, surrounded by 75 acres of orchards and walnut groves. Raised in the home were Edward L. Rives, Robert C. Rives, Lawrence H. Rives, and Pauline Rives. Edward Rives married Elizabeth Ball, Robert married Ethel Head, Lawrence married Verna Tweedy, and Pauline married Louis K. Ball. Mary Rives subdivided most of the 75-acre estate in 1930, and in 1946—one year after her death—the property was sold.

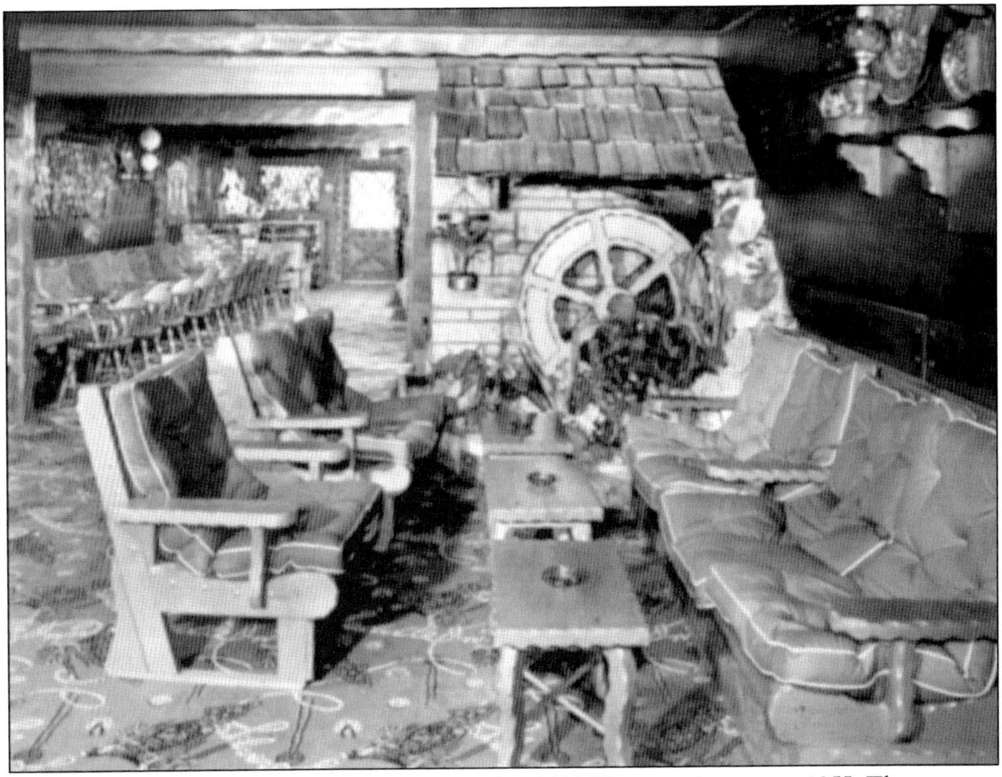

Lyle Williams's Silver Saddle restaurant opened at 7339 Florence Avenue in 1955. The concept of Williams's "saddle" idea was patterned around his large ranch house. The lounge area had a large fireplace, and the huge silver-mounted saddle turned round and round in the front window. An "Indian Show" was staged in front of the barn, west of the main building. A brochure reads, "The water wheel is nestled in a natural setting of flowers and greenery. The wheel is powered by water flowing from the rocks and the entire area is beautified by the lighting effects."

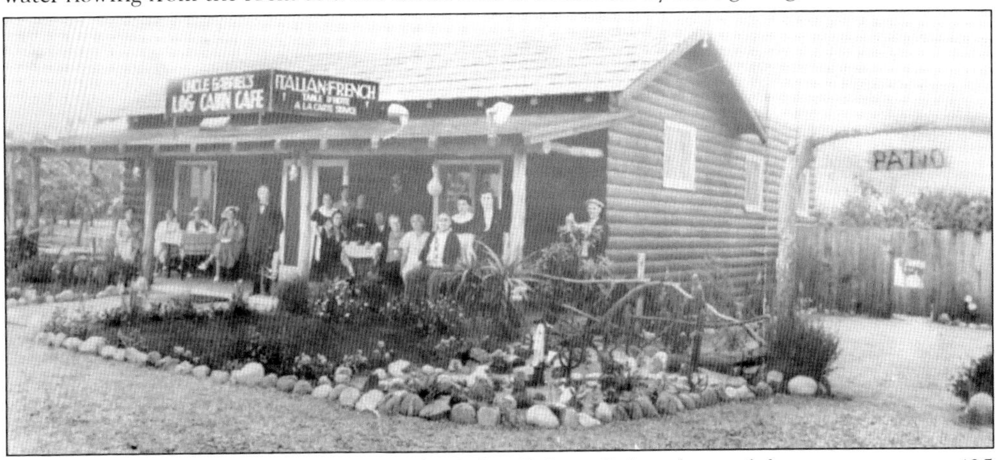

This is an undated photograph of Uncle Gabriel's Log Cabin, located for many years at 425 South Paramount Boulevard—across the street from Warren High School. The proprietor, G. Ispidi, added additional space for a large banquet room in the late 1930s. In November 1938, a Thanksgiving dinner at Uncle Gabriel's cost $1.25 per person. The Merchant lunch was 50¢. In the 1970s, the Log Cabin became Abott's Restaurant.

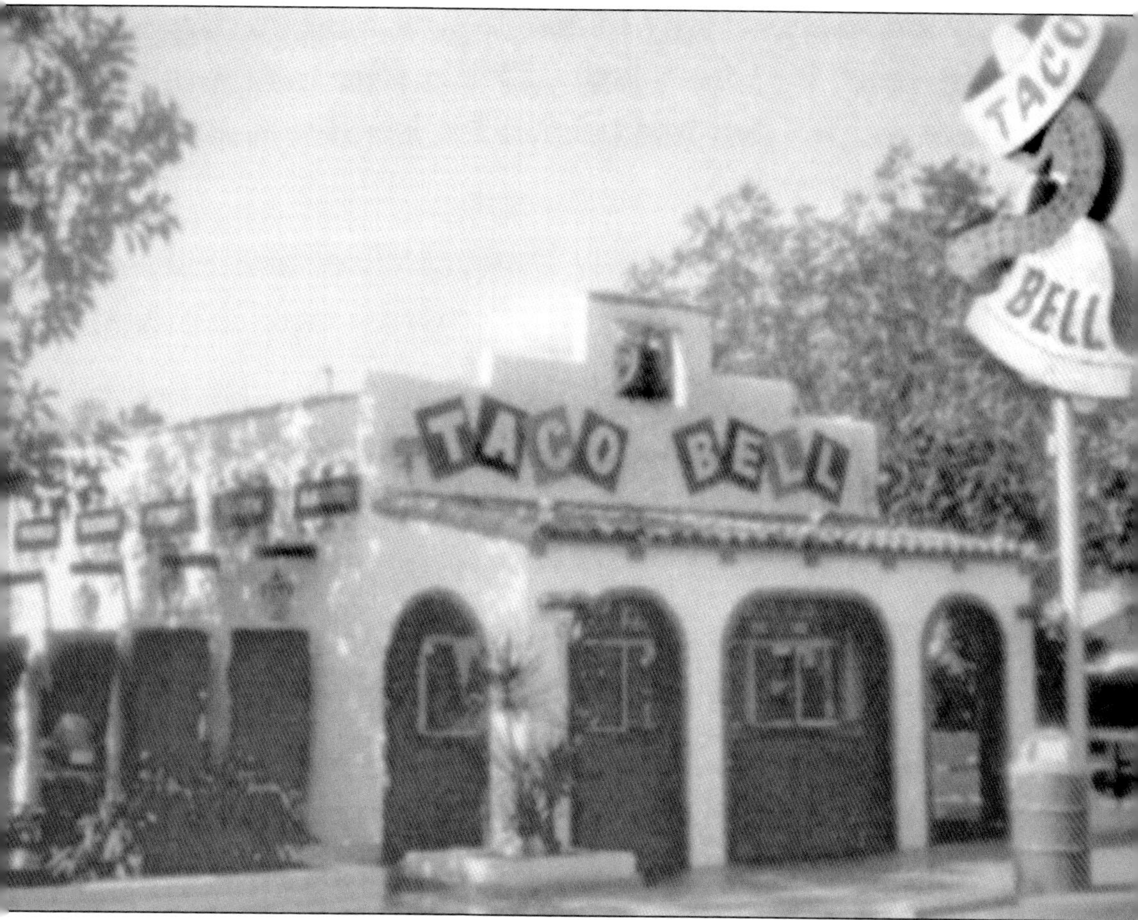

This was Glen Bell's first Taco Bell. A Marine veteran of World War II, Bell started out with a hot dog stand called Bell Drive-In and learned the business as he went. By the early 1950s, Bell experimented with Mexican food, developing a stainless steel, deep-fry basket for taco shells. During 1954 and 1955, Bell built three Taco Tia stands in San Bernardino, Riverside, and Redlands. His wife, Martha Bell, provided the name "Der Weinerscnitzel" to their friend John Gallardi, who worked for El Tacos, to use for his new fast food enterprise. She helped with the menu, too. Glen also owned interest in four El Tacos, but sold out to build the first Taco Bell in 1962. (Image courtesy of Taco Bell.)

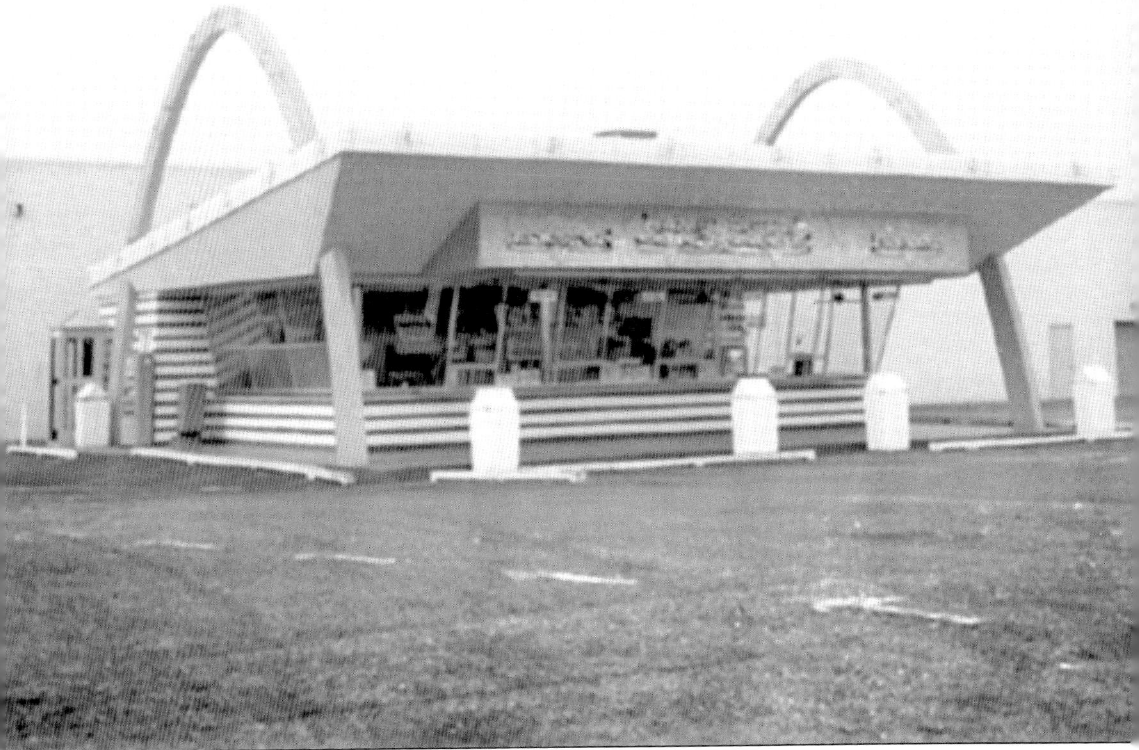

Built in 1953, the McDonald's Hamburgers at Lakewood Boulevard and Florence Avenue was one of the first of the chain. The original owners were Bud Landon and Roger Williams, but they did not consent to the purchase from the McDonald brothers by Ray Croc. Landon and Williams were granted the right to buy food from McDonald's and continue using the name. McDonald's, Harvey's Broiler, Richie's, and many other burger joints were popular with teenagers, particularly from Downey High. The Downey McDonald's was preserved as a landmark by Joyce Lawrence and others attentive to the Downey story.

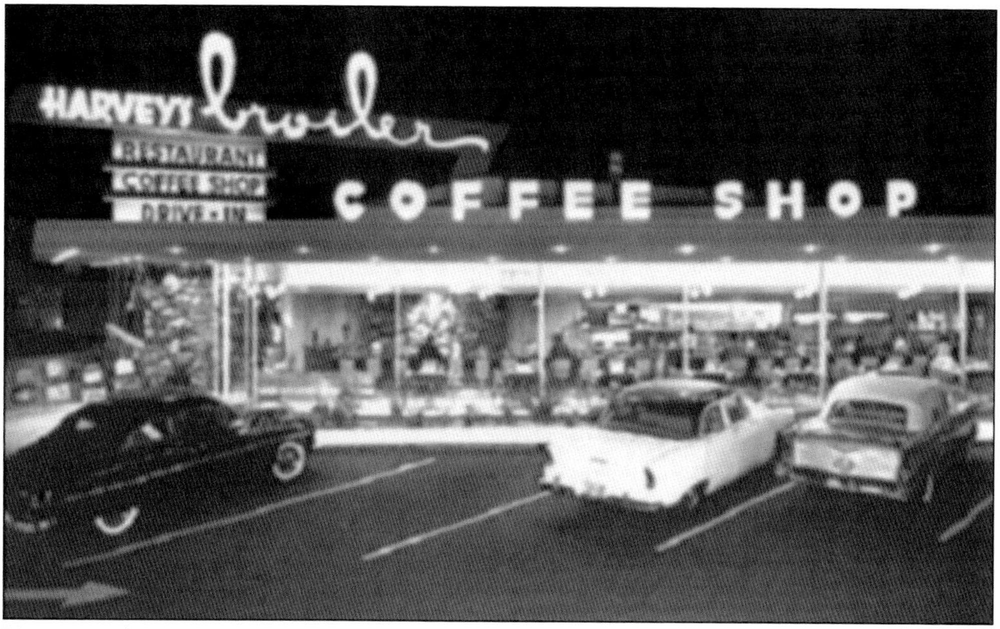

Harvey and Minnie Ortner founded Harvey's Broiler, the landmark 1950s Downey drive-in restaurant and coffee shop. It soon became a Southern California car-culture magnet and was later renamed Johnie's Broiler. In the 1950s and 1960s Harvey's was *the* hangout to cruise to for a burger and milkshake. The property and building have been remodeled and the restaurant is now a Bob's Big Boy Broiler, but the look and feel that Harvey and Minnie Ortner established has been retained.

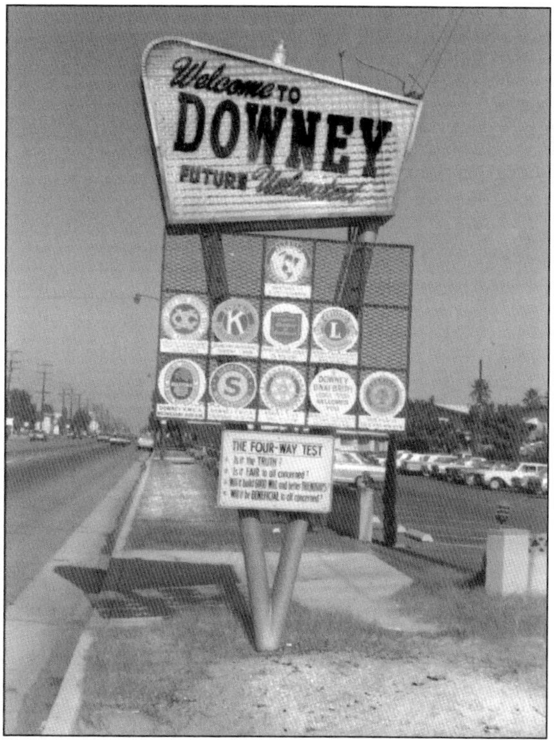

Many Downey residents remember the "Welcome to Downey, Future Unlimited" signs at the borders of the city. The slogan "Future Unlimited" was submitted for a contest sponsored by the Chamber of Commerce in the late 1940s. The winner was G. Gonzales of Downey Home Bakery, 11139 South Downey Avenue. A great place to call home, Downey has been, and remains, one of the finest residential communities in Southern California.

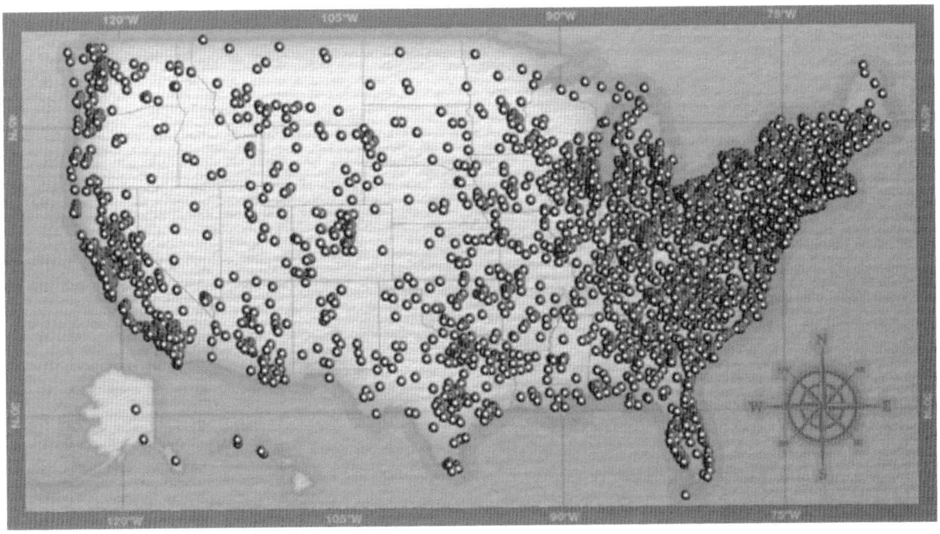